Quality Management for Law Firms

Quality Management for Law Firms

Matthew Moore
LLB MCIM MCIPD C.Dip.AF Solicitor

law society publishing

ISBN 1 85328 715 6

Published in 2001 by the Law Society
113 Chancery Lane, London WC2A 1PL

Designed and Typeset in Stone Serif by
J&L Composition Ltd, Filey, North Yorkshire
Printed and bound in Great Britain by
TJ International Ltd, Padstow, Cornwall

For Eleanor, William and Charlie

Contents

Foreword

Whether your firm is large or small, good practice management and excellent standards of client care are the key to success. Many firms already know that this is how they will thrive in the future, by adopting management structures and best practice to ensure a quality service.

These principles, and the frameworks that implement them, will help practices avoid leaving to chance the key factors that underpin delivering excellent client care.

To illustrate all of this, Matthew Moore's book outlines a number of frameworks for firms to consider, saving them the need to invent one of their own. In addition to ISO 9001 and the Legal Aid Franchise, (both of which my own firm possesses), or Investors in people, the Law Society has contributed its own quality initiative, Lexcel.

Lexcel has been developed as a management tool to address the particular business needs of all legal practices, as well as demonstrating a strong commitment to quality of service.

As President of the Law Society, I therefore commend Lexcel, as I commend this excellent book, to all practitioners and practice managers. I am sure they will reap the benefits in adopting the quality management approach to the business of law on behalf of well cared-for clients.

Michael Napier
President of the Law Society 2000–2001
Senior Partner, Irwin Mitchell.

Preface

It is roughly 10 years since quality management principles were first applied in a structured manner to law firms. There have been significant developments in the area since and this text accompanies the Lexcel initiative of the Law Society of England and Wales in particular. Lexcel has the great advantage of being specific to the legal profession and is capable of being applied to any type of firm or legal department. The book is a general text on this subject, however, and the other principal quality standards are also covered.

One of the main features of law firm management is that there should be weak boundaries between the different management disciplines. For quality one can read client care, better marketing or generally enhanced management effectiveness. Above all quality means better business performance through the provision of an improved service to clients. The emerging area of risk management also relies heavily on quality procedures. This text therefore covers most areas of practice management in line with the areas dealt with under the Lexcel scheme.

In addition to the acknowledgements which follow I would like to pass particular thanks to Alan Henry, with whom I had the pleasure of working in New Zealand a few years ago, and to his wife Alison for their hospitality. My introduction to quality management principles was through Pannone March Pearson as they then were – later Pannone & Partners – with a remit to assist in their early quality programme. My experience is also based on many other training and consultancy clients who are too numerous to mention. Most of the writing was undertaken at my mother's while building works continued at home. My thanks are also due to my wife Angela for her love, help and support. The book is dedicated to our children.

mattmoore@charis.co.uk

Acknowledgements

Figures 5.1–5.4 reproduced from *Understanding Organizations* by Charles Handy (Penguin Books 1976, fourth edition 1993) copyright Charles Handy 1976, 1981, 1985, 1993, 1999: 'The power culture' (p. 178 of original edition), 'The role culture' (p. 179), 'The task culture' (p. 161) and 'The person culture' (p. 184). Performance by permission of Penguin Books Ltd.

Extract from *The Empty Raincoat* by Charles Handy published by Hutchinson. Used by permission of the Random House Group Limited.

Figure 12.3 reproduced with the permission of Blackstone Press Limited.

Thanks to:

Graham Le Roux in relation to Quality in Law and Bryan Frew for permission to reproduce Figure 3.3;
The European Foundation for Quality Management for permission to reproduce Figure 3.4;
Andrew Otterburn for permission to reproduce Figure 4.3;
Aman Rajan and Penny Van Eupen at the Centre for Research in Employment and Technology in Europe for their permission to reproduce Figure 8.4.

Particular thanks to Chris Trott of SGS Yarsley; Simon Young for assistance with limited liability partnerships; Mike Dodd in relation to finance; Peter Shearer for suggestions on strategy; Peter Johnson, Andrew Baker and Mike Frith of the Office for the Supervision of Solicitors; Ben Rigby, Tracey Stanley and the Lexcel team at the Law Society; Steve Reed and Sarah Foulkes at Law Society Publishing; Michael Moore and Martin Moore for checking various chapters and Mark Moore for help with references.

List of abbreviations

CLSQM	Community Legal Service Quality Mark
CPD	Continuing Professional Development
EQ	emotional quota
IIP	Investors in People
LAB	Legal Aid Board
MDP	multi-disciplinary partnership
QIL	Quality in Law
SIF	Solicitors' Indemnity Fund
TQM	total quality management

From professionalism to commercialism

- Supply and demand
- Staffing implications
- Commodification
- Block contracting: productisation in practice

The practice of law has changed dramatically in recent years. It would be comforting to think that some degree of stability might now be achieved, but this appears unlikely. It seems certain that significant change will continue to be the order of the day for the foreseeable future, to the extent that the organisation and delivery of legal services may be unrecognisable in 10 or 20 years' time to many of today's practitioners. The law will continue to regulate how we go about our business, claim compensation from each other and society in general, but those who practise law will need to develop their business operations to remain involved. Those who can adapt will be able to look forward to their future with confidence, but others will struggle to survive. Change presents challenges and in this respect the legal profession is no longer different to any other business sector. Some will cope better than others. There will be, and already are, winners and losers.

There is a considerable degree of unease within the profession with the amount of commercial risk that solicitors are now exposed to. Practice management is more time consuming and demanding than ever it used to be. At a time when fee earning has become more pressured there has therefore never been more to get in its way. Furthermore, our status as a profession seems to be under attack as never before. Small wonder that unease turns to resentment on the part of so many.

Professionalism is the key to understanding these changes. The fact that legal services are professional services sets the parameters for the way in which advisers deal with clients. Most writers describe professionalism as a series of characteristics of which self-regulation and a privileged market position are the most obvious elements. Most professions enjoy some degree of privilege, as through monopolistic protection of certain work areas. Self-regulation protects clients from abuse by both the members of the profession and the controlling body itself. This is necessary since one of the essential characteristics of a professional service is that the consumer is usually ill able to judge their needs. When the doctor or dentist recommends treatment the patient has to believe that the advice is primarily in their best interests and not the adviser's. So too with legal services: a firm's business plan may suggest that more medical negligence work should be sought, but if instructions show no cause of action the work will have to be turned away. Our most basic understanding of professionalism is that the client's interests are paramount even though the adviser has a business interest in the action that is taken.

The professions have always expected to be left to regulate their own activities in recognition of the responsibility which they show to clients. In his presidential address in 1993, Rodger Pannone made a call to all solicitors 'who wish to be part of a self-regulating profession'. Solicitors as professionals should be trusted to regulate themselves, whereas others may need to be subject to independent supervision. In recent years self-regulation has come under attack from an increasingly hostile political environment. The Access to Justice Act 1999 contains provisions for the Government to take complaints handling away from the profession should it ever wish to. A proposal during proceedings on the Bill to prevent the Law Society from using practising certificate income for 'trade union' activities seemed to be inspired by advertisements on legal aid which the Lord Chancellor had objected to. The move was described by one prominent City lawyer as 'a fit of pique' and it was difficult not to agree.

In the former scheme of things there was a basic distinction between business organisations and professional concerns. Our commercial clients might have had mission statements, business plans, cash-flow forecasts and the like, but we did not. Business pursued profits, but we were interested in higher values – in serving our clients and the interests of justice. Take, for example, this quote from *The Conveyancer* (1972):

> Law is not a business, nor merely is it a profession . . . but is one of the three learned professions . . . No profession worthy of its name has ever been impelled merely by monetary reward. It expects, and has a moral right, to be paid properly for its skills and services.[1]

Our traditional ideas of the role of lawyers in society depend on this bargain between the profession and the society that it serves. On the one hand the profession would provide the services needed to enable society to function and regulate itself, but in return individual practitioners should be entitled to social respect and a decent living. It is this bargain which seems to have broken down of late, largely because of changing social attitudes. We are now part of a society that is both less hierarchical and less deferential. We are more likely to complain and are less likely to show loyalty to those we have dealt with before. The consumer is now king and he or she will not adapt their attitudes simply because they happen to be dealing with solicitors.

This has produced a very different view of the role of the profession in society. Robert Sayer, president of the Law Society from 1999 to 2000, addressed a Solicitors Property Group conference in 1996 as follows:

> Unless things change radically, I don't think we will see High Street firms survive . . . We must stop dithering about what we are in business for . . . We are in business to make money and must recognise that it is a business.[2]

In the former scheme of things politicians acquiesced with the professions in their special place in society. The Thatcher era put an end to this cosy relationship even if her and most other governments were heavily populated by lawyers. Anti-competitive restrictions would not be tolerated, whatever their source, and lawyers started to see their privileges progressively withdrawn. The issue is not one of party politics. It may have been a Conservative administration that published a 'name and shame' list of the main firms claiming from the legal aid fund but it was a Labour Lord Chancellor who famously quipped that the success of his legal aid reforms could be judged by the 'squealing of lawyers', to the understandable fury of committed legal aid firms throughout the land.

Politicians have also changed conditions for lawyers through the continuing simplification of legal process. The Woolf reforms of the civil justice system are the best recent example of this trend, but it could be argued that the seeds of the problems for the high street firms were laid when the property legislation of 1925 created the concept of registered conveyancing. Simpler legal rules and procedures are bound to be seen as beneficial to society, but have a clear subsidiary aim of restricting the role of the legal adviser wherever possible. Never was this more apparent than the attempts of late to develop mediation in place of divorce.

'Thatcherism' was blamed by Martin Mears in his presidential address to the Law Society conference in 1995 for the transformation of the profession's place in society. Society's bargain with its professional advisers became 'conspiracies against the public interest'.

3

Speaking of the recent social trends that have so affected the practice of law he pointed out that opening out the professions to free competition may have negative consequences even if prices tend to fall:

> Only a few years ago, conveyancing fees were charged in accordance with fixed scales. It may well be that the fees charged then were too high. Now they are undoubtedly too low. In the short term, the consequence of this is the multitude of high street firms who can barely pay their way. In the longer term, it will mean that a number of them will be eliminated altogether and domestic conveyancing will be carried out by second rate corner cutters who will rely on the rest of the profession to bail them out (via the Solicitors Indemnity Fund) when their mistakes eventually emerge. Meanwhile, the all-round service provided by the traditional high street practice will have disappeared. Now, I ask how such a state of affairs can possibly be in the public interest.

The choice would therefore seem to be between professionalism, where society enables its advisers to pursue their calling cushioned from the discipline of running a profitable business, or commercialism, where the profit motive drives the business without restraint. There has been a blurring at the edges of both creeds. While the professions have been dragged into the world of commercialism, businesses have been forced to confront their social responsibility. The Cadbury Report on corporate governance urged better management of large companies as part of their responsibility to society. What was once famously referred to as 'the unacceptable face of capitalism' is less common today, with public companies at least. Viewed in this way the professions and business have both moved towards a common ground of what might be called responsible commercialism.

There remain differences of degree, mostly regulatory. The specific Law Society rules of professional conduct with their accompanying sanctions are likely to remain limitations on free commercialism for the foreseeable future. The Solicitors' Publicity Code may have removed in the early 1980s the former restriction on 'touting' (a fact which a surprisingly high minority of solicitors seem still not to realise) but there are still some fairly significant restrictions on the contents of advertisements and on identifying clients. As long as such rules remain the law cannot fairly be said to be simply a business like any other.

Supply and demand

From all these factors the larger picture of legal services over the last 20 years or so can be argued to be one of liberalisation of supply and demand. Traditionally, recruitment patterns into the profession encouraged greater protection for the status quo and slower growth. Some of the factors were social attitudes, though no doubt discrimination also played a part. The 1980s saw the introduction of compulsory salaries for articled clerks and very real increases in rates also, making recruitment more genuinely open to a wider class of entrant. When the recession of the late 1980s took hold, and hit the service sector in a way that previous recessions had not done, the profession was thrown for the first time into more ruthless competition between members for available work. The publicity rules may have been relaxed in the mid-1980s to permit advertising and more overt promotional tactics, but it was not until this recession that a marketing mindset was adopted by most. This has continued through the more benign economic conditions since: we may be busy enough today, but can we be sure that we will be in six months' time?

John Hayes was Secretary General of the Law Society from 1986 to 1995. When he left the position he delivered a lecture to the European Policy Forum entitled 'The Future of the Legal Profession'.[3] Attempts to introduce principles of quality management had frustrated him, specifically the difficulty of introducing a client care regime in relation to costs information, complaints systems and basic management standards. The costs of insurance would force these changes onto the unconverted, he predicted. Elementary suggestions for simple business plans would be regarded as an obvious requirement by most concerns, but were seen by many practitioners as intrusive and as unnecessary regulation. On legal aid Hayes saw as inevitable some reduction of the number of 'outlets' (no doubt a deliberately commercial term) which provide legal aid services but not, he hoped, to the detriment of reasonable availability of advice. Standard tariffs for work and client satisfaction checks were also regarded as likely developments which could not be altogether resisted.

In relation to multi-disciplinary practices, Hayes referred to his illustrious predecessor Sir Thomas Lund. That gentleman's far-sightedness can only now be judged. In April 1966 he predicted a shift to more commercial and less non-contentious work, increased specialisation, increasing difficulties for sole practice and increasing amounts of foreign work. It was, however, his views on the likelihood of multi-disciplinary partnerships (MDPs) that led him into difficulties with his Council and was seen as the immediate cause of his early retirement from the position.

Within the City and commercial sphere there are few more astute observers than Alan Hodgart, long-time specialist adviser to professional firms. A problem that he has commented on in relation to the future of commercial law goes to the root of whether legal services represent value for money for clients. The cost of legal advice does not sit easily with our cost-conscious times where earnings per share and costs in relation to turnover have become subject to ever closer review.

Writing in a practice management journal in March 1996 he saw the problems as being on both sides of the client transaction, building to a worrying downward cycle from the legal supplier's point of view.[4] Clients increasingly see the 'value added' from many services provided as being medium to low, he argued, so that clients were increasingly resistant to the fees requested. The response by firms is to increase value, which is difficult to do on a consistent basis, or reduce fees to win market share. The latter reduces profit unless volume can be increased and a more favourable gearing of staff to partners be achieved. Many feel that the costs base of commercial firms is too high for the service on offer. Other than a handful of exceptional advisers who can show increasing value for money year by year, the only viable strategy for remaining profitable is to reduce costs, consistent with ensuring the quality of work performed. Viewed in this way, management will remain challenging for many years to come.

Staffing implications

Traditionally solicitors enter private practice with an expectation of eventual partnership. Prospects of partnership could, of course, be stymied by dishonesty, incompetence or general ineptitude, but the normal expectation was of elevation to partner status somewhere, usually the firm where training had occurred.

Most forecasts see a dwindling number of persons as equity partners and a changing role for those who are. Continued profitability will require partners to confine themselves to the top level of work for their firm and to spend more time supervising the efforts of more staff. Unarguable though this trend may be, it is already proving problematic. At the most personal level many of the best lawyers are not motivated by supervising others. Good lawyers like fee earning and got to their position by doing it well. They are then told to put that to one side and become instead supervisors of others. Many struggle with the required transition.

Most of the profession seems to have more difficulty with staff retention now as opposed to recruitment. In larger firms in particular, partnership can seem to be an ever more distant carrot, with the result that increasing numbers of able solicitors are electing to work in-house or retrain to use their legal skills more widely. Successive reports have shown high levels of dissatisfaction amongst assistant solicitors generally, with one in three from the large firms planning a move to work in-house according to one survey. Interestingly, in this survey the work itself was seen as stimulating and rewarding, but the rewards insufficient to compensate for the hours to be worked and the resulting pressure on quality of life.

Calls for a more rational approach to partnership can be made by those who are not affected by it, or those who have achieved it already. So far as Hayes was concerned:

> the current obsession with reaching and retaining equity partnership status undermines the sensible use of resources and a more realistic order is now painfully needed.[5]

This may be right, but it is important to remember how unattractive this argument is likely to be to a young solicitor, recently admitted, who is ambitious for his or her future. There will be disillusionment for many on being told that they are unlikely to be made a partner even where there would have been little issue over it a few years beforehand. On another level we are likely to see the continued growth in the number of paralegals, in part as an attempt to manage more appropriate staff structures.

Commodification

There is one trend in legal work which seems to affect all sections of the profession in varying ways (see Figure 1.1). Alternatively described as the 'productisation' or the 'commodification' of law, it draws a distinction between traditional patterns of work and new efficiency-based systems which usually depend upon bulk services for profit contribution.

Under type A work the distinguishing element of the service is the expertise. The service works best, and stands to make the adviser concerned the greatest level of profit, where there is something distinct about the expertise: the fewer the alternative providers, the better the fee potential. Looked at another way, premium work will support premium rates. Since there is likely to be some novel element to such

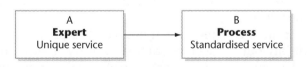

A	B
Expert	**Process**
Unique service	Standardised service

Figure 1.1   *The productisation of law*

work, the risk of error is higher and professional insurance has to be adequate to cover the risks that the firm is exposed to.

Type B work is a very different proposition. The service is likely to be a mature service now lacking its original 'cutting edge' characteristic. Competition is greater and there is little that is distinctive about the expertise on offer. Consequently the service takes on elements of a standard product and pricing becomes more sensitive. It is not so much that there is no expertise in this range of services, but that the expertise is no longer distinctive in the marketplace.

In recent years various firms have harnessed the business potential of bulk process work and have derived considerable benefits from it. It produces new challenges, however. Traditionally law firms were not capital intensive businesses to run. All that was needed was premises, stationery and communication equipment. The real assets of the firm were the brains and skills of the advisers and staff. Process work changes this picture, however, with substantial investment now becoming key to enabling firms to pitch competitively for such work.

There are those who take a pessimistic line on such developments. Many regret what they see as the 'dumbing down' of legal services and continue to seek to provide what they regard as a proper professional service notwithstanding changing client expectations. Domestic conveyancing forms a useful illustration of the case in point. A gulf has grown in many firms between the way that many partners wish to conduct conveyancing and the service that clients are willing to pay for. In many cases things have gone wrong already at the estate agents' office: 'Phone these solicitors and see who's the cheapest'. The client has been encouraged to see conveyancing as a standard off-the-shelf product, in which case the cheapest is likely to be the most attractive. Claims by the firm that things really are more complicated than that and need senior lawyer time and attention will often, though not always, fall on deaf ears. If fees cannot be brought back up to reasonable levels, the service has to change. The involvement of paralegals working under supervision and other changes to increase the return on each transaction may be unpopular, but have to be faced if the firm is to continue to be viable. The choices seem to be to productise to some degree, or make too little profit to continue.

It is not just the high street which has seen this phenomenon. The management buy-out – the clever new deal of the 1980s – has gone down a similar route. Once the domain of certain firms only, with able lawyers applying great skill to bring the deal to its conclusion, the buy-out is now standard fare for any self-respecting commercial department. There is still skill and expertise involved, of course, but this has become systematised so that any individual concerned will have more of a plan to follow. The result is a very different deal with clients. As one managing partner of a provincial commercial firm commented:

> We get the call and are asked who's available and how much. We have to work out a sensible and competitive deal fee and make sure we don't take a hit. We either do this or other firms get the work.

Any segment of the profession has to have different strategies for its work-type range. For those that are able to do so efforts should be made to seek out the new services and develop expertise before the competition in order to charge premium fees in the short to medium term. As the service becomes more mature, and competition grows, the appropriate management response is to systematise and stream-line. The search for the next new service continues meanwhile. The role of the lawyer also probably changes. In expert work the key skill is the expertise of the legal team, but in process work the key factor becomes supervision, systems design and experience. It is a role that many lawyers have little interest in. They enjoy being legal experts and probably prefer not to see themselves as process supervisors, prof-itable though it may be, though there are some notable exceptions.

Block contracting: productisation in practice

Quality as an issue for most high street firms has been largely insti-gated by the Legal Services Commission and its predecessor the Legal Aid Board. The exercise provides an insight into the factors behind the process of productisation and the necessary management res-ponses. Franchising was born from an efficiency review of 1986, resulting in the changes which created the Legal Aid Board (LAB). Concerns grew that value for money was not being achieved. By the early 1990s expenditure on the scheme had increased fivefold over a decade but the proportion of the public who were eligible had fallen. Franchising was seen as the means to get better value from suppliers; it has been little surprise that the option of franchising eventually became compulsory for all legal aid firms.

In 1998 the Lord Chancellor wrote to the LAB for their proposals on how the legal aid scheme could be cost-capped. The contracting regime was their response. The Access to Justice Act 1999 addresses the Government's priorities:

(a) national and local planning, largely through the Regional Legal Services Committees, to assess priorities;

(b) contracting: through the rigorous application of the quality standards and the application of management techniques it will be possible to move towards a regime of fixed prices for pre-ordained volumes of work;

(c) a funding code, to control inappropriate expenditure and impose the regime of payments.

Block contracting is at heart an attempt to manage both supply and demand. In relation to civil work, regional committees assess local needs so as to predict demand. Quite how accurate this macro-planning will be remains to be seen, but it is clear that the supply will be determined more by cost than demand.

This poses many of the management challenges to firms that this book examines. Firms that remain within the scheme will be confronted with an offer of a block of work at pre-agreed prices. They have to decide if it is in their interests to accept or reject it. That decision needs to be based on an analysis of how much the work has cost them to perform in the past which, in the absence of true time recording data, they will not have. They then have to be able to manage the work as a commodity, expecting quotas of it to be processed by their fee-earners. It is a regime that many resent, yet is not so different from the arrangements seen elsewhere in bulk personal injury referral work or debt recovery.

Adding to the difficulties of legal aid work will be a continuing squeeze on rates of pay. Rates on legal aid work declined in real terms throughout the 1990s. The Lord Chancellor announced that he was 'not minded' to increase rates in 1999 as there were still more than enough providers performing the work. The Government was clearly treating its legal aid firms as commercial providers to be driven down on price like any other contractor. Another statement that the best lawyers were not necessary for legal aid work did little to improve morale amongst providers. Many firms expected better from government and the resentment has grown.

The legal aid regime may provide the best example of one of the most significant truths facing any legal practice today. Simply being a busy lawyer is no longer any guarantee of business success. The law firm has to be run on increasingly commercial lines or the professional service which it provides to its clients will not be adequate to meet the needs and expectations of its participants. Society no longer owes its professionals a living.

Main points

- Society no longer affords to its professionals the privileges that it used to.
- The professional firm has to be managed with more commercialism than used to be the case.
- Many more legal services are now delivered in a processed fashion, requiring greater investment and different management skills and systems.

Notes

1 [1972] *The Conveyancer*, pp. 81–2. Quoted in Wilson, A. (1984) *Professional Development for Professional Firms*, McGraw-Hill.
2 [1996] *Gazette*, 13 September, p. 13.
3 Hayes, J., 'The Future of the Legal Profession', [1996] *Gazette*, 1 May, p. 22.
4 Hodgart, A. [1996] *Practice Management*, March, p. 10.
5 Hayes, *op. cit.*

The business of law

- Business structures
- Professional bodies
- The future

In 1987 I was taking part in a careers panel talk at Cambridge University. The panel consisted of representatives of a large City firm, large provincial firms, a local high street firm and the Legal Action Group. The comment was made (without condescension) by the City recruitment partner that it was difficult to believe that it was the same profession that was being described by the various speakers. The comment was true then and would probably be even more true today. Increasingly we see the polarisation of legal practice into various groups which, at their extremes, bear no discernible relationship to each other in their day-to-day activities. The tie, such as it is, is membership of the Law Society and being subject to its regime and the statutory provisions that relate to all solicitors. Calls to a united profession continue, but increasingly the reality is that the solicitors' profession is made up of a number of distinct business groups.

There is more diversification in legal practice than in other comparable professions. Accountants tend to provide much the same range of services for clients of a certain background, albeit at differing levels of sophistication. The doctor or dentist deals in much the same way with patients under their care. The problems treated may differ to a degree with social class and sources of funding but the process of diagnosis and treatment differs little. By contrast, the legal needs of a large institutional client are wholly dissimilar from the individual represented on legal aid in relation to a criminal charge or acts of domestic violence.

The category of firms most likely to have difficulty with this diversity of services and client groups is the high street firms. Many have agonised over their reception areas for some time. It was interesting to note that the *Guide to Client Care* issued to firms by the Office for the Supervision of Solicitors in 1997 included a recommendation of separate waiting rooms in appropriate cases. Partners are often uncomfortable about the messages that this may give, but it can be an expedient solution to a practical problem.

The 1999 annual statistical report from the Law Society revealed that:

(a) there were just over 100,000 solicitors on the roll;
(b) 37 per cent of all solicitors worked in London;
(c) there were 8,561 firms, of whom 3,641 were sole principals;
(d) the profession had a wider ethnic balance at the junior end;
(e) women accounted for the majority of solicitors under the age of 30;
(f) among solicitors 10 to 19 years admitted 87 per cent of men were partners as opposed to 63 per cent of women.

Within the high street, the story of the last 30 years has been the decline of income, however measured, from domestic conveyancing. Traditionally this was the 'cash cow' that funded other more speculative areas of practice, often litigation. This also meant that the geographical network of solicitors firms could be wider than it would otherwise have been. A special working party of the Law Society reported in 1994 that whereas in 1966 some 50 per cent of the income of the profession derived from domestic conveyancing, this had fallen to under 10 per cent by 1993. Over the same period numbers of solicitors with practising certificates in private practice rose from under 19,000 to just over 51,000. The most marked effect was not so much in the 1980s, when fees per transaction fell, since this was off-set by the tremendous growth in conveyancing activity, but as recession took hold at the end of that decade. Between 1986 and 1993 prices fell in real terms by 45 per cent, but much worse was that the volume of transactions halved between 1988 and 1992.

It need not be stated how dramatic this change has been. In para. 2.8 the Report observes:

> it is clear that some small firms with a high historic dependence on domestic conveyancing will have been unable to find other sources of income to compensate for the reduction in their income from conveyancing.

Nonetheless, numbers of solicitors in the high street have continued to rise and many do make a good living from their endeavours. What has compensated in the better, or the more fortunate, firms for the conveyancing shortfall? For most, the answer is litigation and divorce. Since the 1960s society has become more litigious and, of course, the Divorce Reform Act 1969 freed the process of dissolving marriages. The repeat divorce client may still be a rarity, but is no longer exceptional. Personal injury work has also snowballed, in part as a result of the ever-growing traffic which congests our streets and greater 'claims consciousness'. Meanwhile the politicians' attempts to reduce crime seem more soundbite than substance.

The future for any given firm seems largely to be dictated by which sector of the profession it comes from. Increasingly it is possible to predict the key strategic issues being faced by a firm from the profile of what sort of firm it is. Most firms should be able to identify with one or more of the following groupings.

Sole practitioners

Sole practitioners have been the endangered species of the profession for many years yet their numbers have remained mostly unchanged for the last decade. More than half of sole practitioners make no claims on indemnity insurers at all but some of the others give the group a bad name. Increasingly sole practitioners find themselves removed from lenders' panels and unable to perform enough work to be granted a franchise. There are nonetheless rewards and satisfaction in sole practice and it is likely to remain an option that many will pursue. It is the concept of the 'jack of all trades' general practitioner which becomes more difficult to support. The individual solicitor who provides a specialist service should be able to prosper and may even have advantages over many larger, more general firms. Certain practitioners work as much on referrals as their own client base. Such practitioners should be able to benefit from lower overheads and should therefore be able to offer a cost-effective and specialised service.

The high street firm

It is the high street firm, the backbone of the profession for so many years, which is likely to see the greatest upheaval in its professional practice profile over the next decade. The trend elsewhere on the high street is towards fewer, but more dominant, suppliers. Solicitors' firms are unlikely to escape the relentless drive towards lower costs and stronger brands. The closest precedent may be the opticians' profession. Just a few years ago opticians were independent professionals, often practising from unimpressive facilities above shops in the high street. Now we have three or four dominant national chains which advertise extensively on television to create in the public a sense of warmth, friendliness and expertise. Ease of joining into 'law retailing' chains may be the enduring legacy of certain national groupings of solicitors which concentrate on the small to medium firms around the country.

Commercial provincial firms

The growth and rise to national prominence of large provincial firms has been one of the success stories of the last 20 years. It has been fascinating to see how certain small traditional practices have metamorphosed, sometimes, into national firms. Even 10 years ago groups such as the M5 or the Legal Resources Group could function on the basis that there was minimal competition between large firms in different regions. A major issue will be relationships with accountants and towards multi-disciplinary partnerships (MDPs) generally, as this group provides a more general range of largely commercial services than the City firms and the overlap with other advisers is therefore greater.

Within this band there are increasingly two tiers of large firms, in the provinces in particular. Certain firms have built successful practices on a slightly lower tier of commercial work, but a substantial private client and litigation practice also. These firms stand to benefit from the increasing productisation of law. Many of these firms can best be described as 'multi-niche' practices, with involvement in a number of distinct areas of legal business.

General commercial firms in London

There is as much anxiety in this group as any other, feeling that they are squeezed at one end by the seemingly relentless growth of the larger City firms and by the wider territorial coverage of provincial firms at the other. Recent increases in salary rates for junior lawyers are a further pressure on such firms. There will no doubt be a need for many firms in this category in years to come, but almost certainly not the need for the current number. One observer, Henry King, formerly the Chairman of Denton Hall, commented in an interview for the Law Society's *Gazette* on his retirement in 1996 that there would be a reduction in the number of firms as has been the case in recent years with accountants.[1] Conflict issues with legal services will, however, mean that the group of 'megafirms' will need to be larger than the accountants. He is one of the many commentators to suggest that it will settle at about 10.

As with high street firms, the alternative business stance is to be 'niche' in terms of services provided or clients served. There are strong practices which are focused on information technology work,

15

entertainment clients, shipping work or other such areas and these will face the future with more confidence than most.

City and international firms

We have seen in recent years the growth of a privileged elite of firms that are generally dubbed the 'magic circle' firms whose levels of profit performance are outstanding by any measure. There are, of course, parallels with other large London firms and it was the drive to join this elite that King was describing in the article mentioned above. Increasingly, most of these firms are becoming international and will be at the vanguard of what is increasingly called 'post-nationalism' in business, where domestic origin becomes of secondary importance. Already we see competition between the London and US firms, in the City and New York and elsewhere around the globe. Mergers between firms from different jurisdictions are now clouding the original allegiances of certain major practices.

Business structures

An issue much discussed in recent years is whether the partnership structure remains appropriate for today's firms. Partnership was originally designed for essentially small concerns where the participators did not only know each other but owed each other a higher duty of good faith in their dealings with each other. This seems to have little relevance to international practices of many hundreds of partners. It is therefore mostly amongst the largest firms that incorporation, along with limitation of liability, is a concern.

Incorporation was in fact made permissible for solicitors in England and Wales by section 9 of the Administration of Justice Act 1985. Acting on the basis of that section the Law Society passed its Solicitors Incorporated Practice Rules 1988, since amended. From 1 January 1992 it has been possible for solicitors to practise through incorporated status as opposed to partnership or sole trader. The take-up of the possibility has been negligible. There are various reasons for this, of which the innate conservatism of the profession is no doubt one, but the precedent of surveyors and architects was for the most part not encouraging.

From its inception in the last century, incorporation has always been of most appeal to businesses for the protection of personal liability which is then possible. Why create a new legal person, distinct from its members? The Salomon principle enables the separate legal person to have its own separate debts – an attractive option for most of the business world. Rule 14 of the Solicitors' Incorporated Practice Rules effectively removes this benefit: the individual shareholders have to enter a compensation fund covenant which puts them in exactly the same position as they were when they were partners. Therefore, why bother?

One advantage of the incorporated firm is likely to be greater flexibility on staff management issues. Rule 7(1)(c) allows the partners to enter staff benefit arrangements as long as they are not an underhand means of avoiding normal profit-sharing rules. More firms now publish their accounts even though not required to do so while partnerships, but most do not and staff benefit schemes are less likely to work well in a climate of financial secrecy. The incorporated practice will almost certainly introduce more openness to the functioning of the largest concerns.

Staff promotion will also be likely to benefit from incorporation. The ambitious assistant solicitor will reach a stage in the conventional firm where promotion depends upon investment, not just in the format of taking a few shares, but becoming a genuine part owner of the business. Promotion without the degree of investment required by partnership could introduce more flexibility.

Under the incorporation model existing partners become shareholders. In the largest firms not all would become board members, but this would continue the management structures likely already to be in place in such firms. Partnership arrangements and relationships would be converted to a shareholders' agreement which would deal with the critical issues of profit-sharing, promotions and departures from the organisation.

Financially there could be benefits from incorporation since partnership is a good model for creating profits year to year, but usually discourages long term investment. On the other hand, problems of fair allocations of profits do not disappear in a corporate business but they usually become less problematic to administer. Problems of retirement probably would remain. If the company is quoted, and it must surely be a matter of time before that becomes the case with the largest professional service providers, there is a ready market for second-hand shares. In the private company (which is always likely to be the norm), however, valuation would still be difficult and there would need to be arbitration procedures in the shareholders' agreement.

The general view in recent times has been that incorporation with limited liability was only a matter of time, but this has not been without detractors. A further claimed advantage for incorporation is often stated to be better and more streamlined decision-making within the business. It was this argument in particular that inspired one of the most forceful papers of the anti-incorporation camp, an article 'Partnership: Dinosaur or Phoenix?' by David Temporal.[2] Differing from John Pritchard's view in *Legal Business* (December 1991) that 'partnership is a dinosaur whose day has been and gone' he argued that the anti-partnership line was misguided.[3] Poor decision-making had not so much resulted from the organisational framework that firms find themselves in, but the drastic increases in competition and the more unfavourable trading conditions at that time.

Limitation of liability

There has always been a belief that a professional person should pay their debts and should not hide from personal liability through the vehicle of incorporation: thus the argument that limitation of liability is unprofessional and therefore inappropriate to firms of lawyers. As Michael Matthews pointed out in an article in the Law Society's *Gazette*, however, this might have been all well and good in the past when claims were few and far between and the services themselves were simpler, but it has become unrealistic in modern commercial conditions.[4]

The issue of business structures and limitation of liability will change with the implementation of the Limited Liability Partnership Act 2000. In the normal partnership all partners have joint and several liability for the full debts of the practice, whereas in the limited liability partnership (LLP) the contribution of the individual member will be limited to his or her share of the assets unless there is a specific agreement to the contrary or a claim for wrongful trading or preference. Provisions for the clawback of profit for the two years leading up to an insolvency have been restricted during the passage of the Bill and will not now be relevant if the partner reasonably believed at the time that the firm would be able to trade its way out of difficulty.

In relation to outgoing partners the main effect will be to offer the possibility of relieving any individual partner from liability without limit. The duration of risk in the normal partnership could be anything up to 15 years in relation to latent damage claims. Retirement does not affect this situation. The change is proving highly topical with the abandonment of the Solicitors' Indemnity Fund (SIF) 'run-off' cover in 2000, notwithstanding the fact that the usual indemnities of continuing partners would suffice in most cases. Within an LLP a member can only be held liable for acts of negligence for which he or she has assumed sufficient liability. A further factor to take into account is that, since the demise of SIF, any indemnity insurance arrangements are only as good as the cover of that insurer; there are no back-up provisions for the situation where an insurer defaults on cover as through its insolvency.

An LLP is created by a process of registration with the Companies Registrar which will identify the 'designated members', of which there will need to be at least two at all times. There is no need for anything which is equivalent to the memorandum and articles for companies and in this regard the LLP seems, not surprisingly, to be a hybrid of registered company and traditional partnership.

In relation to taxation the stated aim was to make the transition to LLP tax neutral, with the result that the charge remains on a personal tax basis as opposed to any variation of corporation tax. The accounting requirements are more in line with company provisions, however. In return for protection from liability the accounts will become publicly filed documents, but the division of profits between members will not need to be disclosed. Simon Young has commented on the reluctance that many partners may feel in relation to making their performance public:

> Anyone concerned should simply ask themselves would they rather keep their secrecy or keep their income.

It will be interesting to see how many firms pursue the option of limited liability and the profiles of those that do so. Recent changes to the indemnity insurance market may well make it a more attractive option than might otherwise have been the case.

A related issue which is bound to need radical review at some stage is the concept of a profession that cares for its own defaulters through a compensation fund. In more favourable times when all solicitors, more or less, prospered, the profession was smaller and less competitive, the whole concept of mutual indemnity made sense. Now increasing numbers of solicitors are asking why they should pay for the errors or misjudgements of those who are, in some cases, little more than their business rivals.

Multi-disciplinary partnerships

The prospect of sharing profits, or losses for that matter, with individuals from outside the profession ceased to be an issue for most other professions some time ago. Chartered accountants have been permitted to enter partnership with others for over 20 years and surveyors have followed suit, as have chartered patent agents. Doctors and solicitors remain the special case – barristers, with their insistence on sole practice, even more so.

Reform here is likely to be driven by a political perspective. The case for reform was put by Paul Boateng while legal affairs spokesperson in opposition:

> We look forward to working in partnership with the Law Society and the Bar Council to eradicate restrictive practices. We are, however, committed to reform and will not hesitate to legislate should this prove necessary.[5]

The reason for this interest in reform is again the view that consumers are better served by the breaking down of privilege and the freeing of every market rather than the protection which can otherwise be afforded. As Boateng continued:

> Structural reform of the legal profession, the judiciary and the legal aid scheme is part and parcel of Labour's policies to cut costs, improve access to justice and demystify law.

A Law Society poll of solicitors' attitudes to MDPs showed greater acquiescence than many at the time predicted. Of the 675 solicitors contacted a majority (just) of 51 per cent thought that the Law Society should support such a change. Larger firms were more likely to think that they would change into MDPs, though only 14 per cent of the 72 per cent of respondents who thought that there would be major changes in the organisation of private practice in the next five years anticipated MDPs.

The traditional argument against MDPs is that separate representation ensures greater integrity and specialisation of service, but this seems to be a factor which is more important to advisers than clients.

A fused profession

The issue of fusion surfaces from time to time, evokes some fairly strong defences of the current division within the profession, and then retreats until the next outburst. As president of the Law Society, Robert Sayer produced just such a reaction when he called for 'one code of conduct and one regulator for one profession' at the 1999 Law Society Festival and then in the Law Society's *Gazette*.[6] It was not a move calculated to endear him to the Bar Council who responded in predictably terse terms.

There may be too many vested interests in a major decision to fuse the profession. What seems more likely is creeping fusion by degrees. As long ago as the 1970s a Commission recommended the scrapping of separate training programmes for barristers and solicitors. The need for common training increases all the time. The Access to Justice Act

1999 provides that all solicitors and barristers should gain rights of access to all courts on admission. The *Financial Times*, not usually one for hyperbole, reported the story as the 'final nail' in 'the coffin of an independent Bar'. Whether it will be in the interests of most solicitors, with their higher overheads, to conduct as much advocacy as is sometimes thought is a moot point, but clearly the relationship of the two wings of the profession continues to develop. The Bar's reaction to increasing solicitor advocacy is 'Bar Direct', an initiative whereby major clients may by-pass instructing solicitors and so end what the government would no doubt see as a restrictive practice ensuring little more than two sets of fees for professionals.

There are certainly very real concerns for the future by many at the Bar, but these are not just inspired by the encroachment of solicitors on advocacy. Of greater concern to many are the changes to the litigation system which seem to encourage dispute resolution in place of traditional litigation, for which the Bar is almost certainly better suited. The Bar stands to suffer from the Woolf reforms of the litigation process through its streamlining of pre-trial work and limitation of trial lengths. Legal aid reforms also give very real cause for concern. The 'writing on the wall' seems to be for less litigation at lower fee rates.

With the commercial Bar the concern is different. The top solicitors' firms continue to refine teamworking systems and strength in depth, but the structure of chambers remains doggedly independent. There may be fellow counsel sharing chambers, but it is expenses that they share and not income. One of the most cherished regulations of the Bar prohibits the sharing of income by way of partnership, a rule inspired by the need to retain only the best practitioners. Those who cannot find their way to sufficient work should not be supported by partnership arrangements, it is argued. The consequence can easily be gifted individuals who do not have the collaborative arrangements needed to provide truly cutting edge services.

Ultimately the Bar can only survive if it can continue to attract more than its fair share of the best brains entering the profession and can then continue to support them. The salaries now on offer to trainees and junior staff in the largest firms will be an attraction that many such people cannot afford to ignore. This may mean that appointments to the judiciary at the senior end become more heavily drawn from the solicitors' profession, in which case the barrister route to seniority may seem increasingly unattractive.

Meanwhile the activities of some of the top sets in the country seem increasingly like solicitors' firms. In many chambers the pressing issue is 'corporatism', the extent to which chambers as an entity can instruct the members on how they conduct their practice. This has reached such dimensions in certain sets that calls for partnerships are increasing.

The picture seems to be one where all lawyers will soon have advocacy rights and the Bar will share rights of direct access with solicitors' firms. Barristers will be allowed to share profits as well as expenses. All will have the right to choose whether they accept instructions from other lawyers or only act directly for clients and the judiciary will be peopled by member of both sides of the profession. At that stage separate training regimes will seem odd and the division of two controlling bodies will be unsupportable. It may well be, however, that the position settles soon afterwards into something remarkably like the previous status quo. In the much smaller profession of New Zealand all solicitors and barristers acquire dual qualification, the net effect of which is that there are still solicitors' firms functioning as such and there are specialist advocates who limit the client facilities that they offer, but there is more flexibility in who does what and how careers in the law may develop.

Professional bodies

If professional firms diverge into different sectors the job of regulating them also becomes more complicated. The Law Society of New South Wales, for example, argued in 1996 that solicitors in any permitted MDP should have overall control of it, while non-legal partners should be registered with a local law society. As reported in the *Gazette* in August 2000,[7] the Canadian Bar Association voted for much the same position: in late 2000 similar proposals were put to the Council of the Law Society of England and Wales.[8] Opposition remains, however, as evidenced by a joint letter from the presidents of the Law Societies of Scotland and Northern Ireland in the *Gazette* reminding all that there is a wider dimension to the issue within the British Isles as a whole.[9]

A further complication is that different member groups may have conflicting interests. The issue of bulk conveyancing provides a good example. Certain larger firms operate bulk conveyancing services in conjunction with major finance companies, inevitably at the direct cost of many smaller high street firms. If competition becomes institutionalised by practice type and size the implications of the controlling body are uncomfortable, to say the least. Evidence of the difficulties of the Law Society emerged in a report in 1996 which analysed opinion of the Law Society by its members. Respondents were asked to express the extent of their agreement or disagreement to the following statements:

(a) The Law Society is a friendly and helpful organisation.
(b) The Law Society does a good job of promoting the profession to the public at large.
(c) The Law Society does a good job of representing the views of the profession to decision makers and Parliament.
(d) The Law Society pays too little attention to the views and problems of the membership.

The only issue on which most respondents agreed was the final one. In other words, the Law Society was seen to be unfriendly and unhelpful, poor at promoting the profession and representing the views of the profession and insufficiently attentive to the views of its members.

A preliminary question from this report, however, perhaps revealed how impossible is the task facing the Law Society. Asked what was the main purpose and the single most important purpose of the Law Society 43 per cent of respondents thought that regulation was the most important function, while 33 per cent considered the main purpose to be providing a collective voice to decision makers. Both elements of these dual responsibilities apply in very different ways to the different sections of the profession identified above. Regulating the activities of what have become international businesses is a task that is made all the more difficult when the competition for those firms may be from another jurisdiction. The difficulties of national organisations regulating international concerns was one of the major comments to emerge in the report that followed the collapse of Barings Bank from its disastrous, and unauthorised, dealings in Singapore. Likewise, if we are to see the advent of genuine MDPs the issue of supervision is one that will need to be resolved, or the risk will be that firms will choose simply what they perceive to be the most benign, or perhaps even the cheapest, regime.

The difficulties of advocating the interests of the profession are even greater, an issue on which 66 per cent of respondents did not agree that the Law Society was doing a good job. To represent a membership group effectively there is a need for a commonality of interest or activity, and this could not be said to be the case with the profession as it now is. Suppose the profession were to determine that a mass advertising campaign should be instituted, as has been suggested from time to time. The immediate problem is what to portray. Should the making of wills, domestic conveyancing and private client litigation be chosen? These may be mainstream for high street firms, but are irrelevant to the activities of those firms that would proportionately pay the most, the large City practices.

How then should the Law Society of England and Wales meet this impossible task? The suggestion several years ago which featured in a presidential contest, that the two tasks should be separated, would simply have shifted the problem rather than address it. A more radical solution would be to split away the representational function into several interest groups to which firms would be required to subscribe. A group such as the Legal Aid Practitioners Group could no doubt represent the interests of its members better if granted real funding and more formalised status, for example. City firms may already have the necessary institution in their own livery company, but other organisations might need to be established for high street firms and larger non-City practices. Such a development would leave a slimmed down Law Society free to concentrate on its core regulatory role.

The future

Given all these factors, what will be the shape of the successful law firm of tomorrow? It is helpful to examine this in relation to each segment of the profession, but the one principal business response which runs as a thread between all groups is that of market positioning. The successful firm, be it the large international finance practice or the high street practitioner, will be clearly focused on its clients and their needs and will have resourced its practice to make the most of the opportunities on offer. Too many firms at present lack this sort of focus. The partners will 'turn their hand' to whatever comes through the door: it might be sensible to drop one work category in favour of specialising in another, but that might involve upsetting a partner or staff member, so the decision is fudged. A successful approach to market positioning involves:

(1) clear analysis of the environment in which that firm practises;
(2) sound decisions on how best to survive and prosper in that market;
(3) a determination to pursue that course putting the needs of the business above the reservations of individuals; and therefore
(4) qualities of flexibility and adaptability by those concerned.

Another major consideration will be to maintain and enhance the motivation of partners. Gauging the priorities of the firm's key personnel to the following choices may assist with some of the structural changes that now present themselves as options.

24

Main points

- The solicitors' profession consists of very different types of practices which can be grouped according to the services provided and the clients served.
- Regulating the profession and representing its interests becomes ever more complex.
- We are likely to see further fundamental changes to business structures in the next few years.

Notes

1 [1996] *Gazette*, 27 November, p. 14.
2 Temporal, D. (1993) 'Partnership: Dinosaur or Phoenix?', *International Law Firm Management*, December 1993/January 1994, p. 12.
3 Pritchard, J. (1991) 'Legal Business', *Legalease*.
4 [1996] *Gazette*, 13 November, p. 18.
5 [1995] *Gazette*, 28 June.
6 [1999] *Gazette*, 17 November, p. 16.
7 [2000] *Gazette*, 31 August, p. 5.
8 [2000] *Gazette*, 9 November, p. 4.
9 [2000] *Gazette*, 17 August, p. 19.

Concepts of quality

- The management responses
- Quality assurance
- ISO 9000
- The development of legal schemes
- Investors in People
- Quality in Law

There can be little argument that quality management has been one of the principal practice management issues of recent years. Many firms will feel that they have little choice in their involvement in one or other of the systems. Legal aid firms have had to gain a franchise from the Legal Services Commission to continue to perform publicly funded work, while many insurance companies have imposed an obligation on their legal suppliers to have a quality policy in place. Others have seen in quality improvement programmes the opportunity to address management issues which needed attention in any event. Quite what is meant by 'quality' remains puzzling for many solicitors, however, and many feel that the main programmes have little to offer their particular practice. Without an understanding of the business view of what quality means a coherent policy will be difficult to agree upon.

To most professionals, 'quality' is an issue of expertise. A 'quality job' implies that the technical content of the work has been to the highest standards possible. By contrast the business world tends to concentrate more on delivery than content. Being right on the law is the very least that a client should be entitled to expect. What will distinguish the excellent firm from the average is how well it tailors its advice to the particular requirements of the client. This is not to demean the importance of expertise, but the context of that expertise is where firms are more likely to be able to 'add value' and provide a service which is clearly superior to its competitors. Given research which suggests that clients tend to presume quality of content, it is the quality of service delivery which offers true differentiation.

There are therefore two distinct elements to quality, both of which will have to be addressed:

(a) advice which is technically competent and effective;

(b) delivery in a mode that is appropriate to the client.

This formula can have some rather curious implications. The concern of many legal aid lawyers is that with continued cutbacks in real terms to legal aid rates they can no longer perform a 'quality' service for their clients. The challenge is to limit the service level to appropriate proportions. If a firm is allowed three hours in most cases for a standard legal aid divorce, for example, how can it so standardise its systems and procedures to enable the client to receive appropriate professional advice while at the same time making a profit on the work? The firm that chooses to lavish more time on the client than it will eventually be paid for is not providing a 'quality' service in business terms.

In another case a City firm was instructed on a potentially difficult employment problem. The board members wanted to know what would be involved in removing a senior manager with a long service record with the company. They stressed that they wanted outline advice and a general impression of the likely issues. The employment department set to work and, finding the issue to be more complex than it first seemed to be, worked in more detail on it. The result was an impressive letter of advice which could not be criticised for its technical content, but a bill for several thousands of pounds more than the client had envisaged. As a matter of business, quality had not been achieved.

The more prestigious commercial practices seem to have the greatest difficulty in understanding how quality could relate to them. In an unguarded moment a partner from one of the top 10 City firms discounted any interest in quality assurance as it would risk 'lowering themselves to small firms' standards'.[1] In the same paper as this quotation the managing partner of American firm Thompson Hine and Flory expressed concerns that 'the requirements of certification would restrict the individual nature of the practice of law'. Outstanding lawyers, he thought, 'could not be expected to conform to rules required by certification'. This is in contrast to the experience in Australia where the quality movement has mostly been driven by the largest and most prestigious firms, Clayton Utz being one of the first to gain certification to the ISO 9000 standard.

Quality for lawyers is probably best seen as a balancing act between the technical needs of the situation and the client's preferences on service delivery. There will be many situations where the two cannot be reconciled. The work can only be done within the constraints imposed by putting at risk the effectiveness of the advice provided, in which case the work should be turned away. On the other hand there may be situations where the service expectations are excessive for the problem in hand, as with the client of one West Country firm who insisted on a conference with a top QC on a mundane neighbour dispute. The fee of many several thousands of pounds for the meeting was worth it to the client and so was quality in his eyes, but on any objective assessment would have been judged excessive.

Business therefore teaches us to look more to our clients when we examine 'quality' rather than the advisers. In his book *Quality is Free*, Philip Crosby examines the management misunderstandings of quality, of which the most persistent is the idea that quality implies goodness – the idea, for example, that a quality car has to be more of a Rolls Royce than an economy model.[2] A common example is to ask what 'quality' glass is. Thick glass that does not break easily is perhaps the most obvious response, but what if the glass is required for stunts on a film set? In such situations 'quality glass' would be the thinnest product possible. The key is to see quality as an issue for customers or clients more than for providers. A quality law firm will have the flexibility to adapt its services for the preferences of its clients. Thus the formal definitions are either based on the idea of conformance to specifications or on consumer expectations. In the view of the International Standards Organisation, quality is: 'the totality of features and characteristics of a product or service that bear on its ability to satisfy stated or implied needs'.[3] Likewise, according to Juran: 'fitness for purpose or use'.[4]

The quality system that any firm needs to have in place should therefore ensure that:

(1) in all instructions there is clear focus on what the client wishes to achieve and how much they are willing to pay for it;
(2) the firm is properly focused throughout the matter on delivering what the client wants and expects in a manner that is satisfactory to them;
(3) the strategy being pursued by the firm on the client's behalf is viable, both technically and as a matter of business;
(4) there is clear continuing communication throughout the retainer to ensure that firm and client remain agreed on the steps being taken and their implication for the outcome and the expenditure that will eventually be involved;
(5) the client achieves their objectives at the end of the matter.

The management responses

Management consultancy has often been dogged by its perceived 'faddism'. No sooner have organisations bought into one concept than it is declared out of date and replaced by another, therefore requiring more consultancy services to address the new needs now in vogue. A few years ago, all business was 're-engineering', a process that many leading advisers described as a 'must'. It is seldom heard of now. In its place came 'outsourcing' and 'change management', with 'empowerment' an additional choice or a means of achieving either of these.

Professor Tony Eccles of Cranfield School of Management wrote in 1996 that there had been only two true management concepts to have emerged in recent times: total quality management (TQM) and the considerable improvements in information systems which can make services more reliable and specific.[5] TQM is a creed that looks to improve the competitive performance of any business. It originated in Japan over 50 years ago as the country sought to rebuild itself after the devastation of the Second World War. The Americans co-operated and provided know-how as part of their aid package. This included the services of W. Edwards Deming, a doctor of mathematical physics, who is still generally regarded as the dominant authority on the subject.[6] Deming was born in 1900 and died in 1993. Right up until the time of his death he was still conducting week long master classes on the quality techniques he refined first in Japan and then in the USA. In the pre-war years he worked in US Government service and was largely responsible for statistical sampling initiatives, particularly with the Department of Census. Rigorous application of scientific measurement techniques were to be a hallmark of the Deming message throughout his long and illustrious career. In Japan he worked at first with the Japanese Census, but then became involved with the Union of Japanese Scientists and Engineers and thus entered the business world.

Although he collected quality awards throughout his career, it was not until the 1980s that Deming became better known in his native country. By then American business was suffering at the hand of the Japanese industries that he had helped to shape. The uncomfortable truth was dawning that Japanese products were better and that encouragement to consumers to buy American would not work where these goods were seen as being second best.

Deming teaches us that whilst management has the wherewithal to improve quality, only by being ruthlessly determined to do so will improvements happen. He distinguishes between 'common cause' and 'special cause': the constant aspects of a process and special causes of variation, such as those related to change of operators, for example. If the objective is to improve consistency it has to be understood that management have control over both types of causes and must deal with each in different ways.

It is all too easy to discount the successes of Deming and others on grounds that they were merely concerned with manufacturing and that there is little in common with the professional office. Differences of application there may be, but basic patterns continue nonetheless. Every law firm will have a basic discipline to its work: common cause in Deming's terms. Then there are the myriad variations of department to department, fee-earner to fee-earner: the special causes. Harnessing the creativity of advisers while maintaining sufficient discipline is a useful insight into the job of managing partner or head of department.

Most of Deming's creed was condensed into 14 main points for organisations to consider and apply.

(1) Create constancy of purpose to improve what you do as an organisation.
(2) Management has to take the lead by learning, adapting and leading.
(3) Cease dependence on inspection to achieve quality.
(4) Do not award business on price, move to single suppliers.
(5) Always look to improve the systems of production.
(6) Make training job-based.
(7) Institute real leadership to inspire people to do better.
(8) Drive out fear so that all may work more effectively.
(9) Break down barriers between departments.
(10) Eliminate slogans and numerical targets.
(11) Put leadership in place of quota and management objectives.
(12) Remove barriers that prevent people from taking pride in their jobs.
(13) Institute a vigorous self-improvement programme.
(14) Get everyone involved in the transformation of the firm.

Deming also identified what he dubbed the 'seven deadly diseases' of businesses waiting to undergo the quality transformation. Later in his life he described his 'system of profound knowledge' as having four interrelated components:

(a) appreciation of system and the need for process;
(b) the need for statistical theory in shaping business improvements;

(c) theory of knowledge: pragmatism in shaping improvements;

(d) knowledge of psychology and how to inspire people to perform.

Total quality management can be summarised as an obsession to improve wherever possible and continual measurement of that progress. Others took the creed further. Two contemporaries of Deming who shared his work in Japan were Joseph Juran and Armand Feigenbaum. Juran was an engineer by background whose main message was that quality would not happen unless it was planned.[7] The planning needed in companies was:

- identification of customers and their needs;
- establishing the best levels of quality goals;
- creating measurements for quality;
- planning processes capable of delivering what is required;
- producing continual improvements and reducing errors wherever possible.

Feigenbaum is associated more with quality control, as in his seminal work *Quality Control: Principles, Practices and Administration*.[8] One of his notable contributions is to stress the importance of human relations in quality. He also analysed the various 'quality costs' which would affect business performance, concentrating mainly on internal failure costs through work not being done correctly and external failure costs with complaints and warranty claims.

Other Japanese authorities also developed the philosophy of quality initiated by the early American authorities. Ishikawa[9] is associated with the development of statistical techniques while Taguchi[10] developed concepts of the routine optimisation of product and process as opposed to quality through inspection. Shigeo Shingo[11] developed the idea of manufacturing without errors so that the organisation could become 'defects free', a concept later popularised by the more flamboyant Philip Crosby whose book *Quality is Free*[12] was published in 1979 and was based on the slogans of 'right first time' and 'zero defects'. Tom Peters[13] tells us to strive for the 'wow' factor, but these later authorities have perhaps done little more than popularise a philosophy that was in place some time beforehand. Although there are some minor differences the thinking of all the so called 'quality gurus' can be summarised as follows.

- Management commitment and employee awareness are essential.
- Facts and figures are needed: planning and data collection are essential for the process of improvement to be managed.
- Teamwork will be needed to improve communication, customer

focus and problem-solving: management alone cannot effect the improvements which will be needed.

- There needs to be attention to process and to the tools for improvement.
- Organisations should seek to move from inspection for errors to their prevention. This is often achieved by seeing colleagues as internal customers and suppliers.

Quality assurance

Quality assurance developed from the total quality management school but concentrates more narrowly on process. Although it is often portrayed as an alternative philosophy to quality management it is best seen as an integral part of it and, as such, a necessary component of the management systems that will need to be in place. Unfortunately various advisers have taken entrenched positions for or against different components of quality management, of which quality assurance is one. The truth is that all elements of quality are interdependent. People need systems but systems need people.

ISO 9000 is the most generally accepted form of quality assurance and is the most direct origin for quality management schemes in legal practice. The concept of quality assurance originated in the Second World War with the manufacture of munitions – clearly bombs cannot be tested in the way that other products might be. The idea grew that it would be necessary instead to define the exact steps that had to be followed for a reliable product to be made. By following these instructions the products would be more reliable and testing would become less important.

Quality assurance was a major element of the American space programme in the 1960s. With many thousands of components in the space rockets there had to be confidence that all would function as they should. In the 1970s the principles of quality assurance were consolidated into an internationally accepted standard resulting in the publication of ISO 9000 in 1979. Since then over 100,000 organisations have registered under the standard throughout the world. In many industries certification is essential, though there has been a reaction against this type of pressure in recent times and it is uncommon within the professions. Many outstanding companies, whilst insisting on ISO registration at least in their suppliers of parts, will not extend these same requirements to professional advisers.

The adaptation of the original manufacturing wording of the standard to professional firms is a more recent departure. Reading through the original wording of the standard is not easy, but fortunately there are adaptations to make the code more relevant to law firms. All organisations have a core process which will follow much the same sequence irrespective of the precise nature of the service or product in question. Regardless of the nature of the business – be it widget manufacturer, glazing installation or solicitors' firm – there will be a beginning, middle and an end to that organisation's 'process'. At the outset instructions are received, the firm ensures that it is able to do the work and it confirms its understanding of the instructions. The work is then carried out and eventually it should culminate in a clear and tidy manner. If these stages can be successfully predicted and planned, instances of failure should be minimised. The major contributions of quality assurance therefore should be:

- improved consistency of client service;
- reduced internal waste: time and effort working ineffectively or 're-inventing the wheel';
- making management more effective, and therefore
- making the firm more profitable.

ISO 9000 plays an important part in ensuring that effective levels of client care are provided throughout the firm. Since, as Deming put it, 'the customer is the most important point of the production line', positive client reaction to the services provided should always be one of the premier goals of any quality programme.

ISO 9000 developed at a time when many organisations would spend considerable time and resources performing their own checks on their suppliers. This type of 'second party audit' continues in the law through the auditing of the Legal Services Commission with legal aid firms. The Commission's decision was not to accept the 'third party audits' of accreditation bodies but to perform their own checks instead. There has developed over the last 20 years an extensive worldwide industry of quality auditing. Registration to ISO 9000 is evidence for all that the organisation has quality systems and procedures in place which meet the requirements of the standard.

The process of securing certification is threefold. First it is necessary to decide what the firm does and this should then be recorded. At this stage it is also important to agree how best to organise the work of the departments, avoiding the risk of forcing onto the firm methods of working which might be deemed unsuitable. Having agreed appropriate procedures the second stage is to ensure that they are implemented and followed with a high degree of consistency. After the commencement date, observing the procedures will be compulsory.

33

Finally, at some later stage the firm will undergo assessment. The external auditors check to see if the firm has adequate procedures in place and, if so, whether they are being followed consistently, where-upon certification will be awarded. The obvious benefits are external – the client statement that the firm has achieved a particular recog-nised standard – but if the process is to have true value the benefits should be seen as being much more internal. The firm that improves its quality procedures becomes a better and more efficient organisa-tion. Those law firms that have been too focused on the external benefits are generally those that have experienced difficulties with their programme and have eventually failed. In order to succeed there has to be genuine commitment to push through changes which not all will like. As Jane Fonda more prosaically put it 'no pain, no gain'.

ISO 9000

The original ISO 9000 (formerly BS 5750) remains one of the prime quality schemes for lawyers. When Pannone Blackburn of Manchester acquired certification in 1991 they became the first law firm in the world to gain the award. They have since been followed by a few hundred firms in this country and others throughout a number of commonwealth jurisdictions. New Zealand, for instance, has over 30 firms which are registered to the standard and Australia a similar number. The limitations within the standard itself meant that ISO 9000 was always likely to be a starting point, however, and at best a useful component of a more general approach to quality principles in the legal environment.

The limitations of ISO 9000 are that it was based on manufacturing and was more concerned with quality assurance than quality man-agement. There have been various edits of the main international text of ISO 9000 to make it more 'lawyer-friendly' both in the United Kingdom and elsewhere. Unfortunately the quality of advice on ISO 9000 in the earliest years was often poor, with firms forced into changes to suit the quality professionals rather than the other way around. One firm recounted the advice that if an error occurred on a litigation file it should be placed in the bin as 'scrap' – an endearing idea but one which showed the radical gulf between industry and service-based professionals. The contents of the standard could be made relevant to law firms, however, and there was therefore great value in the joint code of the British Standards Institution and the Law Society which first appeared in 1996.

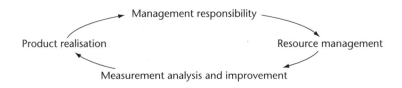

Management responsibility

Product realisation

Resource management

Measurement analysis and improvement

Figure 3.1   *ISO 9000*

A new version of ISO 9000 has recently taken effect, meeting many of the criticisms of the former version. Whereas the former version consisted of a series of 20 apparently random requirements, the new standard is organised into four areas: see Figure 3.1.

A good deal of thought has been given as to which part of the standard law firms should be registered to. ISO 9001 was the fullest version of the standard whist 9002 excluded the element of design. As there was no clear agreement different firms were registered to both, but the standard is now limited to 9001 with 'permissible exclusions' in relation to certain parts of it. Most of the requirements of process will still be found in the new version but there is also more leeway now in the application of the whole of the standard. The standard therefore manages to retain a high process approach to quality management but is now more general in the role of processes to overall business success. The previous standard was felt to be more in line with large organisations and not to reflect the greater informality of smaller firms. The terminology is also less manufacturing based and the new emphasis on measurement brings the standard more into line with a TQM approach.

The development of legal schemes

The major limitation for law firms under both the previous ISO 9000 and the new version is the partial nature of what needs to be in place. Core management processes such as finance controls, business planning, marketing and most of the areas of personnel management are not addressed in the standard. When the Legal Aid Board, as they then were, started their project to improve the cost effectiveness of legal aid provision they looked first to ISO 9000. Would simply requiring firms to have this in place meet their objectives? The possibility was discounted at an early stage because of the gaps that would have been left. The Franchising Specification therefore took shape to set out provisions on all the aspects that were important to the Board. This process occurred in tandem with the Law Society who hoped for many years that they would be able to convince the Board to accept their scheme through the Practice Management Standards. Eventually the Board did develop its own auditing service but the legacy was in part the development of the Practice Management Standards which have since been revised and which now form the basis of the Lexcel certification scheme. The Franchising Specification has also continued to develop, receiving a major overhaul in late 1998 with the publication of the Legal Aid Franchising Quality Assurance Standard (LAFQAS) which now forms part of the Community Legal Service Quality Mark (CLSQM). There are now plans by the Legal Services Commission (the successor to the Legal Aid Board) to widen the scheme and offer it to non-public funding areas of work. Clearly there are many areas still to develop.

The parentage of ISO 9000 can be found very clearly in the Practice Management Standards and CLSQM. The sections on case and file management show a very clear debt to the original standard with all the major provisions finding their origin within ISO 9000.

The Lexcel scheme came into being in mid-1998. It was to be based on the Practice Management Standards which had been approved in 1991. It has the advantage of being the only standard which is designed specifically for law firms and legal organisations and is capable of being applied to the whole operation. It selects the areas of management that are known from research and experience to have the greatest potential to improve performance. The task of assessing firms and organisations to the standard is undertaken for the Law Society by representatives of various approved certification bodies all of whom have to be trained in the scheme. Most organisations registered to date have undertaken Lexcel in conjunction with at least one other standard but it is likely that we will see the development of the scheme as more of a stand-alone standard. The great advantage of the scheme is that it has been designed purely for legal practice and is therefore a particularly attractive option for legal departments in organisations committed to quality management standards.

Investors in People

The Investors in People (IIP) award emerged from a Government White Paper of 1988 *Employment in the Nineties*. Research had suggested that the performance of the United Kingdom was falling behind other European states through a failure of employee development and participation. A new national management standard was proposed by which organisations could measure themselves in relation to training and developing people and the achievement of business goals. Industry seemed quicker to invest in plant and machinery than people. New technology would be an investment but spending on training was seen as a cost. Developments in the economy meant that a higher skills base was needed; unless management attitudes and practice improved, further decline seemed likely.

The same initiative created the network of training and enterprise councils who subsequently did so much to develop and sell the IIP award to the business community. IIP was always seen as being distinct from ISO 9000 and its approach. IIP would not be systems based and would look more to the culture of an organisation and whether systems truly worked. There was never the emphasis on a manual and compliance with it, although various personnel systems such as performance appraisals had in practice to be in place. Whereas ISO 9000 concentrated in the main on the processes of the organisation, IIP looked to the role of people in achieving the results that were hoped for. Most businesses will agree that people are their most important asset and IIP challenges all concerned to make this a reality.

IIP has just undergone a major review and the training and enterprise councils are no more. The standard has now to make a way for itself without the benefits of the funding that initially enabled it to establish itself. The signs are encouraging, with widespread recognition in the commercial world. Research shows that active involvement of employees and improvement of personnel management techniques do contribute to business success.

The new standard is simpler and less prescriptive than its predecessor. There are now just 12 'indicators' or standards which organisations need to achieve. Each is explained in the wording of the standard itself. It is still based on a four stage process which can be traced right back to Deming's early work: see Figure 3.2.

An investor in people first commits itself to support the development of its people in order to achieve its aims and objectives. It then plans on the development that it wishes to implement by ensuring understanding and involvement with those aims. It will

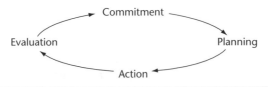

Figure 3.2 *Investors in People*

then seek to put into place the necessary strategies to succeed and will then measure what has been achieved and what needs to be worked upon. The whole process then repeats itself in a manner not unlike the philosophy of continual improvement from TQM. Particular strengths of IIP are that it has a hard business edge to it. It does not require organisations to be better employers for the sake of being so, but because they need to improve in order to achieve better results. Likewise, there is no blanket commitment to train people for the sake of training. Training is only obligatory if it moves the organisation towards its aims and objectives. Most of all, systems must actually work. If an appraisal shows that training will be needed for an individual to meet their objectives, does this training actually happen? That should not be the end of the process however, since the training may not have been effective. There needs to be testing to see if the training has produced the necessary benefits. If it has not, then different steps will need to be taken.

The main consequence of IIP recognition in most law firms seems to be one of culture rather than of systems. It will be the case that many firms first developed appraisal schemes or better training programmes in order to meet the requirements of the standard, but the change in how people relate to each other is probably the most enduring outcome. The essence of the standard is that firmwide goals have to be translated down to team and individual levels, suggesting a much greater degree of involvement than is otherwise likely.

Quality in Law

The Quality in Law (QIL) movement in Australia is the legal quality initiative which is closest to the philosophy of TQM and its methods. The standard was inspired in part by government with a major drive for quality by both the federal and the state governments in the early 1990s. This coincided with a pronounced recession in commercial legal services and a recognition that business techniques had to be taken on board in the management of law firms as with any other commercial concern. QIL started with a group of enthusiasts in Sydney but soon spread to other states and to neighbouring New Zealand, with over 200 accredited members by the end of 2000. QIL, as it is generally known, is closer to some of the original TQM methodologies and has always put great emphasis on measurement. It has six areas of provisions and examines these from the perspective of the internal and external client, thereby focusing attention on those that are affected by the systems required for recognition.

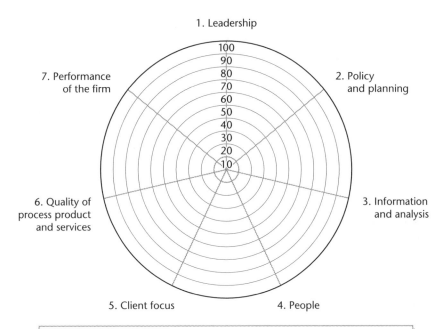

1. Leadership

7. Performance
of the firm

2. Policy
and planning

6. Quality of
process product
and services

3. Information
and analysis

5. Client focus

4. People

	Result		Plot
1. Leadership		× 14% =	
2. Policy and planning		× 8% =	
3. Information and analysis		× 8% =	
4. People		× 20% =	
5. Client focus		× 22% =	
6. Quality of process, product and services		× 18% =	
7. Performance of the firm		× 10% =	

Source: Copyright Global Strategies Pty Limited

Figure 3.3   *Quality in Law*

An initial benchmarking test (see Figure 3.3) allows firms to score themselves for an initial assessment. They can then undergo their 'quality journey' with clear goals and measurable improvements in mind.

The model developed by QIL is along the lines of different approaches to rationalise TQM more generally. In the USA the Baldridge awards produce a similar scorecard of measurement of all the key processes for success. In Europe the European Foundation for

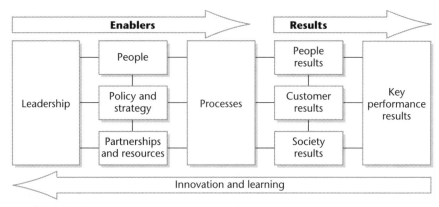

© EFQM. The EFQM Excellence Model is a registered trademark.

| Figure 3.4 | *European Foundation for Quality Management Model* |

Quality Management developed a similar business excellence model (see Figure 3.4). This compares 'enablers' with 'results', stressing the cause and effect of change management.

How great, therefore, is the task of complying with the requirements of the Lexcel standard? The answer depends on the firm's starting position. For the thousand or so firms that have obtained a legal aid franchise the task will mainly be to spread the discipline of compliance to the non-contentious departments. This often proves to be more difficult than it sounds: over recent years litigators have been faced with some compulsion to change practices if they wanted a franchise, but the non-contentious areas are more problematic. It may also be that litigation lends itself more to a regime of compliance than certain other work type areas. Most litigators run files on the basis that any one might need to be assessed for costs, and are probably more assiduous in recording information as a result.

The first task is to produce a manual which addresses all the contents of the standards. This may be time consuming, but is easier than the stages that follow. When the firm is ready for external audit the process will often start with a 'desk audit' consisting of a read-through of the procedures to ensure that all requirements have been dealt with. More difficult by far is then to get everyone in the firm to observe these procedures. This will often mean asking people to change ways of working that they have developed over decades, so the task should not be under-estimated. Some partners will need careful explanation that these new rules are not merely for the staff and that partner compliance is also expected!

To make compliance more likely it is advisable to:

- ensure full commitment by the partners generally and any management executive board: all the authorities stress the need for effective leadership with any quality programme;
- involve a number of people in the first drafting stage to increase 'ownership' of the procedures which follow;
- avoid standardisation for the sake of it: be clear on points over which there can and cannot be any option; file reviews, for example, are compulsory and need to be done, but the frequency of file reviews should be much less in a partner-heavy commercial department compared to a litigation department with a considerable throughput of files where there is heavier reliance on more junior staff;
- talk to people about the procedures and do not merely require them to read through the manuals: partner and staff training meetings should be compulsory.

One of the main tasks for whoever co-ordinates the project is to make it relevant to the future success of the firm. Accreditation is more likely if the firm has a clear goal throughout the process of application, such as, most obviously, the improvement of internal efficiency and consequential gains to profitability. The firm that complies reluctantly out of some sense of obligation will always be more likely to struggle.

A quality plan

In many ways quality involves most areas of practice management. How well these different elements support each other will be one of the challenges of a quality programme. The 'five rings of quality analysis' is used as the basis for the organisation of the contents of this book (see Figure 3.5).

The analysis has various implications:

(1) First level: the heart of any successful organisation is its values, purposes and sense of direction. Issues go beyond the mere compilation of a business plan and involve such issues as the culture of the practice.
(2) Second level: law firms are, more so than most other service businesses, people businesses first and foremost. The financial success of the practice depends not only on the know-how and expertise of the key personnel, but also the efficiency of all elements of the organisation.

41

Figure 3.5   *The five rings of quality*

(3) Third level: this might be called 'operational' management: how well does the organisation fare in terms of its day-to-day implementation of policies? Each of these areas is examined in the Lexcel standard.

(4) Fourth level: this concentrates on areas of case and file management and is inspired by the principles of quality assurance.

(5) Fifth level: finally comes client care. The analysis shows that good client care is not achieved through short term 'quick fix' solutions, but rather through careful management of all the factors of management that form the smaller circles within. An effective client care programme is built from within and will prove disappointing if approached superficially.

Main points

- Quality can have different implications for advisers and clients.
- Quality principles from business need careful application to the legal environment.
- Lexcel is specific to the legal profession and has origins in ISO 9000.

Notes

1 Oliver, M. (1993) 'What American firms can learn about quality from their British colleagues', MBA Europe Institute, Weatherhead School of Management, p.19.

2 Crosby, P. (1979) *Quality is Free*, McGraw-Hill.

3 ISO 8402, 1986.
4 Juran, J.M. *et al.* (1974) *Quality Control Handbook*, McGraw-Hill.
5 Eccles, T. (1996) reported in Abram Hawles Client Review.
6 Deming, W.E. (1986) *Out of Crisis*, Massachusetts Institute of Technology/Cambridge University Press.
7 Juran, J.M. *et al. op. cit.*
8 Feigenbaum, A. (1983) *Quality Control: Principles, Practices and Administration*, McGraw-Hill.
9 Ishikawa, K. (1985) *What is Quality Control?*, Prentice Hall.
10 Taguchi, G. (1986) *Introduction to Quality Engineering*, Asian Productivity Organisation.
11 Shingo, S. (1985) *The Sayings of Shigeo Shingo – Key Strategies for Plant Improvement*, Productivity Press, Cambridge, Massachusetts.
12 Crosby, P. *op. cit.*
13 Peters, T.J. *et al.* (1982) *In Search of Excellence*, Harper & Row.

Many references in this chapter are based on *The Quality Gurus*, a DTI Publication published as part of the Enterprise Initiative.

For more details of Quality in Law see **www.qil.com.au**

43

4

Business strategy

- Management structure
- Fee earning structures
- Business planning
- Steps in the planning process

There should be a well devised strategy for the future at the heart of any successful business, law firm or other. It is likely that those who manage the firm will regard the production of a challenging but realistic plan as being one of their prime responsibilities. Most firms will have adopted some form of business plan over recent years, even if only in response to external pressures from banks or the demands of the various legal quality standards. The strategy should be seen as being the foundation for a programme of improvements to produce a better and more profitable firm. Unfortunately, many firms seem to regard the preparation of a plan as being simply one more bureaucratic requirement of the new quality regime and do not therefore gain the benefit from the exercise that they should.

The reluctance to engage fully in business planning inspired some of the more significant changes to the LAFQAS standard. Whereas the previous franchising specification had provided that business plans did not need to be 'complex or voluminous' the requirements in H1 are very much more specific. The future business strategy has to be detailed for the next 12 months and then available in outline for the two years after that. The main emphasis is on the plan being a document which is 'alive', in the wording of the guidance note, and subject to regular reviews. The requirements of Lexcel are broadly similar and add the requirement for an IT strategy as part of the overall strategy and a consideration of the skills and resources which will be needed. The creation of a business plan is essential for IIP as most of the action to be taken within the organisation and the setting of personal objectives will depend upon it. IIP also stresses the need for people in the firm to know about it and share the partners' commitment to making it work: 'The organisation has a plan with clear aims and objectives which are understood by everyone' (indicator 5).

Management structure

Responsibility for management within the firm and the planning exercise which will be needed are important initial considerations. This forms the first requirement in Lexcel that: 'Practices will have a written description of their management structure which designates the responsibilities of individuals and lines of accountability' (A1).

There is, of course, no one correct structure for all firms. The range and diversity of law firms is part of the challenge for all those who manage law practices. What might be appropriate in one practice could be unwanted elsewhere. Many firms have the added complication of branch offices, with the result that issues of the right management structure become in part a balancing act of ensuring proper representation for all work areas and office locations within the practice.

Whatever the size or complexity of the practice, the starting point for most firms in relation to management structures will be the partners' meeting. There might be loose agreement on the extent to which any individual partner may commit the firm without the express agreement of his or her partners, or restrictions might be set out in the partnership deed. For many firms this basic model of decision-making has proved to be inappropriate to the realities of managing a modern law firm. Decisions can not only be slowed if consent to each one by a meeting is needed, but can also be subject to the 'lowest common denominator' problem, in which decisions are based on compromise and the line of the least objection. A further problem is the amount of time taken on management. The time taken in meetings might not necessarily be lost fee-earning time, since most firms arrange meetings as an additional part of the day and not in normal working hours, but the time will almost certainly be at the expense of the partners' personal lives. The combination of time taken and the quality of decisions made causes many partners to explore different models of delegation (see Figure 4.1).

> 3. Executive board
> 2. Committees of partnership
> 1. Partners meeting

Figure 4.1   *Delegation of management*

The next level of sophistication in management is to devise various committees that will report to the partners' meeting. This can prove to be effective in many firms, but is again not without its drawbacks. The total partner time per decision made may be greater than before, and if the aim of the system is to produce good decisions quickly the lack of responsiveness is likely to cause frustration.

An increasing number of firms have experimented with the concept of the full time managing partner. It will almost certainly be unfair to expect a partner to combine sole responsibility for management with a full fee-earning load but this is often the case in smaller firms. The problem is often one of suitability for the role: the obvious choice for managing partner is also likely to be one of the best fee-earners. Some reduction of hours is the most common solution, though in the larger firms the managing partner is more likely to be put under pressure to surrender his or her practice, even if only temporarily. The only circumstances where this would tend not to be the case are where management is given a fairly low priority and is seen as being very much subsidiary to fee earning, as is the case in certain of the large American firms.

The disadvantage of the full time managing partner role is that credibility in the eyes of partners and staff can soon be eroded. Challenging fee income targets are met with the response 'you don't know how tough it is these days' and the self confidence of the individual can soon be affected. This may be one reason why those who have been full time managing partners for some time often develop an increasing enthusiasm for returning to fee earning as time goes by. Since the core activity of any law firm is to produce fees by providing services to clients, those removed from doing so can soon feel isolated. Depending on the priority given to management, the 'stars' of the firm are more likely to be the highest billers and not those who manage the practice.

One of the benefits of creating a managing partner position is that the firm makes a clear commitment to recognising the seriousness of the management role. Where the right person cannot be found to assume this responsibility it should be possible, in theory, to recruit a specialist manager to whom the role can be delegated. A convincing case can be made for the appointment of a practice director in even the smaller firm:

- the firm bills an average of £100,000 per partner;
- the going rate for a senior manager locally is roughly half of that amount;

- the net loss to the firm of a full time managing partner can therefore be said to be roughly £50,000;
- it would seem to be the case that a lesser qualified partner man-ager will cost the firm twice as much as a trained specialist.

Unfortunately, such examples are not as simple as they may seem. First, they rely on an assumption that there is a loss of the fee-earning value of the partner when they become a manager. In practice their work is likely to be absorbed by colleagues. To the extent that this is not possible an assistant might be recruited so the loss of profit is min-imised. More fundamentally, however, management is not improved if the decisions of the manager are not acceptable. If partners will only accept one of their own as their manager the costs savings of the man-ager can soon seem theoretical.

For all of these reasons the appointment of senior employed managers has proved difficult in many firms. The logic of entrusting decisions to those better qualified and able to make decisions has not always been matched by the psychological acceptance of an abandonment of power by the partners. The steps needed for a senior man-ager to succeed in any firm are:

(1) a clear designation of responsibilities and authority, matched by a clear agreement by the partners as to the terms of reference under which they have delegated decision-making, culminat-ing in either a job description for the individual or a detailed appendix to the contract of employment;
(2) a close and supportive relationship with a senior equity partner, preferably one who occupies the role of managing or senior partner, or both.

Difficulties are particularly likely to arise when decisions which have a major impact on the partners' investment in the practice are being considered. In such circumstances the partner responsible for man-agement must appreciate the boundaries to the true power of the manager if the role is to succeed.

It is helpful when examining the issue of high level appointments to distinguish carefully between management and administration. Firms that are truly willing to delegate responsibility for top man-agement are the exception. Many more firms are willing to delegate administration, however. For this reason the 'Director of Admini-stration' who has an involvement in management of the firm, but line management responsibility for office practicalities only, is more likely to be acceptable. For many firms, particularly the medium and large firms, the combination of administrative manager and managing partner is the key to the best arrangements. Free of the daily barrage of more menial problems, the managing partner can concentrate on issues of personnel, finance and marketing which are more worthy of a partner's time and consideration. The expert manager is in a position to influence decisions but the partners will still feel that they are responsible for important issues, even if the manager then has the responsibility for their implementation.

A management committee, as seen in most of the larger firms, forms a logical extension to developments such as the appointment of administrative directors or the delegation of particular responsibilities to managing partners or committees. As with the board of directors in a registered company, the duty is to exercise delegated powers of day-to-day management in a fair and skilful manner, reporting occasionally to the body of partners as a whole. In many of the larger commercial firms partners' meetings have taken on many of the characteristics of general meetings of shareholders, often occurring quarterly or even less frequently than that. For this management model to work, regular communication must be maintained or it will be unrealistic to expect partners to abandon their involvement in management. Where a board structure exists there must be regular reporting of what is happening. Communication methods will vary between firms, but in most the distribution of minutes is too much paper for not enough information. A weekly summary report is likely to be preferable. In many cases this is better if delivered personally, perhaps at a weekly partners' lunch meeting, while in others it might be a short written summary report. Experience shows that those who still feel involved in decisions being made about them and their practice are more likely to accept these decisions.

The work of Professor Meredith Belbin may be helpful to firms in deciding which management structure to adopt.[1] In his extensive research on the workings of groups he came to the conclusion that groups of more than seven persons have different dynamics from smaller ones. This seems to be the experience with many firms where there is reluctant acceptance that something has to change as the partnership grows in numbers. It may be reassuring to know that it is principles of group structure which are involved and not necessarily the particular personalities concerned.

Having decided what the management responsibilities should be it is necessary then to set them down into a readable form (see Figure 4.2). Organisational charts, which are often referred to as 'organograms' in

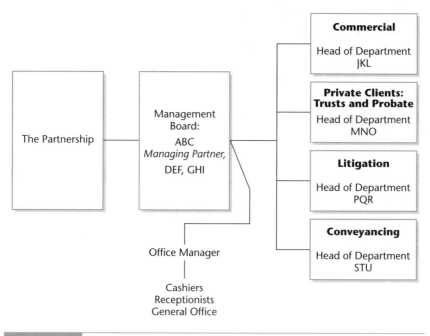

Figure 4.2 *Organisational chart*

current management jargon, are useful in summarising the picture at a glance. The structure should be apparent to anyone within the firm and so should be set out in the office manual, or an edited version of it at least.

Fee-earning structures

Whatever the range of work undertaken by the firm, profit potential is enhanced if the partners are able to employ fee-earners whose work generates a contribution to profit. The ideal ratio of partners to fee-earners is much discussed. A common recommendation is one partner to three assistants, but this will be easier to achieve in certain areas of work where teamwork will be expected by clients or where there would not be preference for partner involvement. Those involved with the defence of professional negligence work typically need to have low ratios of fee-earners to partners since most defendants will find advice on sensitive issues to be more palatable from partners. On the other hand, firms undertaking substantial amounts of legal expenses insurance claims work can achieve very high ratios of fee-earners to partners and consequentially high profit contributions for the practice.

Research conducted in 1998 by Andrew Otterburn showed how the gearing of assistant tends to increase with partner size (see Figure 4.3).[2]

Profit management means that most firms aspire towards a form of pyramid where there are more staff fee-earners than partners, and therefore more support staff, secretarial or otherwise, than fee-earners (see Figure 4.4).

The recession of the early 1990s forced a re-think on this ideal structure. With less work to do most firms preserved most of the work for most of the partners, with the result that recruitment slowed and redundancies became commonplace. Various firms realised that unproductive partners could not be tolerated, the result being changes in the partner line up. The slimmed down firms often assumed a squarer shape (see Figure 4.5).

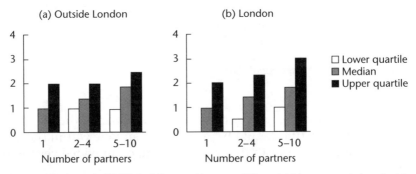

Source: Otterburn, A. (1998) Cashflow and Improved Financial Management, *Law Society*

Figure 4.3   *Number of other fee-earners per equity partner*

Figure 4.4   *Fee earning structures – the pyramid*

Fee-earning structures – recessionary firm

The ideal shape of the law firm may continue to be a matter of debate for some time to come. Increasing use of word-processing equipment by fee-earners will almost certainly mean a reduction in the total numbers of support staff for most firms, but this may be off-set in many by an increased role for paralegal work. It is also quite likely that the rigid distinction which tends to exist in many firms between fee-earners and support staff will reduce, making traditional categories difficult to draw.

Business planning

The strategic plan is the document which sets out an analysis of where the firm stands at the start of the process, where it wishes to be at a fixed stage in the future and the principal steps that it will have to take to achieve this goal. The key ingredients are that it should be recognised as a plan, as opposed to a discussion paper, and it must therefore have the agreement of the partners to be bound by it. The distinction between where the firm is likely to be if it does not inter-vene as planned and its desired position is called the 'strategic gap' (see Figure 4.6). The plan's prospects of success will be greater if the partners are involved in its creation and many firms now widen the involvement to staff as well. If nothing else, staff should be briefed on any plan, as their efforts will be key to its success.

The amount of detail in a plan is much debated. I was once given the analogy of an aeroplane that leaves Sydney for London. It leaves at a precise time with the goal of landing at Heathrow at a definite arrival time. In the 24 hours or so which intervene it may be on course for only about 5 per cent of the time, yet it will generally land on time nonetheless. The passengers are unlikely to be concerned with minor deviations but will be concerned with major changes to

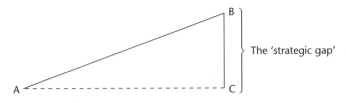

A Where are we now
B Where we want to be
C Where we might otherwise be

Figure 4.6   *The strategic gap*

the itinerary. So too with the business plan. There needs to be sustained progress towards stated objectives and deviations will generally be capable of being corrected. This implies that there will need to be regular checking or 'variance analysis' to see how the firm is doing and to make the adjustments which are needed. In the event of substantial changes new objectives will need to be agreed.

Styles of business plans have changed over the years. The plans that many firms first experienced were funded by an earlier government initiative through the Department of Trade and Industry. This resulted in long and detailed plans, but as the boom days of the 1980s gave way to the 'nervous nineties' greater flexibility was needed in the process. The original version of IIP required of organisations 'a written but flexible plan' and the choice of styles was often represented as a continuum (see Figure 4.7).

Opposition to planning emerged with various successful concerns attributing their fortunes to the fact that they did not have to work within the limitations of a plan. In its place they had the freedom to benefit from a more opportunistic approach. One of the most damning critics of detailed plans was Ralph Stacey, who stated in his book *Dynamic Strategic Management for the 1990s* that:

> long term plans are flimsy, unrealistic, impractical and essentially static. The real cutting edge of management is handling the unknowable. Strategic management offers some useful insights into problems, but as a form of control is of no practical benefit.[3]

Planned   Emergent

Figure 4.7   *Style of business plan*

The best line of advice is to plan, but to be realistic about what can and cannot be planned for. The firm's performance will be shaped increasingly by outside developments over which it has little control. It will need to be focused on its main goals and it will need to know the key indicators for its success, but it should not delude itself into thinking that it can plan its destiny in great detail, especially beyond the next 12 months. This level of detail appears to be suggested by Lexcel where it requires:

key objectives for 12 months and an outline strategy covering a further 2 years to provide a background against which the practice may review its performance and may take decisions about its future (B1a).

Within the accompanying guidance note there is further advice on the type of issues which are likely to be addressed:

capital expenditure (including computers), office location, staffing, strategic and business risks facing the practice, changes in the external environment and targeting new business, but need not be written in considerable detail.

Other aspects on finance and information technology are considered in later chapters.

Steps in the planning process

There are various main steps in the full strategic planning process. The sequence in which they are followed is determined by how clear issues seem at the outset. The fullest sequence where little is obvious might be shown as in Figure 4.8.

Aspirations

There is little point in being involved in any form of organisation unless the individuals know what they expect to achieve from it. The main issues for most partners are likely to be lifestyle and income. There will need to be discussion on what sort of hours the partners are willing to work, how long they expect to take by way of annual holidays and what other interests in life they expect to be able to pursue. A major worry of many practitioners is that they are unable to achieve the balance that they would like because of the pressures of fee earning. Many feel that they are locked into a cycle of long hours for relatively little reward because of the way that legal work has changed. In such situations it is necessary to examine carefully whether the

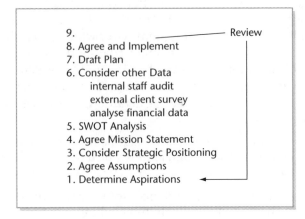

9.   ———— Review
8. Agree and Implement
7. Draft Plan
6. Consider other Data
        internal staff audit
        external client survey
        analyse financial data
5. SWOT Analysis
4. Agree Mission Statement
3. Consider Strategic Positioning
2. Agree Assumptions
1. Determine Aspirations

Figure 4.8   *Steps in the planning process*

appointment of more assistants, perhaps coupled to an effective marketing strategy, could break the pattern.

The other obvious consideration will be to set the rate of profits that are hoped for. The implications of these figures are the next major issue. Subsequent stages of the planning process may well suggest that the level is unrealistic, in which case it will be necessary to think again. Alternatively, higher expectations might mean that commitment to work must be greater than might be hoped for, or that personnel must be employed to whom work can profitably be delegated, or that costs must be trimmed to preserve profitability. Any decision will have its implications which will need to be thought through in terms of the best option for the firm.

Problems often flow from setting an arbitrary level of profits which the firm will struggle to maintain. The risk is that misguided management decisions will follow simply to achieve this goal. Many such decisions will involve counter-productive attempts to cut overheads. Staff cuts or pay freezes not only lower morale, but also reduce the resources of the firm to do the work that it has to do. Aspirations in the planning process must be like any other objective of management – specific and achievable. If the evidence is that the firm in question will not produce the level of income desired more fundamental decisions have to be made about what is to be done with the firm, or those objectives will have to be reconsidered.

Assumptions

Since any plan is a version of future events that the participators wish to bring about it is important to state the assumptions that the partners are relying upon in making the plan.

This area of the planning exercise seems to grow in its difficulty year by year. Until relatively recently it was possible to make various fundamental assumptions about the future of legal services with a good deal of confidence. Increasingly, however, the involvement of the lawyer in areas such as divorce, all forms of personal injury fault-based litigation and property work is being questioned. It is no longer possible for any firm to assume that simply because it provides services in a certain format today that there will still be a willing market for those services in the future.

One of the best ways to analyse this is to consider the complexity of a service and the stability of its provision. Four options therefore emerge, see Figure 4.9.

Legal services are sometimes identified in management texts as fitting the first of the boxes in Figure 4.9, but this would appear to underestimate the difficulties of running a modern law firm. For firms offering a standard list of services, 'simple' may be the better description of their service offering (simple here should not be regarded as being the opposite to learned or professional), but in others it will be complex. Without doubt, however, the environment within which law firms practise has moved from the benign to the competitive over the last 15 years. This makes planning both more important and also more difficult.

In times of greater volatility, opportunities and threats become more abundant. Inevitably, many will concentrate more on the possible threats facing the firm in question and the profession in general. These considerations might occur later in the exercise as part of the 'SWOT' exercise (see p. 60), or at this earlier stage in setting the ground rules for subsequent discussions. The standard method of

Simple service Stable environment	Simple service Unstable environment
Complex service Stable environment	Complex service Unstable environment

Figure 4.9   *Assumptions in future planning*

looking at external, or 'environmental' issues is the so-called 'STEP' (or alternatively 'PEST') list:

- social environment;
- technological environment;
- economic environment;
- political environment.

Looked at more widely, Michael Porter's five forces model is the standard way of examining threats and influences from outside the organisation.[4] These can be summarised as:

- competitive rivalry;
- threat of entry;
- threat of substitutes;
- power of buyers;
- power of suppliers.

Competitive rivalry

Competitive rivalry is more of a concern than used to be the case. In years gone by there seemed to be more than enough work for all firms to survive and, since marketing activities were subject to extensive restrictions before the lifting of the Publicity Code in the early 1980s, it was difficult for any one firm to gain any clear advantages over others. Now that firms are free to promote themselves within a much more liberal marketing code, changes in market position can be more readily achieved. There may often be distaste for the open competition which has become more commonplace, but it has become part of modern professional practice.

Threat of entry

A distinction should be drawn between threat of entry by other solicitors, and by non-solicitors which is examined under the heading of substitutes. Predictions of how the shape of the profession will change in future years are difficult to make. The trends in recent years show continued growth within the profession which will need to be matched by growing demand for legal services.

Threat of substitutes

The threat of entry to legal business by non-solicitors seems to increase with time. Of late, there has been widespread concern over the growth of will-writers, claims advisers in personal injury work and human resources consultancies in employment law. Legal services make an attractive option for many service-based businesses and increasingly the solicitors' profession will have to compete as a collective brand to retain many of its traditional areas of work.

Threat of buyers

We have seen in recent years the growth of 'funder power' under which those organisations that control the payment of bulk fees are more likely to flex their financial muscles to achieve value for themselves. The relationship with the Legal Services Commission and the move towards block contracting form one such example. Other firms in the area of bulk debt recovery or personal injury work will have been more likely also to be subject to hard negotiating on fees.

Threat of suppliers

Unlike most industries, suppliers do not play a prominent part in the provision of legal services since there is not the same reliance on raw materials but competition from the Bar could be considered a factor in certain specialist fields.

Strategic positioning

The most notable contributor to the thinking of how firms should address the question of strategy is generally accepted to be Michael Porter. Until the publication by him in 1980 of his book *Competitive Strategy*, strategic planning consisted of little more than environmental and SWOT analyses.[5] Although there were a number of main options which could then be pursued, each organisation, it was argued, had to find its individual solutions to its particular challenges.

Porter suggested that the range of options open to firms were in fact considerably more limited. In essence, he argued, there are only two strategies for success: to be the 'cost leader' that concentrates on price as its distinct advantage, or to be clearly differentiated from other firms in some way that is valued by buyers. The alternative, he argued, was to be 'stuck in the middle' with no clear chance of success in any competitive market. Viewed another way, Porter argues that to survive and prosper every business needs to be seen as being different in some material way to its rivals. Cost might then be seen as being simply one potential differentiating advantage.

The three choices set out by Porter are mainly based on industries where a limited number of producers vie for domination in defined markets. Solicitors are not necessarily subject to quite the same factors, and it may well be that the 'positioning' issue for many law firms is to make the best of being 'stuck in the middle' as the only realistic option available. Each of the choices bears further consideration, however.

The 'cost leader' choice is one to use with the greatest of caution in legal services. The risks of this strategy are set out in detail in Porter's writings. Clients of law firms are usually ill equipped to judge the quality of the advice provided since the usual reason for instructing a professional is for assistance with a problem which the client is unable to resolve for him or herself. The lack of familiarity with legal services means that the client's view of what is good advice becomes clouded by those aspects that they can evaluate – most notably price. Any firm which is clearly cheaper than others may be preferred by some, but will also be mistrusted by others. The risk of the cost leader position is the risk that most people believe that they get what they pay for, and the firm that offers services at well below the going rate may be presumed to be technically inferior.

Other firms seek to differentiate themselves in other ways. The clear line of advice is to be definitely one or the other, and not the sort of firm that is confused whether to offer quality or cost. It is interesting to note that Porter goes to some lengths to warn of the dangers of being the cost leader in a market, even if a successful one. The main risks, he argued, were that an over-emphasis on efficiency results in the firm losing touch with the requirements of its clients. If the demands of clients become more sophisticated the cost leader firm may well be slow to respond, insisting that price is the issue while quality of service becomes more important to its clients. Likewise, staff morale can often be poor in such firms. Since personnel costs are viewed as one of the principal overheads standing in the way of further efficiency, the value placed on staff can be inadequate. Above all, he argued, the product provided by the cost leader must not be considered cheap or low quality. The distinctive appeal of the cost leader is that they provide competitive prices with no compromise on quality. Law firms aspiring to this position can achieve this by explaining to clients that investment in information technology and other management systems are the means by which they achieve savings which are passed on to clients in lower fee rates.

If cost is not to be the strategy of the firm, some form of differentiation should ideally be sought instead. The key to differentiation is to be clearly distinguishable in a manner that is perceived as being of value by clients. Accessibility might be one such feature: partner access is often mentioned. For many it is the particular reputation with a certain client group or area of work, of which media and high technology firms are common examples.

What of those firms that could be said to be 'stuck in the middle', however? Where a town or city has numerous law firms this may be the reality for most. The risk of profiling the firm in one distinct way is that it might provide a negative message in relation to other work that the firm would value. There may be little point in portraying the office as being specialists in divorce if the net effect is that estate agents stop recommending conveyancing work, for example. The reality for most firms is that they do provide a general range of services and that the distinction between firms is largely to do with the personalities involved. For this reason, clear market positioning statements are often difficult to achieve.

A term often used in this area, which can serve to crystallise the issue of differentiation, is that of the 'unique selling proposition'. What is it that separates the firm from all others? The response might be cost, or quality of advice as through specialisation, or personality and accessibility. The firm that has reached a conclusion on this is in a better position to describe itself in any promotional literature and might even be able to formulate a 'unique selling proposition statement' such as: 'Specialists in divorce law providing, in addition, the full range of services required by private clients'.

Mission statement

A 'mission statement' should summarise the aims and ambitions of the partnership. Mission statements – or 'practice purpose statements' as they are termed in the guidance notes to B1a of the Practice Management Standards – have the potential to promote the identity of the practice. Sadly they often have the potential also to be seen as little more than a meaningless formula of words devised for little apparent purpose. The effort involved in developing a mission statement is likely to prove fruitful where there is, or could be, conflict on issues such as the positioning of the practice. Other than this they might be useful for any promotional literature that the partners wish to develop.

Many mission statements hold little value since they are so bland or distanced from the true values of the firm in question. Disappointment with mission statements is not confined to the legal profession:

Good mission statements or 'visions' are inspiring and exciting. They need to be specific enough to act as a 'tie-breaker' (e.g. when it comes to the crunch quality is more important than meeting delivery targets), whilst at the same time it should be general enough to leave room for people to exercise initiative. Where mission statements have not been effective it is usually because either they do not inspire people (for example they merely consist of a series of bland statements that apply everywhere and nowhere); or they are not evidenced in the actions of management. For instance, the mission statement stresses the importance of customer service and caring for the environment, but the managers' behaviour reinforces a different set of priorities, like cost control and capacity utilisation.[6]

As with much of the strategic plan, ownership is the key. Attempts should be made to develop any mission statement in conjunction with as many people in the firm as possible. There should also be a commitment to making the statement a reality in the experience of insiders to the firm and others. Ideally it should be seen to shape decisions made by the firm and be of true relevance to management.

SWOT Analysis

There should now be a thorough examination of internal perceptions of the practice. Either through open discussion or through a previously distributed questionnaire, each of the participants should comment on how they perceive current strengths and weaknesses and, looking to the future, opportunities and threats. In larger firms this might be done collectively through the departments, with each reporting its agreed view at the discussion meeting.

The normal manner in which the factors, both external and internal, are collated for consideration is through the assessment of strengths, weaknesses, opportunities and threats, invariably known as 'SWOT' (see Figure 4.10). Areas for SWOT analysis will generally

Strengths	Weaknesses
Opportunities	Threats

Figure 4.10   *SWOT analysis*

include premises, people and the firm's client base. SWOT works best as a brainstorming exercise and is also very useful in relation to planning the marketing for any given group.

The aim is to compare each family of factors. How should strengths be used to capitalise on opportunities or weaknesses minimised so as to prevent threats? Although in widespread use, SWOT as a technique is not without its detractors. The fact that the same factors can often appear as both strengths and weaknesses, for example, shows that SWOT is often imprecise. Take, for example, the common situation of the firm having one important client that accounts for a high percentage of instructions performed. Is this a strength to have such a good client, or a threat that the supply might end at some stage? This subjective assessment will probably be largely to do with the temperament of the individuals undertaking the task. If the quest is to produce an objective business plan the subjective nature of the SWOT must be regarded as a disadvantage. It has to be recognised, however, that the SWOT discussions do often provide an invaluable focus on issues of importance to the participants.

Surveys and Data

Other sources of information will have a bearing on the planning at this stage. This might most obviously include:

- analysis of income, expenditure and other finance trends;
- internal audit of staff opinions;
- client survey to include the views of referrers of work.

The objective of the financial analysis is to confront issues of profitability. The criticism can often be made that solicitors are quick to quote billing figures month by month, but seldom have a clear idea on how much it has cost them to generate each pound earned. If analysing costs by departments, a partner profit should be allowed for representing the 'notional salary' which could be expected by a partner. Issues of unit cost will then need to be addressed. Partner-heavy departments might bring prestige to the firm but could even be shown to be loss-making under this manner of examining the figures. Changes of staffing structure and/or reliance on computers often become clearly relevant in this part of the exercise.

The aim of the internal audit is to identify any gap which might exist between the partners' view of themselves as managers and the view that the staff have of them. Typically partners will describe a position where they communicate well and maintain an 'open door' for all personnel. In practice few organisations of any description communicate as well as they should and the normal response to any form of internal staff audit is a plea for better communication. Likewise, the client audit should provide evidence on whether a distinction exists between the level of service that the firm aspires to and the level of service as actually perceived by the clients and any referrers of work.

The report stage

Having answered the first basic question of business planning – 'where are we now?' – the partners should then be able to agree on direction and objectives. In most firms the report will go on to suggest the methods to be used to achieve these goals. The larger the firm, the more likely it is that separate strategies will be devised for marketing, information technology, personnel development and quality. Budgets are likely to remain on an annual basis but be subject to some longer-term overall profitability targets.

By now the collection of information and views should be complete. The discussion of this data, preferably at the meeting arranged for it, should result in a clear sense of direction for the practice. It should now be possible for the co-ordinators of the project, be it one or more of the partners or the external consultants, to prepare a draft strategic plan. This will then be reviewed, perhaps first by a small management group, but then by the partners as a whole.

The draft plan

The range of options open to a firm should emerge from the consideration of the factors identified in the strategic analysis and the need to meet the objectives and aspirations which were identified at the outset.

There is a fair amount of advice on the setting of objectives. According to Drucker in 1974 they should be 'specific, measurable and unambiguous'.[7] It may well be easier to observe this approach in manufacturing where output can be quantified more readily than in the service sector, but the value of having a number of well considered goals as guiding principles throughout the period of the plan should not be under-estimated.

The personal objectives for a sole practitioner might therefore read:

> To produce £60,000 of income for each of the next three years at minimum, rising to a preferred £65,000 in year 3.

In many cases, objectives and aspirations might be drawn more widely than just the issue of money. Objectives are usually defined in commerce and industry by reference to market share:

> To become the largest volume supplier of widgets to the European market.

Objectives might also address client count or reputation, both of which are formats favoured by many firms:

> To secure 10 new clients producing over £20,000 of fees each over the course of the next 12 months.

> To be profiled as the leading entertainment firm in the region as measured by appropriate listings in the main legal directories.

If such objectives are to be achieved they will have to then be made reality for the groups, departments and individuals within the firm by general briefings, meetings and at appraisal interviews.

Implementation and review

Arguably, the implementation of the strategy is the hardest part of all. Certainly this would appear to be borne out by the numbers of organisations who seem to breathe a sigh of relief when the planning exercise is over and they can return to normal operations. The business plan is consigned to the appropriate shelf for review at some stage in the future. There is, of course, only any point in undertaking any form of strategic exercise if there is a real intent to make it work.

It is advisable that there should be a main review of the plan at least annually, with six-monthly checks a requirement of both Lexcel and CLSQM.

Main points

- Attention has to be given to the management structure. The main choices are partners' meetings, the introduction of a committee system or an executive board. All may be in conjunction with a managing partner.
- Management appointments, especially at higher levels, need direct support from key partners for them to be effective.
- There are various steps to producing a strategic plan which should result in a series of objectives for the practice.
- The greater the commitment to the plan by all concerned, the greater is its opportunity to succeed. Regular reviews and changes if appropriate are important.

References to Lexcel

A1 Management structure
B1 Services and forward planning

Notes

1 Belbin, R. Meredith (1981) *Management Teams – why they succeed or fail*, Butterworth-Heinemann.
2 Otterburn, A. (1998) *Cashflow and Improved Financial Management*, Law Society.
3 Stacey, R. (1990) *Dynamic Strategic Management for the 1990s*, Kogan Page.
4 Porter, M. (1980) *Competitive Strategy*, The Free Press.
5 Porter, M. (1980), *op. cit.*
6 Bowman, C. (1990) *The Essence of Strategic Management*, Prentice Hall.
7 Drucker, P. (1974) *Management: Tasks, Responsibilities, Practices*, Heinemann.

Culture

- The ingredients of culture
- The management of culture
- An analysis for firms

Culture can be defined as the values and beliefs which shape attitudes and behaviours within the firm. It has alternatively and more simply been described as 'the way we do things around here'. The issue of organisational culture is much in vogue at present. Many practices have recognised that they have changed in recent years, usually in a manner of which they approve. 'We have become more open and we communicate better' are frequent comments. The process of change is one that they feel that they have little control over, however. Culture can be prompted, but at a slower pace than some would hope for. In this respect culture has been likened to the ocean liner: it can be pointed in the right direction, but sudden changes of pace or direction are unlikely.

The loss of culture is one of the most commented-upon problems of mergers. On many mergers the distinct feel of the predecessor firms is lost at an early stage, but the development of a new combined replacement culture is a much slower process. There are various agencies which have targeted law firms with culture change programmes, deliberate management interventions to change the outlook and fabric of the recipient firm. Such programmes seem generally to struggle. Culture seems to change most effectively as a by-product of other changes rather than as the central theme.

In this context, culture is an important topic for any who orchestrate a quality programme in a firm or department. There will almost inevitably be some change to the prevailing systems and values as a result of the programme. It might be difficult to control the precise nature of this change, but it is possible to plan actions with an idea of the likely outcomes.

The ingredients of culture

The main shapers of culture are, or will include:

- firm's history;
- management structures;
- values;
- attitudes.

Firm's history

History is a very obvious starting point in uncovering the culture of the firm. It may not always follow that the longer established firms will be more traditional in their outlook, but many are. The ethos of the 'family firm' is prevalent in practice, especially in smaller high street firms. Where there have been different generations of the same family running the practice, their outlook inevitably has a considerable bearing on the overall culture of the practice. For others, 'family firm' is an idyll which they aspire towards. 'At heart we are a family firm' announced the managing partner of a large provincial practice to me on one occasion. This was a curious remark, since the last remaining member of the families that had named the practice had died or retired many years beforehand. He was referring to the social fabric within the practice. This was a close organisation where partners and staff related to each other in a more friendly and open manner than might be expected. Sadly, this was not a view shared by many of the staff who felt that the firm was uncommunicative and secretive. Perhaps it is as well to remember that families are often dysfunctional and it advisable to guard against complacency.

A different view emerges in newly formed firms, especially in the commercial sector. These firms can be characterised by their considerable verve and determination to succeed. The work ethic will be high in such firms and people will not question long hours. This has an obvious bearing on client demands. Whatever the client wants in service delivery is likely to be agreed to. Here is a firm which is on a mission to prove that it is superior to the predecessor firms that the members have left. This is an environment that will not appeal to all, especially when the initial growth curve is exhausted. As new people join the firm they do not necessarily share the pioneer spirit of the founders. In their eyes they may have joined an establishment firm which has no reason to be any different to any of the others that they might have joined. Cultural change in such an environment is mostly then an issue for the founding partners who may have to adapt their expectations of the staff in particular. There may be issues of external orientation also. The firm may now need to see itself as no longer the 'new kid on the block', but as part of the establishment that it has competed with since its inception.

Management structures

In his bestselling book *Understanding Organisations*, Charles Handy outlines four structures which describe organisations.[1] Each has its own merits and disadvantages. Recognising which best describes any particular firm can be helpful in determining the issues which management must address.

The Greek temple

In the Greek temple (see Figure 5.1) there are distinct pillars which are only joined at a senior level of the organisation. In law firms the pillars could equate most obviously to departments or offices. Most people in the firm relate predominantly, if not exclusively, to their immediate colleagues in their own area of involvement. There may be occasional encouragement from management for them to feel part of the wider scene, but daily experience does not encourage a wider view in any real sense. The Greek temple is a solid edifice built upon classical design, but may lack flexibility in times of rapid change. Since organisation-wide attitudes are uncommon, cross-selling usually happens poorly. There may even be opposition to cross-selling, with departments looking to performance figures competitively; far from helping other departments they will stifle opportunities to pass work on so that their own figures seem better.

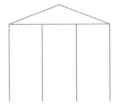

| Figure 5.1 | *The Greek temple* |

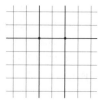

Figure 5.2   *The net*

The net

If the Greek temple best symbolises what is called a role culture, where status in the firm determines views and expectations, the net is the best example of the task culture (see Figure 5.2). Here the predominant issue is not so much where the person falls within the organisation as how they can best relate to others in order to achieve results. There is likely to be more flexibility in this type of firm with the formation of new work teams much easier to implement than in a more traditional role culture. There is less of a sense of control. The head of department, for example, will more readily accept that members of his or her team may need to work elsewhere if the needs of clients so dictate. Given that there is probably more emphasis on external priorities, usually client-dictated, and less on internal politics and status, the task culture is more likely to be focused on quality of client service than the role culture.

It should be stressed that the task culture is not necessarily hierarchy-free. There will still be partners and managers, but there will be less emphasis on behaviour being determined by role alone. If a more junior person is the best qualified to take on a position, they will be more likely to be given the opportunity to do so.

The spider's web

In the spider's web (see Figure 5.3) there will be a central point of control, with the powerbase radiating outwards by degrees. Information tends to flow mostly to and from the centre. In such a firm, knowledge power is often a defining issue in the culture. Who is allowed to know what and when is one of the ways in which people assess their position in the practice. Favouritism may lead to privileges for some and their being withheld from others. The environment may well feel somewhat 'Machiavellian'. This type of law firm is often the firm that draws its name from one partner only, usually the founding partner or the most clearly senior of them. The values of that partner become,

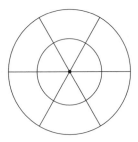

Figure 5.3 *The spider's web*

initially at least, the values of the firm, especially in relation to sources of work. This may initially be a strength, but can become a liability. The strength of many firms will be the diversity of its participators. A strong branding in terms of the work done by the firm can be a source of strength within the business strategy but may well then limit further growth. In many such firms, therefore, there will eventually develop a power struggle with a group of younger partners competing for a more open and participative environment.

The cluster

The point of this organisation (see Figure 5.4) is that it is largely amorphous. The organisation, such as exists, is simply a device for the participators in it. The best example will be any chambers set-up, whether barristers or solicitors. The systems are very much secondary to the members rather than vice versa. It is interesting to observe that at a time when many of the more forward-looking barristers' sets are becoming more openly 'corporate' in their operations, there is a growth of solicitor chambers along more independent lines. The pressures on barristers to set aside their cherished independence are the quality expectations of lay or solicitor clients and the need for

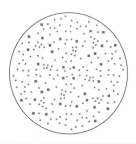

Figure 5.4 *The cluster*

collective promotional activity. It is perhaps no coincidence that many of the solicitors moving into chambers set-ups are often criminal practitioners, needing little in terms of office facilities or central promotion. The individual who feels that their destiny lies in the hours that they work, the rotas that they belong to and the highly personal client following that tends to develop in this line of work, may increasingly prefer this set-up to the more traditional practice.

Values

The development of policies on ethics has been one of the more striking elements of the corporate world over the last decade. There is increasing recognition that business can no longer go about its activities however it wishes, divorced from the society that it is part of. Politicians have been quick to support this development. Margaret Thatcher saw business filling the roles left vacant by rolling back the burden of government, while the later Labour administration has been keen to promote the interests of 'stakeholders' – those influenced less directly by business activities. A striking example was Shell and its attempts to dump a redundant oil platform in the North Sea in 1995. Not only did it face a consumer boycott at the pumps throughout Northern Europe, but various of its outlets were subject to violent and unlawful attacks. Shell's professed philosophy to be a responsible member of the community at large seemed at odds with its decision, and protest followed.

Public protest could also affect law firms, albeit on a smaller scale and often from individual former clients. The senior partner of one general practice explained to me how literally weeks of her time had been taken in dealing with a protester who took up his activities outside one of the firm's offices.

Such situations know little of right and wrong. Whatever the true position, public perception matters. Society expects higher standards of responsibility from business, be it professional or other.

Most firms will have undergone a mission statement exercise at least once in recent years. A similar exercise as an adjunct or alternative to the mission statement may be the drafting of a values statement. In many firms this will be a more fruitful activity than drafting a mission statement since the issues which will arise under it will often seem to be much more pressing. The values which can be analysed include the following.

Clients

The Office for the Supervision of Solicitors recommends that firms should have a 'client charter' – a statement of the values that firms will show in their dealings with clients. Some may go as far as stating response times, whereas others will be less specific. The client charter makes a useful component for any brochure text and can also look effective posted on a noticeboard or display board in the reception area of the firm.

Staff

Most organisations will trot out on occasions that their staff are their most valued asset. A hot potato in the accounting world is that if this is so, why do people not appear as an asset on the balance sheet? The indicators in the Investors in People quality standard lay great emphasis on clear leadership within the firm and clear values on training and development. If the firm declares itself committed to the development of its people, for example, on what grounds would it agree to or reject an application for a training place on a local legal executives' course where the secretary would be away from the office one afternoon per week?

Other issues for staff would include dignity at work. Are the partners prepared to commit themselves to the express prohibition of the types of behaviour that could be described as abusive or demeaning? What of the very common situation where clients, or even representatives of other law firms, are abusive by telephone to secretaries or others? Does the firm react, in which case how? Ideally these are issues which should not be determined by which partner is involved. A clear policy would be preferable.

Community

Does the firm see itself as an active part of its local community? To do so might be justified on grounds either of social responsibility or commercial expedience. There will be causes where gain to the firm seems unlikely and others which sit well with a marketing policy. The managing partner of one firm set out guidelines for his partners that they should record 400 hours per year in any attributable practice development activities. Sit as a school governor, be active in politics or your church, he told them, do anything that brings you into direct contact with the community that we serve. The rationale was that if 30 or more partners were to do this there would have to be very real benefits to the marketing programme. Other companies – Boots are one example – encourage community involvement by their personnel. They have less direct reason to do so but are anxious to be seen as good corporate citizens.

Profession

The degree of support for local law societies varies greatly across the country. Involvement on the Law Society council is also a considerable commitment. It is a matter of concern that it has been difficult to get candidates to stand for certain constituencies around the country, but understandable given the hard business pressures to record hours on the one hand and the nature of the commitment to the Law Society on the other. Does the firm see itself as an enthusiastic supporter of the professional bodies or does it seek to have as little as possible to do with them? Again, it is a useful discussion to have.

Attitudes

The prevailing attitudes within a firm are often highlighted by the choice of its terminology. Are clients described as such or 'punters'? Is the firm that receives a complaint quick to label the complainant as a 'nutter'? The criminal world has its own distinct terminology, where clients become 'crims' who will look to their 'briefs' to avoid 'bird'. Clients may object to being labelled punters or nutters, but most hard core recidivists seem happily to acquiesce in the language of the criminal world and share its use. Jargon is only offensive when it is not a shared language.

In their book *The Character of a Corporation* Gareth Jones and Rob Goffee use two types of relationship to define culture – sociability and solidarity.[2] Sociability defines the extent to which people like each other. Through sustained face to face contact people help each other, often without regard for personal interest. The other element of solidarity consists of 'task centred co-operation between unlike individuals and groups'. Such interaction has little to do with affection, rather it is shaped by the need to achieve results where there is a shared interest.

The pairing of these factors leads to four categories.

(1) The networked organisation: high socialisation/low solidarity. Working in such an environment is described as enjoyable and personally rewarding, but poor performance may be tolerated more than it should be. In extreme cases cliquishness blocks policy.

(2) The mercenary organisation: high solidarity/low sociability. This type of organisation will probably be a competitive environment. Work is seen as important, perhaps even an obsession. A former partner in one firm once described to me how he had spent four out of the previous five Christmas Days in the office working on deals. Personal relationships may matter for little in this type of firm, but in the short term there will be a ruthless dedication to the practice and their competitors will take them seriously. In the words of the authors they will have 'a high degree of strategic focus, rapid response to competitive threats and an intolerance of poor performance'. Higher than average partner and staff turnover is often one less fortunate indicator of this sort of firm.

(3) The fragmented organisation: low sociability/low solidarity. In this type of organisation there is not necessarily a great degree of true teamwork and the extent to which people actually like each other also counts for little. It is interesting that the authors place 'law firms and consultancies' into this group: 'You can become the best in your industry by having the best individuals who may not co-operate with each other very much'. This observation seems to accord with the views on teamwork in Chapter 9. In such organisations, recruitment and retention are the concerns of management, rather than the harmonisation of the maverick talents within. It would certainly not be appropriate, however, to categorise all law firms as falling into this description. It may well be that the type of legal organisation that the authors have in mind is the chambers model, rather than the more overtly corporate commercial practice. Law firms most certainly come in all shapes and sizes and, as with any other business organisation, will embrace the whole range of types however they are defined.

(4) The communal organisation: high sociability/high solidarity. These organisations are sociable environments where it is fun to belong, but also highly cohesive with individuals who are not over-calculating about their personal interests. With an air of trust and a focus on achieving success, this seems to be the most desirable of the four categories described.

The management of culture

The firm that wishes to manage its culture can turn to a number of devices to do so. Many will stem from the business planning exercise.

Where do the priorities of the practice lie? Is it maximisation of profit, climbing the partner earnings league, achieving professional prominence for expertise or creating a more sociable environment for people to belong to? These need not be seen as alternatives. The work of Jones and Goffee shows us that it is possible to strive for quality of working relationships and of results, but often there will be a trade-off.

Having determined priorities, the plan can also deal with methodology. Does it see the achievement of ambitious earning goals through the dogged use of current resources or through the development of its personnel?

In many respects it is easier to describe mismanagement of culture than its management. One can point to obvious errors made and hope that benefits will follow from their correction. Most mistakes stem from mixed messages, where partners and staff hear one encouragement but conclude that it is more in their interests to act differently. The most common examples include the following.

- 'Marketing is to be given top priority'. Many firms will stress this, and it is often evidenced by passing high budgetary allowances for client entertaining and other marketing initiatives. Sadly, no allowance is made for fee-earner time, the most important ingredient of the great majority of the most successful marketing. If time on practice development is not measured it will not be rewarded. Even if it is recorded, as more firms now do, it may still be seen as being simply 'non-chargeable time' and therefore subsidiary to the main fee-earning activity of the firm. One assistant in a large provincial firm who was an unusually gifted sportsman, and very well connected as a result, described to me how he tired of continually excusing himself for a perceived shortfall of time recorded. The excuse was always accepted, but the issue would not go away. His conclusion was that it was more in his long term interests to downplay the client relationship building to which he was well suited in favour of simply recording chargeable time. Partnership followed. What the firm said it did not seem to mean.
- 'Teamwork and delegation are to be rewarded'. A similar contradiction often emerges in relation to how work is performed at different levels. Partners in particular will be encouraged to delegate work and become true managers, yet the firm will continue to measure, circulate and discuss performance figures that are far too personal. There is therefore institutional pressure to record time and 'squirrel' work, hording it to ensure that the

individual's personal figures look good, especially in times of recession. The response is to restrict personal details and circulate for discussion only group or team data. Better concentration on the profitability of teams is more likely to produce the required results.

The other obvious way to influence culture is through staff involvement and communication systems. The firm that seeks a greater contribution from its personnel will be likely to change the prevailing attitudes within the firm. This would tend to make the likely development of culture more open and more participative. It is an orthodoxy which various commentators have described. The philosophy of performance management, which we examine in Chapter 12, sees the organisation and the individual as fellow players in improvements and is an attempt to break down the traditional 'them and us' of most organisations.

The trend in progressive organisations is likely to be:

- from machine to organism;
- from hierarchy in problem-solving to a network;
- from status-driven managers to facilitators;
- from military command structure to employee commitment.[3]

The impact of this way of thinking on Investors in People is clear to see. The first indicator states that 'the organisation is committed to supporting the development of its people', while the planning indicators are introduced by 'the organisation has a plan with clear aims and objectives which are understood by everyone'.

An analysis for firms

The firm wishing to define its culture and then state how it would like to see it develop will need to examine a number of trends and factors. The analysis of sociability and solidarity is very helpful and lines up loosely with a comparison that is commonly made within legal practices. This can be summarised as the difference between the collegiate (sociable) environment and the harsher (solidarity) environment. This distinction has been thrown sharply into focus by the attention lavished on the American firms who have moved into London and various other European centres in recent years. The American firm will tend to be more focused on narrow business goals. Earnings per partner are likely to be the sole indicator of substance and there will be enormous attention to all issues of time capture. There is unlikely, however, to be any allowance against fee-earning targets for involvement in management and the firm will be unlikely to support management positions in areas such as marketing. Faced with recession and declining income, partners and staff will be dismissed. The maintenance of profitability is all important.

The traditional British firms differ in many respects. The collegiate practice will see the maintenance of effective teams in good times and bad as being a priority. There is therefore a greater degree of job security for all within the firm. When faced with declining income, rates will be cut to maintain market share. Wider issues of practice management are more highly valued.

A further distinction arises in such firms in relation to partner profit-sharing. The collegiate practice will be likely to have some form of lock-step arrangement in place whereby the profits to each partner are shaped more by general factors than personal performance. The American firms generally look aghast at such arrangements. Surely, they argue, you must pay the top performers top rates, or they will leave. The greater the commitment to the collegiate ethos, the less finance is the only reason for belonging to a firm. At the extremes there are two very different philosophies on practice management and culture. A well researched piece in *Commercial Lawyer* (July/August 2000) showed that there was a move by many firms to more of a 'halfway house'.[4] Modified lock-step was more likely in the largest commercial practices, especially those that have recently undergone transatlantic mergers. Between the purists at either end of the spectrum many will now allow for a top slice of profits to be allocated for unusual contributions, or a super-plateau for consistently higher performers, or a number of other arrangements.

For the sake of a shape, the culture of any given practice can be seen as three converging circles which are defined as finances, relationships and working patterns (see Figure 5.5).

| Figure 5.5 | *Culture of a practice* |

	1	2	3	4	5
			Relationships		

(1)	Supportive	Competitive
(2)	Team-driven	Individualistic
(3)	Hierarchical	Task-driven
(4)	Formal	Informal

Finances

(5)	Collegiate lock-step	Merit-based
(6)	Service-focused	Profit-driven

Working patterns

(7)	Traditional	Experimental
(8)	Techno-resistant	Techno-receptive
(9)	Office-based	Flexible location

Figure 5.6   *Culture assessment chart*

There is a loose correlation to the collegiate, sociable firm on the one hand and the corporate 'solidarity' firm on the other, but it is not a precise variation, especially in the area of working practices. The chart in Figure 5.6 may enable readers to assess their own practices and, in so doing, produce data for discussion.

Main points

- The culture of the firm will be likely to change in any quality improvement programme.
- It is important that the culture is conducive to the aims of the firm and that there is consistency between what is said and what is valued.

Notes

1 Handy, C.B. (1976) *Understanding Organisations*, Penguin.
2 Jones, G. and Goffee, R. (1998) *The Character of a Corporation*, Harper Collins.
3 Pascale, R. (1990) *Managing on the Edge*, Viking, London.
4 [2000] *Commercial Lawyer*, Issue 39, July/August, p. 23.

6

Personal organisation

- Inefficiency and business performance
- A plan of improvements
- An organised working environment
- Dealing with the worst time-waster problems
- Action for the quality programme

The job of the lawyer is to marshal facts and evidence, apply legal principles and so to achieve as positive an outcome as possible for the client. The administrative aspects of this process are critical. Only through achieving good levels of file and information management can the adviser hope to perform well for the client. The personal organisation skills of the fee-earner are crucial for the service provided. It therefore seems ironic that so many solicitors are such poor time managers.

The malaise of poor organisation also affects internal relationships. Analyses of the output of secretaries in law firms show that their productivity can be frustratingly low, in their opinion, because of the chaotic working routine of so many of the lawyers that they work with. Similarly, many trainee solicitors feel that they could be considerably more useful to their firms if only time were made to supervise and control their work. The reality of work in many firms is a self-perpetuating pattern of inefficiency. The result is disproportionate effort having to be made for the results and outcomes actually achieved.

Office administration can also suffer. The frustration of many training, finance and marketing managers in larger firms is that their work seems to consist mainly of chasing up fee-earners to reply to e.mails or memoranda or to do what they have said that they will. Few firms quantify the cost of this internal inefficiency. There seems to be little point in paying competitive salaries to high calibre individuals only to emasculate their efforts through lack of adequate support.

The issue for a quality programme is the degree of effort required for results achieved. The higher the relationship, the better (see Figure 6.1).

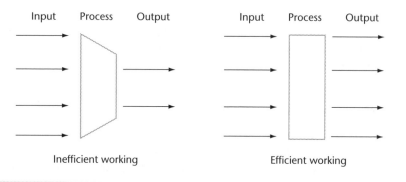

| | Input | Process | Output | | Input | Process | Output |

Figure 6.1   *Inefficient/efficient working*

The appropriate use of time is pivotal to the commercial perform-ance of any practice.

Law firms have only their time, the expertise of their advisers and the effectiveness of their systems to sell to clients. The difficulties of trying to control time as the commodity of production, which in law firms it is, should not be minimised. In their book *The Complete Time Management System*, Christian Godefroy and John Clark point out three facts which underpin this whole area:[1]

- Time cannot be bought: we are all blessed with the same amount of time each day and it is for each of us to use it as wisely as possible.
- Time cannot be saved up: the well prepared precedent bank helps, but client demands can only be dealt with if and when they arise.
- Time cannot be stopped: lost time cannot be recovered.

It is possible to summarise from this the effects of poor time manage-ment in law firms. Where time is poorly managed:

- fee-earners suffer since work intrudes to too great an extent into their private lives;
- support staff suffer through having a chaotic and inefficient working routine;
- clients suffer since inefficiencies result in delays and poor service;
- marketing suffers since the principal barrier to better marketing in many firms is lack of time to do it by key personnel;
- as a result of all of these the firm suffers as profitability will be adversely affected.

The conclusion has to be that everyone suffers from poor time management. This means that achieving a general improvement in personal efficiency should be a priority for any quality co-ordinator seeking to improve the performance of their firm.

Inefficiency and business performance

Studies in the hotel industry suggest that 30 per cent in-built inefficiency is the norm: in other words roughly a third of the effort and tasks undertaken relate to activities which should not have to be done at all, perhaps repeating work not correctly done in the first place, sorting out problems caused by poor communication or locating personnel or items in circumstances which should not be necessary. No similar research appears to be available on the work of solicitors, but it may well be that the proportion of wasted time by all personnel in a typical law firm is roughly the same, if not higher.

Factors to take into account if attempting to measure inefficiency include the ability of fee-earners, and partners in particular, to push inefficiency down the line. Their own routine seems smooth, but the secretary and juniors are left to cope with a state of affairs which can easily be seen to be chaotic and stressful. Secretaries seldom criticise fee-earners directly for this sort of problem. It is, however, in everyone's interests to raise the issue of efficiency at appraisal interviews and to seek improvements where possible.

Part of the time management problem is perception. The principal barrier to improvements to time management is often psychological. Take two solicitors achieving the same output as measured by chargeable hours and billing levels:

- Solicitor 'A' keeps up to date with post and most active files daily. One of the results of this is that a relatively 'clean' desk is maintained since there is little that is out waiting to be worked on. 'A' manages the day to achieve a balance between being available for colleagues and clients and producing the work which he or she is responsible for. 'A' leaves the office most nights at 5.15pm and avoids weekend work.
- Solicitor 'B' thrives on pressure, has a cluttered desk at all times, seldom has time to talk to his or her secretary other than to give out tapes and take messages, has adjusted to working late as a matter of routine and also works regularly during one day of the weekend.

Even if time recorded and billings are roughly equal, all too often the 'martyr' who appears to be fighting a losing battle is the one valued in firms. A change of attitude is needed to ask if the impossibly busy individual is working as well as they should. Where work truly is exceptional it is to be hoped that teamworking patterns can lessen the temporary stress of the situation.

A plan of improvements

Part of the difficulty of improving time management is that the improvements are mainly to be achieved through collective, as opposed to individual, changes. There are various ways in which any individual will be able to improve their routine, but ultimately the real difficulty of time management will be more likely to be how the team functions than the individual. This becomes more so with junior personnel. Secretaries and trainee solicitors have little leeway to organise their routine without the assistance and support of those that they work with. The following suggestions will therefore be more valuable to teams of people who are willing to consider how they work together, but it is also possible for any individual to improve their time management techniques.

Set goals

The most basic starting point of all for the firm or department that wants to achieve improvements in their efficiency is to set goals. The financial performance of firms is maximised by setting budgetary targets which people aim for. The presence of goals improves the performance that would otherwise be likely. Likewise, time management is more likely to succeed if partners and staff have defined what they want to achieve. The improvements might be defined in collective or individual terms:

> Fee-earners in the department should not need to work routinely at weekends.

> Unless there is an exceptional deal going through a department, every member should finish work and leave the office by 6.30 p.m.

> Secretarial overtime should be reduced by a stated percentage.

> The backlog of typing, which is a particular problem of many litigation departments, should be reduced by a stated number of days.

One of the more interesting pieces of data to analyse is the percentage of chargeable time recorded by fee-earners for the total time they work. With assistant solicitors this should be quite high, though it will always tend to be lower when the fee-earner is in an area of practice where they work on many files each day. In many firms the percentage might be less than two-thirds, which most partners would consider disappointing. If this is the case the underlying causes for any inefficiency should be discussed and more challenging goals agreed.

Question attitudes

Another important step is to change the 'martyr' attitude mentioned above. An inefficient routine which eats into personal time should not be regarded as being satisfactory. The role model should be one of efficient and effective working throughout the working day without the need for regular work in what should be personal time.

Complacency is most often observed in relation to backlogs of typing. There are firms where the norm is to accept typing backlogs of a week or more. The risks of allowing this state of affairs are obvious – time limits make no allowance for the fact that the work was done but was waiting to be typed. As delays grow fee-earners have to devote energy to remembering what is still urgent and decisions have to be made about what not to type. Correspondence is often superseded by events and therefore becomes abortive, the result being a waste of time and resources by all concerned. The most remarkable feature of many firms with persistent backlogs is the view that this state of affairs is acceptable or inevitable. It is also interesting to observe how often a backlog is more or less a steady figure. If a department can maintain a backlog of a week for considerable periods of time it suggests that the support staff can keep up with demand, but that fee-earners will never change the pattern to allow the backlog to be cancelled. Alternatively it could be that there is no real commitment to change the situation. Change will only occur when there is determination to deal with a situation which is regarded as being unsatisfactory.

Define the daily routine

The next step is to define what the ideal daily routine should be. This is fairly easy to do as between one fee-earner and their secretary:

> The post is collected/delivered as early as possible. This is always reviewed at the start of the day, along with any diary reminders. A discussion about the priorities for the day ahead ensures that less time is wasted in the morning and both individuals are more focused on the main tasks of the

day as early as possible. The secretary can report on work currently being processed. If this has become excessive there will be little point in more tapes being produced. The fee-earner might agree to telephone more often than write that day, or make arrangements to do work which is time consuming but which does not involve so much typing. Regular communication on an habitual basis of this sort pays dividends as the day progresses and lessens the need for interruptions by one of the other.

Unfortunately the ability to plan the day seems to diminish with time. If the adviser receives faxes or e.mails throughout the day it will be more difficult to assess the total tasks for the day. It is also important to look at the special needs of the work of the department. It is a curious phenomenon, observed in various managerial studies, that people will never quite believe that their current workload is normal. We often say, and hear others say, that life will be calmer in a few weeks' time. For many people this is a myth. Years pass by with the workload more or less constant, but with the individual still certain that the pressure that they are under is temporary only. One of the best studies of this tendency was that of Sune Carlson on managing directors in Sweden:

> The nine persons worked long hours (8.5–11 hours per day) but were surprised by these results when they were made aware of them and consistently thought that the period under inspection was unrepresentative. As a group they realised that their work patterns were unsatisfactory and they criticised themselves for neglecting policy, which in turn meant that they spent too much time dealing with one-off decisions.[2]

The tendency for one-off decisions to multiply if policy is neglected was termed 'administrative pathology' by Carlson. It is a concept which will ring uncomfortably true for many lawyers, both in respect of client work, where details can often detract from the main direction of the matter, and in relation to the ever more demanding managerial aspects of running a law firm. The price of failure to organise a daily routine is an office routine of 'fire-fighting' where all issues become critical before they can be dealt with.

The unstructured nature of the office day in many firms is often a direct result of the climate of fear of clients which has grown in recent years. Clients have become more demanding and to fail to respond immediately can seem to put future instructions at risk. Many will argue that it is impossible to plan a routine to any day since the demands of clients are so difficult to predict. The risk of not doing so, however, is that the day becomes reactive with insufficient attention being given to the more involved work which needs concentration. Those clients that shout the loudest receive the best service: those that respect the time needs of the adviser are penalised. This is turn encourages more clients to be more aggressive in their demands since this is perceived to be the only way to get a sufficient level of attention. For many lawyers this can be seen as the stress cycle of which they are often victims (see Figure 6.2).

It is unrealistic to seek to break this cycle by taking on less work, or increasing charge-out rates, since that would be to stand out against a competitive market. What must happen instead is that the current routine must be improved where possible. The following is an example based on various criminal departments that have attempted to systematise their procedures:

An analysis of the difficulties of their routine would include the following:

- spending mornings in court removes the most productive part of the day for the advocates;
- the advocates have limited time to see clients since they are in court most mornings, usually with multiple commitments;
- court lists mean that different members of the department may well have to pick up colleagues' files at short notice;
- time to dictate routine letters is at a premium: many criminal lawyers only achieve this by working into the evening;
- legal aid rates which apply on most matters mean that work must be delegated to junior staff wherever possible;
- night-time police station visits would be a considerable personal burden for the partners and regular staff.

Recognising these issues, the admitted fee-earners attend court and write the results and decisions onto the file card as they progress. By ensuring that notes always appear in the same place colleagues have confidence in standing up before the magistrates that they will have the pertinent details before them. Files are passed back to the departmental administrator who prepares standard correspondence wherever possible, and

Figure 6.2   *The stress cycle*

attends to all billing requests at the earliest possible opportunity. Dictation of tapes is limited to letters of advice, instructions to counsel etc. An arrangement exists with an independent approved police station attendant who reports pro forma to the firm on all visits.

What is impressive about these arrangements is that the people concerned have taken time to consider the particular problems which they are exposed to. The pattern of work would be in marked contrast to many similar departments, where the criminal lawyers find it difficult to stay on top of the work that they take on.

Handling interruptions

Another common example of possible improvements concerns post opening and distribution. In one firm a busy head of department would see all the post of her department before it was distributed around her colleagues. If a client telephoned after the switchboard opened she would feel that it was essential that she took the call. The client received immediate advice, but meanwhile the whole work of the department was on hold while the post sat on her desk. The change made was that calls were answered when they came in and callers were told that they would be telephoned between 9.30 a.m. and 10.00 a.m. This became the routine for the day every day. In time clients started to ring at 9.30 a.m. instead of 9.00 a.m. Where the will exists clients as well as colleagues can generally be educated into a routine to suit the firm. The issue is not so much to respond to clients whenever the telephone rings but is instead to balance the needs of all clients with the immediate demands of the one who happens to be calling.

It is important to add that developing habits and routines is also important to delegation of work, especially to trainee solicitors. If an individual is to supervise trainee solicitors fairly and to enable them to make the best contribution to the firm's work it is necessary to make sufficient time to supervise their work. This is best achieved by indicating a time of the day when the supervisor will endeavour to be available. Those firms that have 'open door' policies should be prepared to examine this aspect of time management in particular. The open door policy is desirable in principle, but is difficult to apply consistently for the following reasons:

- it encourages unnecessary interruptions where, with a little more initiative or persuasion, the question might not have been appropriate in the first place;

- it can cause delays by the supervisor – an open door makes it easier to suggest that juniors try later; it is not uncommon for days to elapse until the opportunity does actually arise;
- it means that the supervisor achieves little progress with their work as the day progresses, resulting in a tendency to be abrupt with those that need to see them.

This is not to suggest that the day should be rigidly planned in advance, nor that open door policies always fail. The nature of private practice would make any completely structured approach to the day unrealistic. In practice, however, open door policies are often felt to be unsatisfactory by many staff who should supposedly benefit from them. A sensible modification may be to recognise that 'open door' is a statement of intention only and cannot apply all the time. A general plan for the day should be understood to apply where there are always open door periods. This should benefit colleagues and clients alike.

9.00 a.m.   Post arrives.

9.15 a.m.   Review post with secretary and delegate as much as possible to her.

9.30 a.m.   Tasks for the day.

12.00 p.m.   Available for trainees and others requiring supervision.

2.00 p.m.   Return phone calls unable to take earlier.

2.30 p.m.   Tasks for the day/client interviews.

4.15 p.m.   Post signing/supervision starts.

It is worth considering the benefits to the secretary of this plan being in existence. The secretary is likely to benefit from receiving early the post that she or he is required to action. The discussion is a positive way to start the day. The secretary is able to suggest to colleagues that they should try to see the fee-earner after 12.00 p.m. if matters are not genuinely urgent. She or he is able to tell telephone callers that their calls will be returned immediately after lunch. In the good team the fee-earner will recognise the need to back the secretary up in what she or he says. Repeatedly missed telephone calls are minimised.

Prioritise tasks

Too many fee-earners attempt to cope with the work which comes in on an unplanned basis. It is highly unlikely that the day will be capable of being planned precisely, but this should not detract from the simple task of working out the priorities of the day and being focused on them as the day progresses. The point is all the more important for partners and other senior personnel. To supervise others an individual's routine has to be effective. The risk of concentrating merely on the immediate task or crisis is that other work will be becoming more urgent the longer that it is neglected. Such tendencies bolster the stress cycle shown in Figure 6.2 above.

There are various models of planning priorities for the day. What matters is that they work for the individual and it is therefore unwise to claim that any one system is intrinsically better than any other. One which is sometimes encountered in practice is a four box chart which defines all tasks by their importance and urgency, see Figure 6.3. The problem with this system is that all matters become urgent sooner or later, and it is questionable to be encouraged indirectly by a personal organisation scheme to deal with matters only once they become urgent.

The system which seems preferable in law firms is a three column daily planner where the factors are defined by the degree of importance or urgency attaching to them (see Figure 6.4). Any list will only be a snapshot of what has to be done at any time, and most people will tend to rewrite it daily, in addition to amending it as the day progresses.

The best time of day to prepare the list is immediately before the individual leaves the office. This ensures that the fee-earner arrives the next day focused on what must be achieved that day. This also uses the part of the memory that seems to work best at night. Indemnity insurers have recommended that a notepad is kept by the bed for reminders from the subconscious that many can have at night. Many have missed deadlines at work only to remember them somehow while asleep at home. The notepad by the bed may seem a curious

(1) High urgency High importance	(2) Low importance High urgency
(3) Low urgency High importance	(4) Low urgency Low importance

Figure 6.3   *Planning priorities*

Must	Should	Like

Figure 6.4   *Daily planner*

addendum to an office case management system, but it can prove beneficial nonetheless. Having worked out the tasks for the next day most people will arrive for work the next day more focused on them and therefore more likely to make the all important good start to the working day. The day where the first hour is wasted always seems more difficult to make a success.

An organised working environment

A further element of the improvements which can be made is to improve the working environment of members of the team. Many who have opted to pursue registration under ISO 9000 have elected to make a tidy office part of their compulsory regime. There is nothing in the scheme to state that this has to be the case, but it can be a significant improvement to the efficiency of the team nonetheless.

Particularly worrying are those individuals whose desk is chaotic but who can be relied upon to comment 'Don't move a thing: I know where everything is'. This is seldom justified and in those rare cases where it is true it should in any event be a principle of office routine that everyone else should be able to know where important papers might be. The inefficiency of any individual having to sift through piles of papers to find some crucial letter or document should not be tolerated. The worry that the file retrieved from a cabinet is not up to date is a further factor. Everyone is absent from the office sometimes whether planned or otherwise. This makes it all the more important that all information is readily available to all colleagues all the time and that files are best kept properly up to date.

One of the most intriguing elements of the physical environment is how attitudes change to those who 'personalise' their space. Family photographs are a common feature of many offices. These often seem to deter others from making themselves feel too much at home if borrowing the desk for whatever reason. The behaviour of others is more likely to start to change, however, if other accoutrements of the typical home environment are introduced. The story was once told of the typist who sat near the middle of a large typing pool in a large commercial office. Her workload was more or less the same as her colleagues around her. Moving on from family photographs she introduced a soft lighting lamp, at which others approached her less often. Next came a rug which went under her desk and chair. People now started to apologise for intruding and she was often able to read a book while others worked around her.

At the other extreme, part of the interest of various large accountancy offices in moving to 'hot-desking' arrangements where personnel are assigned a work station for the day is to prevent the proliferation of personalised items around the office. This suggests a very different view of the role of the office and the time that the persons concerned should be spending there which improving technology might make more commonplace.

Adopt a logical filing system

A failing of many lawyers is that they file too much information. The consistent filing of letters, notes and other papers on fee earning files is one thing, but the systematic filing of other information, be it mailshots received or internal memoranda, is usually another. Other potentially invaluable pieces of information can often be overlooked or discarded.

The question that should always be asked is 'how useful might this be in the future?' Few internal memoranda meet this test, and one of the most effective methods of dealing with them is to reply in handwriting on the bottom of the paper. This will mean that the sender is freed of the paper and the recipient is reminded of what they asked or commented on and why. A worthy replacement for the voluminous internal files which can easily build up is a 'clippings file' where all sorts of interesting pieces of information are stored for possible future reference. A management device often recommended in industry is to set up files for the internal reports and memoranda that should be kept by reference to sender rather than subject. This can work quite well since most later questions arise from the person who sent the communication or someone asking what happened about a particular memorandum. A file containing all communications from the head of department or personnel manager for the last six months can prove to be much more valuable.

Choose the appropriate format of communication

The easiest thing to do when information has to be communicated is to pick up the dictaphone and put words onto tape. The changing nature of office IT may mean that this does eventually become a thing of the past, but probably not for some time to come in most practices. Written communication is important whenever advice is to be dispensed or confirmed, but is not so important when simple information needs to be conveyed. The time spent dictating is only a fraction of the actual effort required by the firm to send out the letter, a process that will be examined in greater detail in Chapter 14. Secretarial input is required, some delay will usually be inevitable, and the communication is only as personal as the written word can allow. In many such instances telephone contact is preferable in all regards. Telephone contact is two way, so allows the recipient to ask immediately on any points that have been overlooked. Delay is avoided and the secretary can spend greater time on tasks requiring her attention. In many cases the fee-earner could be dodging an issue by not telephoning: it may be easier and potentially less confrontational to write if there is bad news to convey but the letter can merely inflame the situation in such circumstances. It should follow that the need to have written the letter in the first place and the current pressure of work in the team should be issues addressed by supervisors who are called upon to sign or check outgoing post.

One of the easiest improvements to the fee-earner whose work is always subject to backlogs is to cease dictating office memoranda. Likewise there is seldom any compelling reason to dictate all notes of attendance and other file notes: legible handwritten notes are likely to be perfectly acceptable. There are few offices where less but more helpful internal communication could not be a realistic goal. The situation in firms with internal electronic mail appears to offer little hope. It may be easier to 'bin' communications, but the volume seems to increase. Much of the greater output is of marginal assistance to most. In the same way that telephone contact with the client can often be a preferable alternative to a letter, so can a conversation with a colleague in place of a laboriously produced memorandum.

Changes to communication patterns by teams can often be more effective than merely personal changes. One of the best systems, which also offers great potential for marketing effectiveness in law firms, is to have a weekly summary sheet distributed throughout the firm. People within the firm can be encouraged always to concentrate on this information sheet when it appears. By diverting most requests for help and one-off pieces of communication through this channel, the daily surfeit of memoranda is reduced. An example of such a sheet appears in Chapter 15.

Dealing with the worst time-waster problems

The steps suggested above should all help with the problems most complained of by solicitors in coping with their routine. These can be summarised as follows:

- telephone interruptions;
- colleagues' interruptions, whether work or social;
- changed priorities;
- administrative complications;
- personal fatigue.

Telephone interruptions

There is a worrying trend in respect of telephone interruptions which needs careful consideration. Rightly striving for the best levels of client care, the view is increasingly taken by many firms that direct contact to the fee-earner is a priority. The approach adopted by such firms is the external equivalent of the 'open door' policy, but is fraught with similar complications. Those firms that have private direct lines to fee-earners display the problems the most poignantly. In some cases the only prospect of working on any substantial task is to do it out of office hours or to divert the telephone, sometimes contrary to office instructions. If the working day is one long and uncontrolled sequence of interruptions the quality of work suffers, more substantial tasks are postponed in favour of lesser ones and work therefore becomes critical before it is undertaken. The net result of this is that the quality of response on the telephone often leaves much to be desired. Picking up the telephone to unannounced calls may mean that the caller gets an immediate response, but the fee-earner will often have to find the file and return the call in any event, thereby adding to his or her workload and still not producing the immediate service that the partners may aspire towards. Worse still, as the day progresses the frustration grows so that the response can easily become curt as the pressing tasks of the day remain unattended to.

Earlier offers to return telephone calls start to become increasingly difficult to meet.

The better approach appears to lie in the planning of the day into sections discussed above. It is helpful to take into account that true open availability is a myth. Personnel are unavailable because they are in meetings, out at court or absent. Once this is recognised it is a simple matter to ensure that there is good availability every day, but not all day.

> In one West End firm the partners were regularly working at least one day a weekend, which for many meant a long journey into London or taking large files home. They agreed that in half a day on Saturday or Sunday the output could easily be the equivalent of a full day or even two in the week. The telephone interruptions were the greatest difference. Jobs inevitably took longer if the telephone interrupted concentration and the flow of dictation. They resolved to try a system of 'prime time' when they would simply be unavailable. They recognised that it was inadvisable to be negative, nor did they want particularly to lie to callers about the fact that they were in the office and simply working on other matters. 'Prime time' became a code. The receptionist/switchboard operator would say to callers that he or she was unavailable at the moment, but would be free after the stated time (usually 11.00 a.m.) or would the caller like to speak to the secretary. Calls put through to the secretary were noted or actioned by her. If a call was needed from the fee-earner she would say that this would occur between 11.00 a.m. and 11.30 a.m. and would question if the caller were likely to be available at that time. Abortive calls were minimised by this.

The principal findings of these arrangements were that few callers objected to immediate non-availability knowing that they could speak that morning. Most callers preferred to call later rather than speak to the secretary. Weekend working was reduced. The fee-earners felt better able to provide a quality response with their main tape of the day out of the way earlier than would otherwise have been the case.

To those who may read this and consider it heretical to the object of better client care it is important to stress that client care works at levels other than the superficial. Clients are accustomed to not speaking to their adviser at the first time of trying. The direct line is a positive feature of client care but only if the person is there. Many calls ring unanswered or divert to a message machine. In some firms it is not uncommon for the lawyer to 'hide' somewhere in the office to avoid all calls.

Quality of response, coupled to the avoidance of unreasonable delays, should be the aim. The view should be taken that quality of response should be more important than mere speed of response.

What actually leads clients to be highly dissatisfied is more likely to be leaving a message which is not returned as quickly as they are expecting. In most cases the secretary taking a call has little idea of when the fee-earner might return the call so can give little real help. If anxiety increases on the part of the caller as the day progresses they are more likely to call again. Many become aggressive to the secretary even if they revert to normal when speaking to the adviser. More and more of the secretary's day is taken up in taking telephone notes and fielding irate clients. The need for a pattern for the day and for a period of uninterrupted working can be seen to be the best response to this unsatisfactory state of affairs.

Colleagues' interruptions

There are various nuggets of advice available on how to handle interruptions by colleagues constructively. These range from standing when the interrupter enters the room to placing files on chairs when interruptions need to be discouraged. All such tactics are a part admission of defeat. In theory we should all be able to be honest – we do not have the time now but we hope to be free later. A feeling of guilt can easily develop. We are at work in part to socialise and to share experiences in a service profession where the experience of colleagues is an invaluable asset. Our being busy can often cause offence to be taken.

This is a problem where collective action is almost certainly called for. Some code is needed to avoid the embarrassment and potential offence that can easily arise. A 'prime time' arrangement as above can achieve this: there is no reason why prime time cannot include internal interruptions as well as telephone calls from clients. In other firms an unofficially coded system develops – the most common example is that the door to the office is either open or closed to signal availability. On balance it is probably better to put such systems onto a formalised and overt basis. Few might enthuse about the concept adopted in one large open plan office of a major retailer of staff donning a red baseball hat while wishing not to be disturbed, but fewer still could deny that there would be real benefits to self and to clients in allowing for an interruption-free time every day.

Changed priorities

The fact that the working day is so prone to changing and competing demands for attention is both the problem and the challenge of legal work. Coping with a range of clients, most of whom appear to think that theirs is the only matter deserving of attention that day, adds to the problems. The reactive and unplanned day is not the best way to cope with legal work. The daily planning schedule as set out in Figure 6.4, if applied with flexibility, is invaluable. As circumstances change matters may be promoted to 'must' items. The frequency with which this happens might lead the individual to consider if their personal routine allows enough leeway to cope with continual changes to circumstances.

Administrative complications

Collective action is once again called for. In particular it must be recognised that one of the prime responsibilities of the management of any firm is to create an environment which is supportive to efficiency of working. If junior personnel have to scour the firm for a secretary willing to type work, if lack of resources for such services as photocopying mean delays and frustrations or if lack of training mean that facilities cannot be used, management is likely to be regarded as having failed. For their part fee-earning and secretarial staff have to realise that management and administrative personnel also have their priorities and needs. It is test of the quality of leadership in many firms to see if tensions between different sections of staff have been minimised or even, in some cases, contrived at.

Personal fatigue

The greatest platitude of all in law firm management is that law firms are a 'people' business. The implications of this can easily be overlooked. People are different to machines in that they are potentially brilliant and creative, but also prone to error, fatigue and poor performance. It is unrealistic to expect continuous, full productivity day after day and month after month. On the basis that we should eschew the 'martyr' in law firms, holidays must be taken. A balance between private and working lives is the best method to head off stress and fatigue problems before they arise. On a daily basis the discipline of the list of tasks should ensure that more important jobs are undertaken first. The temptation on our worst days is to dither with the least important tasks and become increasingly anxious as the day progresses.

Action for the quality programme

The difficulties to be faced by the quality co-ordinator in this area should not be under-estimated. In many cases real success will involve a change of some cherished beliefs and a willingness by the most senior to alter their ways to make work throughout the office more efficient. The type of time management training which has become commonplace in many firms' internal programmes in recent years plays a useful role, but will probably be doomed to failure if it is not accompanied by the sort of collective changes described above.

Having defined some goals there must be extensive consultation within the team. In this the co-ordinator should bear in mind that those who are most junior are probably in the best position to offer the greatest insights. As the likely victims of any inefficiency in the office they are best placed to suggest improvements to the daily routine. Having elicited suggestions they must be examined. Ideally there should be a departmental exercise to determine how matters could be improved and the quality committee will be invaluable in ensuring that difficult issues are not avoided.

Common suggestions by secretaries in such exercises include:

- appreciate the pressure that we are under too: we deal with the same clients;
- return phone calls: if the client rings several times they will often become angry with us even though they are polite to the fee-earner when they do eventually speak to them;
- do not lie to clients;
- telephone clients more often;
- when dictating tapes provide a list of contents, speak clearly and give precise instructions, do not chew or eat while you are dictating, provide urgent work separately and earlier in the day;
- more shorter tapes are easier than fewer longer ones.

Rules for the department should be drawn up and these should be included in the departmental quality assurance procedures. Breaches of the agreed standard should be treated in much the same way as any other irregularity.

Training sessions are essential, addressing both the personal techniques which can assist and the collective improvements which have been determined. The goals which have been set should be monitored and the process of continuous improvement should be pursued. Much can often be learned from observing the routine of those who have adjusted to part-time working, particularly those who have to leave at a certain time because of child care arrangements. Working to a clear finish time often keeps interruptions to a minimum, and it is not uncommon to find that the same output is achieved in four days where the person used to work five, or where the finish time is 4.00 p.m. daily. A clear sense of the available time and the priorities to achieve within the time available do appear to produce the organisational benefits envisaged in this chapter.

Main points

- Bad time management has a direct effect on business performance.
- Part of the problem is often the culture of 'martyrs'.
- A programme of improvements will benefit from clear goals.
- Better time management is an important response to increasing stress levels within the profession.
- A consistent pattern to the working day benefits all concerned – including clients.
- Organisation of working environment, filing of information and the best choice of communication are helpful.

References to Lexcel

D7 Supervision

Notes

1 Godefroy, C. and Clark, J. (1990) *The Complete Time Management System*, Guild Publishing.
2 Carlson, S., (1951). As quoted by Lawrence, P. and Elliott, K. (1985) in *Introducing Management*, Penguin Business.

7

Stress management

- Responsibility for stress
- From pressure to stress
- Stressors
- The filter factors
- Treatments

The issue of stress is not directly mentioned in any of the main quality standards, yet is increasingly seen as an important component in the management policies of many progressive institutions. There are good grounds for treating the subject seriously in the law. There are two elements that would lead firms to develop a policy on stress management: either to fulfil its values to staff within its strategy, or as part of its risk management profile. There is plentiful evidence of the risks of mounting stress levels and it is clearly a growing concern in relation to personnel welfare. There are also self-evident links between stress levels and the likelihood of errors, as highlighted by the Solicitors' Indemnity Fund Risk Assessment Manual.[1]

There have been numerous surveys in recent years testifying to significantly increasing stress levels. In a report in the *Gazette* the Solcare co-ordinator reported that calls were dividing something like 50/50 between stress and alcoholism.[2] Given that alcoholism itself may be a reaction to stress the position was bleak, however viewed. 'Lawyer burn-out on the increase' was another familiar heading in the *Gazette* in July 1998.[3] The article reported the worries over fee-earner turnover being as high as 40 per cent per annum, the source being a confidential report produced by a number of City personnel departments.

Stress difficulties are endemic in modern business life, but appear to be more pronounced in the law than elsewhere. One report found that stress levels in solicitors were, to the apparent surprise of the authors, higher than junior doctors.

According to Dr Stephen Williams . . . lawyers, who made up 408 of the 2,231 respondents to the poll had the worst profile of the four vocational professions surveyed. He said: 'we expected doctors to be the problem group, particularly junior doctors. In reality it was the lawyers who were the worst'.[4]

The *Gazette* recorded that solicitors reported the worst levels of mental and physical health, as well as the lowest energy levels. If long hours are a fairly obvious cause of stress the law is as pernicious as most areas. The City report mentioned above told the tale of a team of lawyers spending 72 hours 'locked together drafting a £25m agreement'. One solicitor from Dibb Lupton Alsop (as they then were) commented that 'deals are becoming more complex and institutions are spending much larger sums of money, so they are taking longer over their due diligence checks'.[5] Surely any medic would be greatly concerned by another partner from a City firm quoted as having only had a maximum of three hours' sleep per night for three months. The more genteel days of the profession, where the occasional round of golf would follow a few hours at the office, seem to be little more than a fast fading memory.

Three causes were provided for the apparent increase in stress within the profession in an article by Catherine Berney, a solicitor turned consultant and trainer.[6] These were:

(1) a growth in competition throwing greater focus on service quality, delivery and price;
(2) the reduction of traditional client loyalty and an increased tendency for clients to 'shop around' for the best deal;
(3) the increased technological capability so that 'there is no longer any excuse for not knowing the answer'.

In Berney's view lawyers are faced with 'more decision making and less time'.

This trend of increasing lawyer stress coincides with increasing employer responsibility for stress-related illness. There are have been a number of well publicised findings and settlements in recent years. *Walker* v. *Northumberland County Council* [1995] 1 All ER 737, QB remains a landmark decision:

> Mr Walker, a social worker involved in child care, had a sharply increased workload. Increases in the population area for which he had responsibility had not been matched by increases in staff. He had no record of nervous illness, nor did he have any particular features of his personal life which were stressful. After a first breakdown in 1986 he was promised an assistant, but the help did not materialise and his caseload continued to increase after his return. A second nervous breakdown followed later that year. The employers were found responsible for this second breakdown on grounds that it was on notice of the risks after his

first illness, and they had failed to act reasonably in relation to his return to work.

More recently in another public sector case, Beverley Lancaster was awarded £67,000 against Birmingham City Council having shown that her workload had caused her serious illness. Claims are increasing in the private sector also and there have been numerous high profile settlements in recent months, including a settlement of £100,000 by a major bank of a claim against them by a former manager. This latter case produced a sharp response from the CBI. How, they asked, should employers cope in an increasingly competitive workplace when the problem was that certain employees could not cope with pressures that others thrived upon? Where will liability end if an enjoyable working environment for the majority turns out to be problematic for others?

Whether out of fear for legal liability or for genuine concern for colleagues, those responsible for personnel management in law firms should be prepared to look for and help with stress when it does manifest itself. Beyond this, however, the position on stress management becomes distinctly less clear. What the caring or prudent employer should do, and the extent to which the risks can be quantified, is at best a grey area. Various strategies can be employed from stress audits to training and counselling, but the prognosis for resolving the problem is far from encouraging.

Part of the difficulty is defining quite what stress actually is. Stress is not a single recognisable condition, but can include a range of problems and be evidenced by a number of different responses. Common symptoms of stress would include absenteeism and, ironically, its seeming opposite of 'presenteeism', the tendency never to take time off or work regular hours. Poor performance could result, as could irritation, mood swings and bullying of others. Lack of concentration is commonly experienced, often linked to sleep difficulties at night. More extreme medical conditions will also often be related, most commonly digestive problems such as stomach ulcers or coronary failure. The difficulty is that all such problems could just as easily arise in the absence of stress. Cause and effect are difficult to establish, and therefore to protect against and accept responsibility for.

Much is made of the so-called 'fight or flight' reaction. Faced with situations of threat or danger we respond with responses physiologically in place from man's earliest days. Facing a vicious predator we would be conditioned to respond with a near instantaneous set of reactions. The hypothalamus area of the brain triggers the pituitary gland to secrete adrenaline through the adrenal glands on either side of the kidneys. The adrenaline will cause the heart to beat quicker and blood pressure to rise, while breathing becomes short and shallow. The digestive system shuts down and we become partly numbed to pain. Should we be cut, the different blood texture would enable wounds to heal more quickly. We are as well equipped as we can be to face physical danger. We now have the choice to stand and fight the threat or to beat as hasty a retreat as we are capable of.

The problem of modern life is that our conditioning seems much less appropriate to office dangers. Standing up to make a presentation or responding to an intimidating meeting or telephone call could all generate the fight or flight response within us, but this might happen several times a day for pressured advisers whereas the reaction was more occasional for our distant ancestors. Furthermore, we do not have the opportunity in the office environment to work off the chemicals generated by the response through our system. The combined effect is that our bodies could, quite literally, be wearing out at a much faster rate than nature intended. Little wonder, therefore, that 'burn-out' is the concern of so many reports and authorities in the area.

The worries of excessive fight or flight reactions are all the greater as the body may react in this way not just to immediate physical or personal threat, but when we recall past concerns or panic about future risks also. In his book *Managing Stress: the Challenge of Change* Derek Roger highlights the distinction between 'everyday' stress and 'post-traumatic' stress.[7] Post-traumatic stress is 'the aftermath of exposure to events which exceed the individual's capacity for coping' whereas everyday stress is defined as 'the continuous effort of responding to the inexorable change which is the only constant in life'.

Along these lines the distinction could be made between short term stress and long term stress. Short term, or everyday, stress is something that we will all need in appropriate measure as part of the challenge that keeps us occupied. It certainly seems to be part of the make-up of most lawyers that continuous challenge is an important requirement for motivation. Starved of it most professionals have a fairly low boredom threshold. We respond to this daily challenge by adapting to it. This is unlikely to be problematic unless, as Roger puts it, 'opportunities for recovery are few and far between'. What we might call long term stress is of much greater concern. Here the victim is unable to cope, whether through not recovering quickly enough in relation to everyday stress or through mental difficulties of a post-traumatic nature. If we continually struggle to keep our heads above water, or if we are beset with anxieties generated from past experience, the health dangers grow.

Responsibility for stress

A further concern for partners will be who is actually to blame for the worsening position on stress at work. Blame could be attributed amongst three groups: clients, the firm or the victims. Berney primarily highlights changed client expectations and this seems to be the logical starting point. Increased client demands and the need to respond effectively in a consumerist environment may seem to be factors beyond the control of the firm, but there have been moves by some firms to agree more realistic arrangements between advisers and clients and these could no doubt assist. One of the more encouraging trends to emerge in recent years is the American development of 'partnering' for which Dupont are credited.[8] Under these arrangements the client agrees to limit the extent to which instructions will be undertaken in the firm and not to sue for negligence. In return it receives discounted fees. All should benefit from a greater sense of trust and co-operation. Other than through such developments, however, collective stress improvement through better client demands seems unlikely.

At a personal level, individual partners might take the lead in discussing with clients whether there truly is the degree of urgency claimed with particular matters or tasks. To do so could be seen as effective leadership in the terms of Chapter 8. It is the firm that has legal responsibilities for their personnel and not clients. The issue here is part of culture. Is the firm supportive or does it see people with problems as 'wimps'? There was a worrying item reported in the *Gazette* which announced 'Solicitors Stressed, but Firms Uncaring'.[9] Joint research by Solcare and a firm of legal recruitment agents showed that only a quarter of firms actively helped staff with stress. At the other extreme a remarkable 10 per cent had responded to stress difficulties by instituting disciplinary proceedings. A further 5 per cent had been told to start grievance proceedings. Expressing little surprise at the findings, Lucy Winskell, speaking as the Law Society Council member with responsibility for young solicitors, attributed such remarkable responses to the 'macho culture' of many firms where it was considered a weakness to admit to being unable to cope. Perhaps even more concerning was the report of the Trainee Solicitors Group in June 2000 of abuse of trainees by firms based on various 'harrowing' tales to the group's helpline.[10] Little wonder that fee-earner turnover in some firms is so worryingly high.

Complacency and poor management of the issue might be compounded by research that happy workers are not necessarily, it would seem, more productive workers. According to Dr Rob Briner of the University of London:

> The available evidence shows no strong link between stress, satisfaction and performance. Similarly, measures of stress and satisfaction also appear to be largely unrelated to absenteeism.[11]

This would suggest that stressful circumstances might be quite likely to continue to produce satisfactory performance results. However, the firm that permits long term stressful conditions, knowing full well of the dangers thereby posed to the individual, and which has responded to other stress difficulties in a disciplinary manner, will struggle to show that it holds the moral high ground in any eventual stress-related claim.

The third possible source of blame is the victims themselves. The role that the individual complainants play in their own demise is one of the more contentious elements of many stress situations. The psychological make-up of the lawyer may collude with working conditions that are likely to cause problems. Dr Stephen Williams, the author of the report showing the highest levels of professional stress amongst solicitors, commented on the tendency of people to 'buy in' to the 'urgency addiction' of firms.[12] His observation was that 'many of the people attracted to the profession are high flyers with a predisposition to push themselves too hard – they love the adrenaline rush'. The leading stress consultant Dr Ann Fingret has also talked of the lawyer's insistence on perfection being one of the problems: working longer and harder to get things right in a manner that is simply not possible given the workload and time pressures.[13]

The difficulty may well be how close the boundary seems to be between an agreeable level of daily challenge, which is the norm for most fee-earners, and the long term stress symptoms explained above. An analogy can be made with top athletes who will train as closely as possible to their cardiac abilities. Working at this outer level of endurance increases the risks of viral illness. Paradoxically, the super-fit are often less immune from colds and flu than others. So too with the ambitious fee-earner. They may have coped well for years with sustained pressure, but they are likely to be close to their edge of endurance and the pressures that they have always thrived upon can easily switch to become the problem.

The fee-earner can assist by being prepared to ask for help as soon as they realise that they are not coping as well as before. Various commentators have highlighted the need for the individual to take some of the responsibility for their own condition. Penny Moyle of Oxford University has talked of companies asking their staff to become more 'emotionally literate'.[14] Likewise, Andy Guppy of Liverpool John Moores University has talked of individual employees being responsible for their own well-being: 'there is no reason why coping strategies should be kept to the counselling room'.[15]

If clients, firms and individual employees could all be to blame for the conditions leading to stress problems it suggests that all three parties have to be prepared to work together to improve matters. The prime responsibility must surely lie with the firm, however, which should create the conditions where fee-earners can enjoy the stimulus of professional challenge but with a safety net in place when difficulties arise.

From pressure to stress

The firm that wishes to put in place a stress management policy will need to understand a three-stage process: see Figure 7.1. The object is that the 'coping strategies' in the middle column should be sufficient to absorb the pressures generated by the activities of the firm. Depending on how effective these filters are, stress difficulties, as highlighted in the third column, should be avoided.

(1) **Stressors** ⟶	(2) **Filter factors** ⟶	(3) **Stress difficulties**
Client demands	Supportive culture	Emotional: depression, irritability
Fear and anxieties	Organisation of work	Sleep disorders: fatigue
Competing pressures: role stress	Efficiency management	Digestive problems: loss of appetite or eating disorders
	Delegation of work	Loss of sex drive
	Personality: the resilience of the individual	Muscular: head, neck back pains
	Personal lifestyle and health	

Figure 7.1   *Stress management policy*

Stressors

Increasing client demands have been commented upon already, while fears and anxieties are best dealt with under the heading of 'personality' in the filter factors. This leaves the issue of role stress. It is often not simply particular work pressures or an overload of work that causes stress. The interrelationship with our personal life is bound to be a major influence. The wise employer will therefore look to the full range of roles occupied by the person, to the extent that they are known about, and not exclusively the working responsibilities. Psychologists will often approach stress by drawing up a 'role chart' to plot the competing demands upon the individual.

The chart works by looking at the roles and relationships that define our view of ourselves. From each line we may give and take, not necessarily in equal measure. For many people in the modern era the obvious problem is that we simply have too much going on in our lives. We strive to be effective in every role, but there is simply not enough of us to go around. We are suffering from 'role overload'.

Another common difficulty is 'role conflict', in which competing roles can make us feel inadequate in all regards, of which the 'sick child' phenomenon is the most common. We have our commitments to work and wish to be taken as seriously as any colleague, but a child off ill at home can wreak havoc with practical arrangements and make us feel that we are failing as parents. For many this is a 'no-win' situation which is highly stressful. 'Role underload' can arise when there is too much focus on work as there is insufficient stimulus elsewhere, leading to the individual being too highly strung about work issues and lacking in perspective.

The filter factors

The firm that is serious about wishing to improve stress management will make attempts to produce a genuinely supportive environment in which problems are raised as early as possible without fear of criticism or career prejudice. Good leadership here requires the partners to agree new coping strategies to deal with current problems. Effective supervision of this type will almost certainly have a positive impact on fee-earner retention rates.

Those who take instructions, whether partners or assistants, can also assist by questioning with clients unrealistic or unnecessary deadlines which will create avoidable pressure for fee-earners. Good leadership requires partners to be prepared to rise above the culture of 'fear of clients' and negotiate sensible conditions for turnaround of work. Where this is not possible firms will need to be more prepared than they often are to turn work away on grounds that it will not be possible to resource it adequately for its high quality standards.

So far as personality is concerned there are those of us who are worriers and others who take difficulties in our stride. Whether through nature or nurture the differences are as unfair as they are real. Fears and anxieties will be common experience for us all, however, and what varies is how well we deal with them as individuals. Derek Roger includes in his book a questionnaire which investigates the extent to which we are likely to 'ruminate' on previous difficulties.[16] The ability to consign mistakes or problems to the past, to learn from them and then move on to new challenges is one to admire in those who have it. Others will benefit from realising their tendency to add to current difficulties by churning through the past and can be encouraged to talk through problems to lessen their impact. The author also contrasts 'avoidance coping', in which the individual avoids confronting difficulties and 'detached coping' in which he or she may be over-fatalistic about their problems and feel that they have little influence over them.

Other management responses – principally time management, delegation and teamworking – all play an important part in attempts to counter stress related problems.

So far as lifestyle is concerned we seem to be bombarded daily with messages about what to eat and to avoid, how much exercise we should take and which stimulants should be rationed. There seems little argument that better physical health enables us to cope with the demands of work better and it is one of the actions that can most easily be taken to manage stress problems.

Treatments

There is a potential fourth column to the stress management chart, for treatment. Since the objective is prevention rather than a cure, however, it seems defeatist to include it. Briner talks rather disparagingly about most 'stress management interventions', which he lists as:[17]

- reducing exposure to psychologically harmful working conditions;
- instituting stress management training programmes;
- providing counselling therapies.

Briner concludes that changing job conditions does not necessarily improve matters, a conclusion which he describes as 'disappointing and puzzling'. The main conclusion seems to be that changes to work are often only cosmetic and short term – true changes are not the usual experience. He is equally downbeat about the prospects of stress management training working. The difficulty will be transferring the conclusions of the training session to changed arrangements within the job. All too often such sessions provide insights which will not be transferred to changes of working arrangements, perhaps through the non-attendance of key decision-makers and isolation from the true working environment. He is more positive about the prospects for counselling, though observing that they often focus on non-work, personal issues rather than work-related stress.

The abiding conclusion is that the only effective way to manage stress is to change the circumstances that bring it about in the first place – what Briner calls 'specific and focused solutions'. These might relate to volumes of work, the terms under which instructions are received, the support provided to personnel and the culture of the organisation. If all can be addressed in a stress management programme they are likely to be appreciated by talented and valued personnel and will undoubtedly form a useful component to the firm's risk management, personnel welfare and quality policies.

Main points

- Stress is an increasing problem within the profession and will have an impact on personnel welfare and risk management.
- The firm, the clients and the personnel concerned all have a part to play in developing a sensible approach to stress management.

Notes

1 'Self Assessment Risk Audit' (2000) Solicitors' Indemnity Fund.
2 [1999] *Gazette*, 6 May, p. 4.
3 [1998] *Gazette*, 15 July, p. 9.
4 Williams, S. (1999) 'Report by Resource System for BUPA', reported in [1998] *Gazette*, 11 November, p. 1.
5 [1998] *Gazette*, 15 July, p. 9.
6 Berney, C. [1995] *International Journal of the Legal Profession*, vol. 2, nos. 2–3, p. 239.
7 Roger, D. (1997) *Managing Stress: the Challenge of Change*, Chartered Institute of Marketing (CIM Holdings).
8 [1998] *Commercial Lawyer*, Issue 24, p. 27.
9 [1999] *Gazette*, 16 June, p. 1.
10 Report of the Trainee Solicitors Group in [2000] *Gazette*, 22 June, p. 1.
11 Briner, R., and Reynolds, S. (1999) 'On the costs, benefits and limitations of organisational-level stress interventions', *Journal of*

Organisational Behaviour.
12   Williams, S. (1999) *op. cit.*
13   Fingret, A. [1997] *People Management*, 23 January, p. 17.
14   Moyle, P. [1997] *People Management*, 23 January, p. 17.
15   Guppy, A. [1997] *People Management*, 23 January, p. 17.
16   Roger, D. (1997) *op. cit.*
17   Briner, R. [1997] *People Management*, 23 January, p. 17.

8

Leadership

- Thinking on leadership
- Supervisory leadership
- Commercial leadership
- Leadership tasks
- Leadership attributes
- Decision making
- The management of change
- Managing a quality programme

Leadership, it could be argued, has always been vital for any organisation. The pressures of modern practice, however, have increased the importance of leadership within every firm in private practice. In a changing environment clarity of purpose and the drive to achieve are essential. The universal advice for any firm embarking on a quality management project is to have true commitment from the top. Much the same could be said about a review of the business strategy, a new marketing policy or a project to maximise financial performance. It follows that the quality of leadership will be one of the prime determinants of the business success of most practices.

Within the law it is the pace of change in recent years which has thrown leadership into sharper focus. In years gone by the autocratic senior partner would have far fewer concerns. Legislation and changes to the law were more intermittent, the practice of law was seldom an issue for politicians and job mobility was a problem yet to surface. The task of managing a firm was more one of monitoring developments than initiating change. With growing commercial pressures have come greater leadership challenges. Along these lines the distinction is often made between leadership, which has overtones of driving an organisation forwards, and management, which is controlling performance and results. Merely to manage the firm will be to see it fall behind. Leadership must now find the way forward.

Leadership is a role which will be assigned to various individuals, or perhaps a group, within any firm. It is a responsibility which will bear heavily on those assigned to the task. They will judge themselves and be judged on how effective their leadership is. The essence of leadership is how well leaders elicit improved performance from their partners, colleagues, and the department or firm as a whole. It is little surprise, therefore, that the legal press abound with leadership stories. Of greatest interest is the managing partner thrown into a firm that was reckoned to be ailing, only to pull it around and then to be awarded some sort of prize for performance in its category. What strategies were adopted and what internal changes were needed to achieve this? It is an area of practice which has become very much more public in recent years.

Precise advice on what good leadership is and how it can be developed is, however, difficult to find. The unavoidable conclusion from the myriad of management texts dealing with the subject of leadership is that a wide range of styles, values, beliefs and activities can amount to good leadership. Leadership appears to be situational: what may be effective in one firm may be unacceptable elsewhere. It will follow that the culture of each organisation clearly has much to do with it. The authorities can suggest a framework for better leadership, but it is for each person to find their style and approach within their own particular circumstances.

Thinking on leadership

At the outset of management studies there was much greater confidence that steps to better leadership could be prescribed. The American researcher and writer Frederick Taylor considered that management was a science that could be subject to rigorous examination with the aim of distilling the essential principles for general consumption. His book *Principles of Scientific Management* lays down a clear division of leaders and the led.[1] Those who are able to lead should do so and it should not be for subordinates to interfere with the processes instigated in this way. This formula succeeded in his work with the first production lines in the early years of the twentieth century. Taylor had a particular involvement in the automation of the early Ford plants, with notable success. They are views which sit ill at odds with the flatter more democratic business structures of today, however.

On the vexed question of who should be appointed to a management position, Taylor considered that some people stood out for their management potential. He was a believer in the 'traits' of managers for leadership. Good leaders, he observed, were intelligent, articulate, and well educated. They possessed qualities of assertiveness, self-confidence

109

and resilience. What seems more curious to the modern eye is his assertion that certain physical attributes indicate management potential. Good leaders, he tells us, are taller and not overweight. Quite apart from the inappropriateness of such ideas to today's society another very obvious difficulty arises. Exceptions can very easily be found to such bland assertions. Good leaders may generally be intelligent, but not in all cases. Some of the dynamic leaders may be short and many are poor communicators; others are overweight. This analysis of leadership seems to throw up almost as many exceptions as illustrations and cannot therefore be accepted as being of sufficient value. There are certain fairly self-evident values that would be associated with better leaders, but in themselves they are not preconditions of either the role itself or success in it.

Thinking on leadership moved on with the so-called behaviouralists. Various researchers turned their observations away from who and what leaders were to what it was that they actually did. Building on earlier American research the British authority John Adair developed his 'action-centred' approach to leadership.[2] He argued that there are three sets of needs to be addressed, and that the prime responsibility of leaders was to pay proper attention to each category (see Figure 8.1). The best managers, he tells us, are those who intervene and assist whenever imbalance arises.

Helpful though the insight is to better leadership from the behaviouralists, there is still no answer to the main point in issue. How can one determine the best approach to secure the best results in any given situation? The management theorists respond that this must depend on the circumstances particular to any given situation. The contingency theorists show us the aspects to consider and to adapt for success. Most authorities in this area examine the relationship of the leader to the group. According to Fiedler, for example, results were best where:[3]

(a) the leader was liked and trusted by the group;
(b) the task was clearly defined, and
(c) the power of the leader in the group was high.

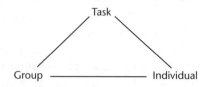

Figure 8.1   *Action-centred leadership*

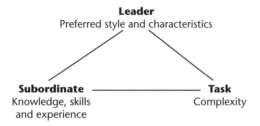

Figure 8.2   *Good leadership – 'best fit' theory*

Specific studies in law firms are hard to find, but the above sounds a fair description of the better performing departments in firms. Another analysis is that good leadership is to be found in a balance between three concepts: see Figure 8.2.

The 'best fit' theory tells us that there is no right or wrong in management practice, only appropriate or inappropriate. Certain factors will influence the balance and the acceptability of styles and can therefore be helpful for analysis in given situations. In his text *Understanding Organisations* Charles Handy includes:[4]

Leader:	preferred style
	confidence in subordinates
	need for certainty
Subordinate:	self assessment of competence and intelligence
	interest in the task and perception of its importance
	past experience
Task:	timescale – urgency
	significance of risk of errors

Supervisory leadership

In relation to supervisory management and the preferred style of the leader one of the most helpful concepts is that of leadership style analysed by direction and support. By taking these two concepts and pairing them alternatively with each other, four main styles emerge, each of which, it is argued, can be appropriate in various circumstances. This model (see Figure 8.3) first appeared in the work of Paul Hersey and Kenneth Blanchard.[5]

The analysis is based on the amount of specific direction or instruction provided (task behaviour) and also on the 'socio-emotional support', or 'relationship' behaviour. One of the most

Low direction High support	High direction High support
Low direction Low support	High direction Low support

Figure 8.3   *Supervisory leadership*

interesting applications of this theory is that it can track the 'learning curve' of an individual. When I first start to learn a new skill I will need specific instruction in what to do at the outset, but gradually emphasis should switch to my understanding and confidence with the issue in hand. My mentor can become less instructional in time and, in due course, less personally involved with me also in relation to that activity. Applied to the above 'best fit' model, the complexity of the task and my knowledge, skills and experience should determine how 'hands-on' my supervisor is. The leadership style appropriate in the circumstances depends more on my familiarity and comfort with the task in hand than their personality or preferred style. It seems fair to conclude that good supervisors are flexible and able to deal with different colleagues in different ways.

Leadership in law firms operates in two distinct respects. At its most obvious level there is leadership of fee-earning work – delegation, in effect. There seems to be a general acceptance for the proposition that lawyers do not naturally make good delegators. Delegation of fee earning work is too often an all or nothing activity, with most lawyers being too prone on the one hand to retain work that should be passed on, and on the other hand to offload too much responsibility on others. The quality of working relationships, which is the central tenet of the contingency theorists, has much of value in this area. Delegation is more likely to work as all agree that it should if there can be better working relationships between the team members, issues that we consider in Chapters 9 and 10.

Commercial leadership

Increasingly, leadership is also vital to the commercial activity of running a successful business. Although technical errors are not so much the concern here that they are bound to be in any area of fee earning

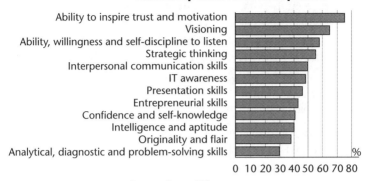

Leadership skills rated as important

Source: Create/Cilntec

Figure 8.4   *Leadership skills rated as important*

work, they nevertheless permeate law firm management since it is from this discipline that senior and managing partners emanate. Within this area, general commercial research into leadership in organisations has much to offer. American research into the skills that respected business leaders see as being important themselves include the willingness to take risks and the willingness to accept losses, entrepreneurial skills that do not necessarily come naturally to the professional.

In recent years there have also been extensive studies into the personal skills of prominent leaders. Reporting in 1997 Rajan and Van Eupen interviewed 49 top business leaders, mostly from the service sector, whom they studied in conjunction with accompanying interviews with human resources directors and other postal surveys. Their conclusions are neatly summarised in the chart in Figure 8.4 from their report *Leading People*.[6]

One of the most striking aspects of their findings is how few of the core professional skills feature in the higher end of the chart. Analytical, diagnostic and problem-solving skills are the stock in trade of the professional adviser, yet are well down the list of priorities. The very term 'visioning' produces cynicism from many lawyers, while strategic planning is seen as being an essentially flawed activity by many because of its implicit uncertainty of outcome. The conclusion has to be that top partner leaders have to show different or new skills to those that they exhibited to qualify for the job in the first place. Moreover, a basic change of attitude and outlook may also be necessary. It may, to a certain extent, be necessary to suppress or 'unlearn' many of the skills that they have had to show to date. Partners willing to embrace such personal changes can generally learn these new skills: those who resist the need to change will not.

In this research and most other like it 'inspirational' is a term which is common currency. According to the authors:

> leadership is about taking people where they have never been before. It is also about developing the essential emotions, excitement and convictions that help people to cope with the journey.

Interestingly, most interviewees downplayed the essentially personal quality of 'charisma'. Ray Treen, chief executive of Cornhill Insurance, was quoted:

> I am a long distance runner, not a sprinter. What I lack in charisma I more than make up for in persistence. If you are passionate about your goals, persistence and patience are the key. But that's not all: you have to balance soft values with hard deliverables. You can't have one without the other.[7]

Rajan and Van Eupen also offer interesting insights into the selection and development of top management.[8] One of their main recommendations in this respect is that the practice of promoting subject specialists 'needs re-appraisal'. Generally in the commercial context a senior purchaser does not necessarily make the best purchasing manager, but there is less leeway on this in the professional services firm than elsewhere. More firms are now introducing highly placed management experts, but they will generally work alongside senior partner managers and very seldom exclude them. Allowing for this the researchers recommend that a high degree of 'people skills' should be a prerequisite of the transition to the management position.

Leadership tasks

Whatever the theory and approach to leadership, the responsibilities of the position can be broken down into a number of areas (see Figure 8.5). This could be used to develop a score card on those in leadership positions: how well do they fare against all the tasks of the role?

Direction

Of all the responsibilities of the leader, direction is probably the most important. We regard 'strong leadership' as being particularly directional and the term would normally be used in a favourable or complimentary tone. The sports analogy is commonly used for practice

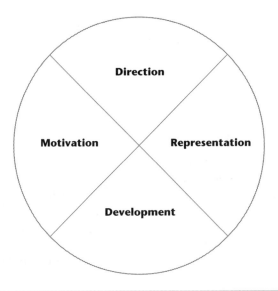

Figure 8.5 *Leadership tasks*

leaders. The job of coach is to select the right team and determine the tactics. They must ensure that the performers know what is expected of them and that there is a sense of teamwork throughout the group. Having created the sense of direction and purpose it is up to others to perform to their true potential. Leadership is more than anything about getting others to perform to achieve the goals determined.

In the practice management arena responsibilities would include the formulation of objectives, conducting whatever discussions are needed to refine the objectives and deal with uncertainty about them, and then monitoring performance and modifying action as necessary.

Representation

The best leaders are those who are loyal and committed to their team members. They will take risks for their colleagues and will argue their case. They will be assertive when it comes to requesting benefits, be they job-related improvements to terms or conditions, or training. This attribute tends to generate loyalty in return.

A wider element of representation is the degree to which the leader, a head of department for example, provides a bridge to activities elsewhere in the organisation. The most effective departmental leaders are often those who go to greater lengths than others to report back to the department on developments generally within the firm, especially if this will have a particular bearing on the department in question.

Development

The theory of motivation tells us that people tend to work best when they are confronted with appropriate challenges. Most in the professional environment need to feel that they are developing in some way, learning new skills or acquiring greater seniority or responsibility. The job of leader must then include a responsibility for developing the individuals within the group and the group itself. This is wider than simply orchestrating a training programme, it is actively coaching members of the team on a continuous basis. To develop the sporting analogy, it is shouting from the touchline and giving the half-time team talk, encouraging both individuals and the group to do better and meet their true potential.

Motivation

The firm or department which is motivated is the one most likely to succeed. It follows that motivating partners and colleagues is a prime role for anyone in a leadership position. We will look at the theory and practice of motivation in greater detail in Chapter 9 in the context of pay policy. Suffice to say for present that there is, of course, much more to motivating people than simply the level of remuneration that they receive, though this is inevitably a major element of the total picture. Psychologists tell us that we have basic needs: to pay for food, housing and other essentials, into which safety needs can also be added. The higher order needs are for recognition, development and the realisation of our ambitions. We have to feel that we are treated fairly in relation to the lower order needs and that our higher order needs are being adequately addressed.

This view of motivation supports two basic responsibilities of the leader. At the lower level of more basic needs is the need to ensure effective business performance. In a high salary environment the margin of error is reduced: profits have to be maintained to satisfy partners and to maintain the salaries of employees. If drawings and salaries cannot keep pace, talent will soon haemorrhage. At the upper level of motivation is the need to coach continuously and keep presenting the appropriate challenges for the personnel concerned. Where it is unrealistic for the managing partner or head of department to do this in person they must ensure that systems are in place to encourage this: reviews and the 'one-to-one' meetings which have become standard in many firms in recent years. Ensuring that the supervisors have the necessary counselling skills is also an important responsibility.

Leadership attributes

The traits theory of leadership tells us that certain individuals can be predicted and chosen for positions on grounds of certain personal attributes. This would be rejected by most because of the frequency of exceptions to the general rules which can be found. There is, however, value in looking at the attitudes and beliefs of the most successful leaders in order to see how any given leader might improve their own effectiveness in the role.

One of the most extensive exercises of this type was conducted by the Gallup Organisation and reported in 1999. This involved conducting face to face interviews with some 80,000 managers in total, including some of the most prominent industrialists and other high profile leaders in various walks of life. The report of the research describes listening to 120,000 hours of tapes and checking through five million pages of transcript for the patterns that could suggest success. The result was a fascinating book, *First, Break all the Rules* (Buckingham and Coffman, 1999).[9] The result of this exhaustive exercise?

> It turns out that great managers don't have much in common at all. If you were to work for them, you would come across different styles of motivation, direction and relationship-building. Yet, in spite of these variations, there was one insight to which successful managers kept returning. People, they said, don't change that much, so it's a waste of time trying to put in what was left out. The answer is to try to draw out what was left in – which is hard enough. This explains why great managers don't believe that everyone has unlimited potential, why they don't help people to overcome their weaknesses and why they break many of the other rules that conventional wisdom offers.[10]

The authors go to some lengths to stress that this does not mean that weaknesses are simply ignored or that training is a waste of time. The analysis is more positive and includes seeking out talent when recruiting personnel. Talent, they stress, is more than experience and is not confined to the skills bordering on the genius level that we see in top performers in the arts or sports. Talent is defined as a 'recurring pattern of thought, feeling or behaviour that can be productively

117

applied'. In this respect talent is differentiated from skills and knowledge. Talent is innate and can be nurtured and employed to good effect; skills and knowledge can be trained.

Within the law there is often a distinction between those who are meticulous on details as opposed to others with higher people skills, with the 'best of breed' combining the two. How best to deploy a details lawyer with poor interpersonal skills? One approach is to use them appropriately, the approach of 'finders, minders and grinders'. An alternative way of developing the person is to define the competences that need to be core to anyone in the role and attempt to train skills that will lessen the areas of perceived weakness. Both could be valid choices. The pragmatic response would seem to be to use people to do what they do best, on grounds that they will enjoy their work more and probably do it better. Work towards the all round expert, but make the most of each individual in the meantime.

In recent years much has been made of so-called 'emotional intelligence'. This sits neatly with ideas on using the talents of each individual and being an effective coach to every member of the team. Given that intelligence is a concept of great importance in the law, and a treasured asset of the professional adviser, it is a useful area to examine further. There is a growing view that we define intelligence too narrowly. In his book *The Empty Raincoat* Charles Handy lists nine variations:[11]

- Factual: the ability to retain facts and figures and shine at quiz games;
- Analytical: the ability to sort out problems and find the right solutions;
- Linguistic: the ability to learn and retain languages;
- Spatial: the ability to see patterns and develop them;
- Musical: the greatest musicians could be unintelligent in relation to the above;
- Practical: the ability to strip down a machine and re-assemble it;
- Physical: co-ordination of body and movement;
- Intuitive: the least intelligible of all, but a real attribute of many;
- Interpersonal: defined elsewhere as emotional intelligence.

Handy defines interpersonal intelligence as 'the wit and the ability to get things done with and through other people'. There is increasing interest in this ability since it, as opposed to more conventional definitions of intelligence, seems to be the major determinant of business or financial success. One study of a cohort in Massachusetts showed that conventional IQ or academic ability related only to 4 per cent of real world success, but that 'EQ' (emotional quota) related to over 90 per cent. This was explained in terms that a high EQ equips individuals to handle disappointment, control and channel feelings and to empathise with, and so influence, others.

One of the principal authorities in this area is Daniel Goleman. His book, published in 1996 and titled *Emotional Intelligence* examines the neurological basis for emotion and so the differences between us.[12] Both he and other authorities in this area stress that there is more to emotional intelligence than simply being a nice person to know. His book examines five domains:

- knowing one's own emotions;
- managing these emotions;
- motivating oneself;
- recognising emotions in others;
- handling relationships.

The good news seems to be that these are areas – unlike IQ – which can be developed. In the terms of the Gallup research earlier, they are certainly talents of some, but are capable of being learned as skills by all. It is little surprise to find that the accolades go to those with high IQ as well as pronounced EQ skills, a view to emerge from Higgs and Dulewicz from their work at Henley Management College.[13] This is also compelling information in relation to the selection of managing partners and heads of department. In the professional sector, knowledge-based as it is, promotion goes most obviously to the senior practitioner. The Bar, with the continuing tradition of naming chambers after the head of members for his or her duration of the office are the best example of this. If nothing but expertise, professional pre-eminence and seniority of experience mattered, this would be an effective way to select people for key leadership positions. The challenge is now more diverse, however, and different qualities have to be recognised and sought.

Decision making

Leaders make decisions, but there is little value in this if the decisions made are unacceptable to those affected by them. One of the elements of effective leadership is getting the balance right between strong and autocratic leadership on the one hand, as opposed to democratic consultation on the other.

The choices open to leaders can be represented as:

1. make decisions and announce them;
2. make decisions and try to encourage their acceptance;
3. present possible decision and generate discussions;
   before deciding;
4. present problems, invite discussion and reach;
   joint decision with team;
5. make all decisions as team decisions.

Which will be appropriate will depend on the variety of circumstances relevant to leadership generally. The culture of the organisation is a major element. There are often particular difficulties when a firm has had a dominant, perhaps founding, partner in charge for many years and then have to survive his or her aftermath. Inevitably in such circumstances, a direct replacement is unlikely to be found. A new system emerges which is more democratic and further down the scale than the previous regime.

Other factors will include the decision in question and its importance to those affected by it. Minor administrative issues generally benefit from a quick decision. Even the wrong decision may be better than no decision. The managing partner who consults on every issue soon loses credibility and support as others will see him or her as failing in the decision-making role of the position. The skill is knowing those sensitive issues on which consultation is important. Major issues require consultation, the extent of which depends on how acquiescent the partners or colleagues concerned may be.

Decision-making style is best seen as an adjunct to the 'best fit' theory illustrated above. The leader should match their style to the decision being made and the persons that will be affected by the issue in hand, all of which is subject to the prevailing culture of the team or firm in hand (see Figure 8.6).

The management of change

Given the pace and frequency of change it is not surprising that there is a great deal of emphasis on the management of change in the business press. How well a leader can pilot a firm or department through change will be the sternest test of their abilities. Research by Alan Hooper and John Potter of Exeter University's Centre for Leadership Studies examines this area and is contained in their book *Intelligent Leadership – Creating a Passion for Change*.[14]

There is widespread recognition that change will be threatening to most affected by it. The status quo is safe and familiar, so change is

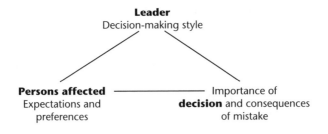

Leader
Decision-making style

Persons affected ———————— Importance of
Expectations and **decision** and consequences
preferences of mistake

Figure 8.6   *Decision-making style*

bound to raise concerns. The crucial skill, according to the writers, is 'the ability of the leader to unlock the potential of their people'. The distinction is made between transformational leadership and traditional command and control leadership. Merely to tell people what will happen and what they will do will not be enough, they have to buy in to that change and have a sense of involvement. Charisma, again, is downplayed: 'it is more about the processes created at the strategic and operational levels of an organisation than it is about the personality of the top person'. The four main areas of advice which follow serve as a useful summary for many of the points covered in this chapter on leadership more generally.

Communicate the reasons for change

Since people tend to be more comfortable in an environment that they understand it is vital to explain why changes are occurring and how it will affect them and their role. Open communication is required, with frequent updates on developments. The leader needs not only to be clear in their own mind on the way forward but to be assiduous to communicate this to their partners and colleagues

Releasing the potential of people

The best leaders inspire people to do their best and provide the right environment for them to do so.

Setting a personal example

Leadership by example is one of the dominant themes of leadership training in the military and is frequently referred to elsewhere.

Hooper and Potter talk about the importance of integrity. They also stress the need for 'passion, praise and pride'. Specifically, the need is to re-inforce the purpose and values of the change and to show the qualities of effort and enterprise needed for success. If instituting a quality programme, for example, the head of department must not be a detractor of it or fail to follow its provisions in his or her own fee earning activities.

Self-pacing

Perhaps one of the most intriguing elements of Hooper and Potter's work is their emphasis on what they call self-pacing. Time management and personal organisation is a large part of this. The leaders that they had studied tended to have a routine for coping with their pressures and were more disciplined in their working practices. Most also had a particular view on the work versus home issue, jealously guarding their weekends. All of the 25 leaders focused in the research leading to this latest book took the view that weekends away from the pressures of work enabled them to maintain energy levels over long periods.

Managing a quality programme

One way of looking at the challenges of leadership is to examine the practical steps that will make a quality programme more likely to succeed. Taking the principles above, the best advice would be:

(1) Be clear about the quality strategy: what are the benefits in mind and is it clear that the strategy adopted will be likely to achieve what is intended? Has sufficient thought and analysis gone into the development of the quality strategy?

(2) Gain commitment: in many firms this will be limited to a partners' meeting. This would be a useful first step, but no more than that. For quality to work throughout the firm it has to be understood and embraced throughout the firm. The quality partner or leader should therefore be as visible as possible on the issue, perhaps attending departmental meetings and meetings of secretaries as well as distributing helpful notes on the process of change.

(3) Secure involvement: many firms have benefited from the establishment of a quality committee, perhaps involving secretaries and administrators as well as fee-earners.

(4) Set a realistic pace: the programme must not be hurried, nor must it be allowed to drag over too long a period of time so that momentum is lost. Periods of six months at shortest to 12 months at the longest are common. Some firms have allowed for 12 months to gain Lexcel, and a further six months or more to gain Investors in People after that.

(5) Keep communicating: encourage improvements and deal as directly as possible with problems.

(6) Celebrate success: thank and congratulate all who assist in the process.

References to Lexcel

A1   Management structures
D6   Communication
D7   Supervision
D5c   Management training

1 Taylor, F. (1911) *Principles of Scientific Management*, Harper and Brothers.
2 Adair, J. (1983) *Effective Leadership*, Pan.
3 Fiedler, F. E. (1967) *A Theory of Leadership Effectiveness*, McGraw-Hill.
4 Handy, C. (1976) *Understanding Organisations*, Penguin.
5 Hersey, P. and Blanchard, K. (1969) *Management of Organisational Behaviour*, Prentice Hall.
6 Rajan, A. and Van Eupen, P. (1997) *Leading People,* Create/Cilntec.
7 Treen, R. quoted in Rajan and Van Eupen, *op. cit.*
8 Rajan and Van Eupen, *op. cit.*
9 Buckingham, M. and Coffman, C. (1999) *First, Break all the Rules,* Simon & Schuster.
10 Buckingham, M. and Coffman, C. *op. cit.*
11 Handy, C. (1994) *The Empty Raincoat*, Hutchinson.
12 Goleman, D. (1996) *Emotional Intelligence*, Bloomsbury.
13 Higgs, M. and Dulewicz, V. (1999) *Making Sense of Emotional Intelligence*, ASE.
14 Hooper, A. and Potter, J. (2000) *Intelligent Leadership – Creating a Passion for Change*, Random House. See also the report in *People Management* (1999) 19 August, p. 46.

9

Teamworking

- Legal teams
- Teamwork
- Team rewards and pay
- Meetings
- Chairing meetings
- Acceptable meetings behaviour

In a quiet bar a handful of people are enjoying a drink. A gunman bursts in and forces them all to move into one corner. They have become a group, not so much through closer physical contact, as through a shared perception of their common predicament. This does not mean that they are yet a team, however, and circumstances may dictate that they never co-operate to a sufficient degree to justify this description. Whether a group is a team is a qualitative assessment of how well a group functions together. Some measure of cohesion and interaction will be required for us to conclude that teamwork has developed.

In the work environment good teams add value: they secure better results than the individuals within the group could otherwise achieve. Little wonder, therefore, that the management shelves in bookshops groan under the weight of texts on teams and teamwork. Getting work-based personnel to achieve better results through enhanced teamwork is one of the most common aspirations of directors, partners and managers in any organisation. Results in law firms, however, often disappoint. Assistants commonly quote lack of teamwork as one of their principal reasons for seeking new positions elsewhere. Teams, it would seem, are unlikely to form without some very clear direction and prompting from those responsible for them.

It is possible to take a jaundiced view of the particular difficulties of forming lawyer teams, like Sally-Anne Hunter in 1998:

> Lawyers are notoriously anal folk; their love and passion for logic and detail is the reason for their commercial being. Like engineers, account-ants and DIY addicts, their satisfaction comes from order and clarity.

Unfortunately, teams and the people in them rarely conform to logic, clarity and order. In fact, the opposite. Like other cautious and rational people, when faced with the need to achieve a task, detailed plans and procedures abound, but sensitivity to personal requirements often remains forgotten. The logical personality of the typical lawyer will assume that everyone will be equally motivated by the task in hand, transparently clear in their communication with other team colleagues and will leave their ego firmly at home.[1]

If lawyers have difficulty in forming teams it may perhaps be that teamwork is more important elsewhere. If teamwork adds value, however, and fits with a model of quality working, how can it be developed and maintained? If there are special difficulties of initiating teamwork in the legal environment, what are they and how can they be overcome?

Legal teams

Groups form for a wide variety of reasons. They may stem from the direct needs of fee earning or may be for managerial or administrative functions and could be permanent or *ad hoc*. Whether a group should be formed at all depends on a series of factors. Considerations would include:

(a) The size of the challenge: is it feasible that an individual should be expected to achieve what is required within the available timescale?

(b) The complexity of the task or role to be addressed: is a range of inputs required and/or different areas of expertise?

(c) Involvement: is it important that there is seen to be a wider base for initial decision-making in order to secure greater support at a later stage?

(d) Originality: the professional may be tempted to believe that, given time, they will be able to work out the appropriate solution to a situation, but the reality is that a group can spark new ways of thinking. 'Brainstorming', for which a group will be needed, is likely to be more creative than solitary thought and will usually produce more originality.

It is tempting to examine the role of groups and teams simply from the perspective of the organisation. What will the firm or department gain from the time spent on this activity? It would be wrong, however, to overlook the personal perspective of groups also, as Sally-Anne Hunter reminds us. Observe any meeting at work and one will see how the ostensible agenda is determined by arguments about the collective good, usually the results to be achieved. Not far below the surface, however, will be the personal interests of those present. They will know to phrase their contributions in terms of the greater good, but much will be dictated by the maelstrom of emotions that make up organisational politics. It may well be that the operations of the group can be likened to the iceberg (see Figure 9.1), with most of the activity out of view below the surface. To harness fully the potential of teams, appreciation and control of the personal perspective will be at least as important as control of the rational common objectives.

There are those who criticise the loose way in which teamwork is used as a concept in the working environment. In recent years a very lucrative circus has developed in which top sports people visit work conferences to lecture on the merits of teamwork. Understand how a rugby or football tournament was won, the reasoning goes, and you will unlock some of the potential of your organisation. This is certainly an attractive concept which may provide a useful insight into the interest in the presenter, and there is probably little harm in it. Such occasions do not always survive rigorous analysis, however. Professor Meredith Belbin, the leading authority on the working of teams, points out that sports-based teams do not provide a direct parallel.[2] Members of sports teams, he reminds us, have a fixed position and have to be selected. Individual players cannot rely on being selected for every match. The head of department will not have quite the same luxury of choosing whose recent performance merits their taking part in the projects of the week, or to a much lesser degree at least.

The sports analogy offers one insight into the nature of legal teams, however. The teams that we naturally think of are teams based on interdependence. Football, rugby or netball teams are the most

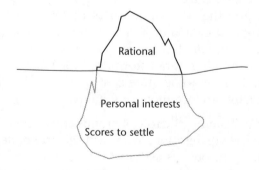

Figure 9.1   *The iceberg*

common to come to mind, the orchestra or drama production for others of a less sporting disposition. In these areas success can only be achieved through the complementary contributions of others in the group. The reality in most law firms, however, so far as fee earning work is concerned, is more of an athletics or cross-country running team, in which the success of the group depends primarily on the individual efforts of many, and real interdependence might be extremely limited. We can cheer on those around us, but it is mainly up to them to perform to their best potential, and there is little that we can do directly to help.

The model of the athletics team leads us to consider how teams should be organised in the law firm and what we should expect from them. The team might not be vital for interdependent activity, but could be essential for co-ordinating the complementary efforts of a take-over team in a corporate department. At a lesser level it might simply be advantageous for motivating people who might otherwise risk experiencing a sense of isolation and a lack of support. It is important to be clear on why a group is formed at all and have clear objectives in mind in relation to the benefits to be gained.

Teamwork

One of the most interesting projects to be undertaken on teamworking in recent years was conducted by Hilarie Owen, who reported in 1996 on her two years of research with the Red Arrows display team.[3] Relying on a trainee solicitor to proofread a document carefully is one thing, but to fly at 500 mph with other aeroplanes a few metres on either side is quite another. Teamwork may be beneficial in the legal office, but is literally a matter of life and death with this widely acclaimed team.

The principal finding, unsurprising so far as it goes, is that trust is essential in highly performing teams. Of more significance, however, is the issue of how to develop such trust.

> My research found that trusting others begins with trusting and knowing ourselves – in other words, self awareness. Another important factor for teams is openness, but this can only be achieved when team members have boosted each other's self esteem and can communicate assertively.

Other key findings were:

(1) During the winter development of the programme for the next season there is open criticism by team members of their own

mistakes and the mistakes of others, including the officers in charge. Rank and hierarchy is not allowed to put excellence at risk. This open environment encourages a view of mistakes as learning opportunities.

(2) The selection of new pilots is a team matter. A shortlist is developed, but those on it spend a couple of weeks with the team, including flying as passengers, with the team then saying who they feel comfortable working with. This is seen as being vital to the early assimilation of the new recruits into the team.

Owen developed a model of teamworking as a result of her time with the group and called it the 'synergy chain process'. It works on the basis of two 'value chains' – one the whole team's objectives and the other the individuals' objectives. Only if the needs of the team as a whole and the individuals within it can be simultaneously addressed, she argues, will you get the level of excellence that the best teams aspire towards.

Behaviour within teams is an aspect much written about by psychologists. There are those who will conform to the needs and norms of the group, and others who will resist or even wreck the collective efforts. Why people fall into one attitude or another seems to depend on the basics of personality – nature or nurture. In order of enthusiasm the choices are:

- internalisation: the individual does not merely comply with the group, but embraces the values and norms and adopts them as their own; they are willing to subsume their individuality for the sake of the group;
- compliance: the involvement is positive, but is more detached and independent. It is more a matter of expedience to conform;
- counter-compliance: the individual may withdraw his or her efforts and may become a silent member, or even seek to withdraw from membership.

The most celebrated work on the effective operation of teams is Meredith Belbin's *Management Teams – Why They Succeed or Fail*.[4] A management team, he argues, can combine all the necessary qualities for success which one individual alone cannot possess. The text provides an analysis of group behaviour, examining how individuals behave when put into a group situation. Get the chemistry of the group right, and better results should follow. If the chemistry is wrong, disharmony and poor results might be expected. The book recounts the long process of working with management training teams to develop the profile of the initial eight roles.

- Chairman: a relaxed, but assertive individual, whose talent is to harness the contribution of others. Tends not to see other group members as threats, but as resources to be used to good effect.
- Shaper: the driver of the group, who likes discussions to go the way that they prefer. Pushes self and others to achieve results. Assertiveness can switch to aggression, can be too sensitive to criticism and does not like to be constrained by rules and regulations.
- Plant: advances new thoughts, often in an independent manner. Usually intelligent, but sometimes a tendency to be too abstract.
- Monitor/evaluator: a good critical thinker and evaluator of ideas, usually objective and perceptive. Requires input of others to show their best, and potentially too self-critical. Sometimes negative to the input of others also.
- Company worker: recognising the rather unglamorous title this role is also sometimes referred to as the 'implementer'. They will accept the rules and conventions of the organisation and will turn talk to action. Often determined, practical and full of common sense. A reliable completer of ideas.
- Team worker: observant of the feelings of others and holds the team together well through their concern for others. Might lack toughness and resolve in difficult situations, and can therefore be a behind-the-scenes worker in many cases. For this reason they often do not get the credit due to them: their goal may be more to achieve harmony and results.
- Resource investigator: a people-oriented member of the team, with a lively enquiring mind. Can be relied upon to do the hard work between meetings to research concepts or form new contacts.
- Completer/finisher: will ensure that details get attention and that matters are not left unresolved.

There is considerable practical application in Belbin's work. His analysis is not simply a matter of observing success or failure and finding a way to rationalise either, it is possible also to use the analysis to improve team performance. This can be achieved either through varying membership to achieve a more complementary balance of roles, or to fill missing inputs through related appointments. Many is the partnership, for example, that experiences ill-tempered partners' meetings through shapers fighting for dominance. Many is the firm that bemoans the lack of activity for want of a completer/finisher.

There seem to be many more shapers than finishers in partnerships, so it can be advisable to carve out clear areas of influence for the stronger minded, and seek to appoint a meticulous partnership secretary or personal assistant to the managing partner to ensure that things get done.

The greatest insight provided by Belbin and others, however, is to remind us that good teams don't necessarily just happen. In some instances, through good fortune or instinctive leadership, they may do, but in most cases careful adjustment of the team, either through its participants, their responsibilities or the support they enjoy, may be needed. The firm that is focused on excellence will also invite its personnel to analyse for themselves how they contribute to team structures, and will seek improvements where possible.

Building teams

Our group of drinkers from the introduction to this chapter have been confronted with a challenge to them all. The situation is not resolved swiftly and a collective realisation grows that they need to function as a team to maximise their collective chances of survival. It is easy to imagine the plot of the drama that could then be written. Initially there is reluctance to help each other and certain characters clash with each other. The mission seems impossible, but slowly agreement is reached on a plan of action. The plan works and the team have succeeded. Later there is talk of a reunion.

This well worn plot of so many television dramas follows the life cycle of the group. The four main stages are stated to be as follows.

- Forming: the individuals come together in whatever circumstances and accept the need to work co-operatively on the challenge ahead.
- Storming: as in all human relationships, some airing of differences at an early stage is likely to improve later performance. The suppression of difficulties at an early stage may be polite, but will probably not prove healthy in the long term.
- Norming: the group that is able to survive initial disharmony and the tensions of formation will agree on the terms of their collective operations. The greater the degree of compliance and internalisation, the better the prospects for the work of the team.
- Performing: the mature team can now deliver to its brief. There may be a sense of cliquishness about it. New entrants did not go through the difficult process of formation and may have to work hard to gain acceptance.

The optional extra stage is 'mourning'. Good teams can be a high-light of our lives, providing the self-esteem which psychologists tell us we all yearn and getting from us the best levels of our personal achievement. That we should have fond recollections for such involvements is hardly therefore surprising.

The four phases of team formation provide a useful basis for advice to those who find themselves team leaders.

Forming

There is widespread advice on how to form the best teams. Most of the principles of good leadership apply to the development of teams. Owen observes that 'you can't make trust happen; it takes time and is based on a leader's behaviour being consistent'. In a report on team-building in Wilde Sapte, Judith Mayhew commented:

> While many factors appear to play a role in creating this dynamism, one stands out above all others: *the skills and behaviour of the practice leader*. In firm after firm, we have observed marked changes in performance from the same group of partners where the only thing that changed was a new individual appointed to the leadership of a particular practice group.[5]

Good leaders clearly have greater prospects of succeeding at develop-ing better teams. Later in her article Mayhew understandably counsels making sure that the right people are put into these crucial positions. What are the criteria for the position?

> Too often we select the best lawyer whether based on technical or rain-making skills. This individual, however, may not be the most able to coach and develop individuals and create a team. A team leader must be trusted by the members of a team as a person who can promote and develop their individual career plans.

Clearly the ideal is the paragon of virtue who can combine the tech-nical skills to lead by example with the softer skills of coaching others, but if a trade-off is needed the better coach should be preferred to the technical expert. In his latest revision of his work group types Belbin added the 'expert' – an adviser to the group who would sometimes be quite aloof from it. It may be a telling analysis of many legal teams that they suffer from putting in charge the person with the most expertise without regard to the interpersonal skills needed in the role.

Apart from the leader or co-ordinator, attention also needs to be given to who can usefully contribute to the other roles to be filled. The available research stresses that consideration should also be given to their likely ability to work well together and offer complementary contributions.

Storming

Into storming we can place the need to agree on objectives. As in decision-making under leadership, it may be tempting for the leader to dictate the agenda and the *modus operandi*. There may be much to be gained, however, from asking for input from the group itself. The natural coach will discuss the inputs of team members in putting together a team to work on a large deal and will not necessarily simply impose them. They will also seek to achieve a wider view of the roles of all, so may well arrange meetings and/or a written brief to ensure that all have a clear view of how their contributions fit into the greater picture.

It is understandable in a fee-earning environment, where time is quite literally money, that there should be a temptation to hurry the newly formed team into action. In the corporate world there is more emphasis on strategic retreats and team-building exercises. More partnerships have 'away-days' now than was ever the case before, but there are good arguments in favour of getting any team to concentrate on its proper formation before results are expected from it. This could be a facilitated workshop on the topic to be covered, with a discussion on the perceived difficulties and issues to be confronted, or it could be more indirect and simply seek to improve the personal cohesion of members of the group.

Norming

A plan of action is now needed. The input of every member has to be understood, preferably by all and not just the person in question. Team communication and reporting has to be clearly established and then made a priority. A common example in major commercial practices is the weekly summary of progress which the partner in charge has created for collective consideration. Standards of behaviour should also be clear. The greater the focus on achieving the best results possible, the more open is likely to be the internal atmosphere. If excellence is the goal, hierarchy should not prevent a junior member of the team raising an error or weakness with the person in charge. Where internal hierarchies are in fact the priority, technical and service delivery problems will be more likely to be suppressed.

Our team, be it an internal committee, or a project-based fee earning team, can now perform. This may be fraught, and it may succeed or not. Where things go well there will be an eventual celebration and nostalgia may even develop. Either way, a de-brief from the client should be sought after projects and fed into the firm's management system to ensure that the lessons of the team can continue to be learned.

Team rewards and pay

One of the most difficult elements of managing teams is to consider pay policy towards them. If the 1980s saw the advance of individual performance-related pay schemes, the 1990s saw the advance of team-based pay in its place. There is a very obvious dissonance between, on the one hand, encouraging teamwork within a department, but then allocating pay bonuses on a purely individual basis. Individual members of the team will soon learn that to gain the highest pay award and, more importantly, the accolade and promotion prospects that will go with it, they should put self in front of team. A selfless attitude that passes on better work to colleagues will simply not pay dividends under the firm's scheme. Individual performance pay schemes are also reckoned to encourage managers to consider team members too much as individuals and not enough as team players.

Understanding the role of money as a motivator is clearly important to understanding how pay schemes should be designed. The main theory is still generally accepted as Maslow's hierarchy of needs: see Figure 9.2.[6]

Maslow tells us that a blocked need is likely to cause demotivation. As we satisfy a need we become relatively uninterested in it and more concerned with the next need up the hierarchy. A satisfied need is less likely to motivate.

An alternative approach was suggested by Frederick Herzberg (see Figure 9.3).[7] He suggested that there were two categories of motivating factors: hygiene and motivators. The first group stand the potential to demotivate but are unlikely in themselves to be positive factors. It is sometimes questioned if his assertion that job security is merely a 'hygiene' factor would be as valid now.

One recent piece of research by Jane Sturges suggests that there are four categories of people with different motivational preferences.[8]

- Climber: strives for recognition from external criteria such as promotion and status: in her research with a group of 36 managers all seven in this category were men. They are very goal-oriented in their view of career progression and are likely to be very competitive.

133

Figure 9.2 *Maslow's hierarchy of needs*

Hygiene factors	Motivators
Working conditions Pay Job security Work relationships Management practices	Work itself Responsibility Sense of achievement Recognition Chances of advancement

Figure 9.3 *Herzberg's two factor theory*

- Expert: sees success in their job as the most important aspect of their motivation. They like to see themselves as specialists and like to receive positive feedback as such. The content of the job is more important than the role within the organisation.
- Influencer: wants to have a positive and tangible effect on the firm. They like autonomy, particularly if they are more senior personnel. Younger influencers are motivated by responsibility.
- Self Realiser: thinks of success in very personal terms and in a way that may mean little to other people. Their desire to succeed in terms relevant to them will override traditional career success.

The picture seems quite clearly to be that money is more a potential demotivator than a motivator. A person who gets the fair going rate for what they do where they do it is unlikely to focus unduly on the issue of pay. If, however, we believe that we are being unfairly treated on pay in some respect it runs the risk of causing demotivation and resentment. This will mean that the overriding interest for management is to achieve perceived fairness in its pay scheme, whatever that may mean. In practice there are advantages in having set scales for many grades and clear criteria by which negotiations are conducted for others.

It is the public sector which has experienced the greatest difficulties in reconciling team systems of work with individual pay bonus arrangements. Typically these ration the number of people who can be graded as 'excellent' and so get the highest award possible. The effect is more often than not to disappoint the majority, if not worse. Research from the Institute of Employment Studies suggests that performance-related pay tends to make people more concerned with money and more mercenary in their dealings with the organisation than they were beforehand.

If a firm wants to prove that it values teams and the way that they function, one of the strongest ways to reinforce this message is to offer some team-based rewards. As throughout pay policy, however, the concept is almost bound to prove much easier than its implementation. The introduction of a team pay system that will be perceived to be fair by all personnel is at best ambitious, and perhaps an impossibility in all but the smallest of concerns.

Some interesting research into team-based rewards was published by the Institute of Personnel and Development in 1996.[9] The survey covered 98 organisations belonging to the Institute's Compensation Forum, a group that is reckoned to be more forward-thinking on such issues than the norm. Around a quarter of the group had already introduced a formal link between performance and pay, with a further 47 per cent declaring an interest in doing so over the next year. Just over a half of the organisations with team-based reward systems in place were confident that it had improved team performance, but only 22 per cent could quantify the gain. On the key practical issue of how to calculate the bonus formula there were three main approaches:

(a) performance related to defined criteria: various corporations (Lloyds Bank and Norwich Union were quoted) had developed specific measures on such issues as sales and measures of customer satisfaction;

(b) performance related to an overall criterion: the Benefits Agency was quoted as paying team bonuses if there had been 'a valuable contribution to performance as determined by local unit managers';

(c) achievement of predetermined organisational and team objectives: these are usually measures of objectives contained in business plans.

Certain organisations paid bonuses as a flat rate to all eligible, while others made the payment a percentage of base salary. One of the best schemes that I have encountered was a progressive two partner firm that stated to its entire staff that if billings for the year were above a certain figure, all personnel would receive a £500 bonus. If billings were £100,000 above that figure, all would receive a £1,000 bonus. In a small office set-up this seemed to support a culture of openness and togetherness.

According to Armstrong and Baron team-based reward systems work best where teams:[10]

(a) are distinct units for which targets and standards will be clear;
(b) have a considerable amount of autonomy in their operations;
(c) have an interdependent pattern of working within them;
(d) are stable, with clearly established patterns of working;
(e) are mature and, in the way that we have already examined, formed;
(f) have good team players within them, as opposed to individualists.

On these criteria most law firms would appear to be on fertile ground. If the department or group is to be the unit for reward, or the team within the group in the largest commercial practices, there will be the clear pattern of operation and membership that seems to be desirable. Although interdependence between fee-earners may not be as pronounced as some would like to believe, there is, of course, considerable interdependence between fee-earners, paralegals and support staff. There is often also the management concern to break down the 'them and us' attitude which can develop between these different levels.

There are success stories with team-based rewards: many organisations report improvements in morale and effectiveness. The converse of the success of some within the firm, however, will be the relative failure of others. The poorly performing groups will risk a greater sense of demotivation when they observe the success of others, and perhaps even alienation. Many personnel managers will have particular difficulties in recruiting for a certain sector of the firm, particularly internally, and these difficulties may be compounded if it is known that team bonuses are less likely in these parts of the firm. If a patchy picture of success under the arrangements is likely, organisational flexibility could therefore be threatened. Other concerns with team-based systems are the risk of undue pressure within teams for members to comply and the perennial problem of assessing in a manner which is seen to be fair by those affected by the system.

The conclusion on team bonuses may therefore be best seen as promising, but there is a need to proceed with great caution. It is essential that the scheme is seen to support the objectives of the firm, be consistent with its culture, either existing or intended, and must be bought into by as many of the participants as possible. A particular danger of the law firm is the risk that the scheme may exacerbate the division between fee-earners and support staff. At the other extreme, fee-earners may be disappointed if they do not receive what they regard as their rightful due. No doubt in many firms, however, the formal implementation of an appropriate system would enhance the effectiveness of teamwork within the practice.

Meetings

The law of meetings starts with an analysis of what exactly a 'meeting' is. A good deal of judicial attention has been given to the circumstances where one person alone can be said to have had a 'meeting', but we do not need to consider such niceties here or the jurisprudence of statutory meetings. For our purposes meetings are where teams come together to discuss their objectives and other points of common interest.

Meetings may not be the scourge of professional life that they are in many commercial organisations, but they can easily become too much of a burden in an environment where time is the commodity sold to clients. It is the responsibility of anyone calling a meeting to ensure that the effort of all concerned will be appropriate. A meeting is used well and is appropriate if:

- a collective view needs to be formed and adhered to;
- the decision will be a better one, either intrinsically or in terms of its likelihood of being implemented, as a result of the joint involvement;
- it advances a sense of teamwork which is beneficial to the work or the sense of well-being of those in the team.

A meeting is used badly if:

- it is a means of hiding from activity – discussion is easier than action;

- the gain for members of the outcome is less than the pain of participation;
- the time taken is disproportionate and frustration results.

In his more recent research, marketed as his 'Workset' project, Belbin colour-coded meetings by reference to people's view of their usefulness.[11] The classification is more general, looking at the usefulness of all activities that we perform:

- blue: work a job-holder has to perform in a certain manner;
- yellow: individual responsibility for meeting an objective (how matters little);
- green: tasks that vary according to the reactions and needs of others;
- orange: shared responsibility for meeting the objective;
- grey: tasks that are incidental to the job (e.g. cover for a colleague);
- white: new or creative undertakings beyond normal daily requirements;
- pink: presence required, but no useful results: time is seen as wasted.

In research in a hospital in Leicester, Belbin found widespread misunderstanding of expectations of roles and tasks. The picture is produced by developing a pie chart of colour-coded activities for each individual following a period of colour-coded time recording. More generally, amongst business executives meetings are identified as being the principal component of wasted, or pink, time.

> One person's useful meeting is another's waste of time. Typically the people who classified their meetings as pink work were those who did not speak or who were not consulted. If there is a general pattern, it is that the larger the meeting, the more pink work figures. This is to some extent inevitable, since larger meetings give less scope for individual contributions.[12]

Belbin recommends distinguishing the various meetings that people become involved in.

- Sub-meetings: two or three people meeting usually do so with minimal formality and it seems to stretch the meaning of the word meeting to describe their gathering. These can be intensive and depend heavily on interpersonal relationships. They are good for green and white work.
- Team meetings: so far as Belbin is concerned 'a large team is virtually an oxymoron: additional members add nothing and get

in the way of real progress'. In smaller teams selection plays a part in people attending at all in that there may be individual and shared roles, but no traditional leader. In slightly larger teams there is a need for more structure. Team meetings are good for orange and green work.

- Group meetings: these are different to team meetings since attendance is a right, rather than down to selection. Departmental meetings are the obvious example. They are the manager's chance to monitor yellow work collectively, but this may be at the expense of pink time for individual attendees.
- Formal meetings: these are meetings from status relationship where seniority may not be clear-cut. The appointment of officers enables progress to be achieved and lessens conflict. The risk is that progress is slow. The chairperson ensures progress.
- Mass meetings: in mass meetings little happens other than the giving out of information: an audience is addressed.
- Unstructured meetings: it may be that new projects need unstructured meetings while matters are still forming. Inevitably there will be pink work for many present, but it will not yet be obvious who should be there and why. There is nothing wrong with this if it is simply a stage of progress as opposed to a permanent state of affairs.

One of the objectives when planning meetings should always be to minimise the amounts of pink time experienced by the attendees. It might be tempting to achieve this by avoiding meetings altogether, but meetings are to be welcomed if they are genuinely useful. It is as well to consider carefully in advance why a meeting should be held at all. Meetings have the potential to:

- share ideas and information;
- allocate work;
- explore or develop ideas;
- resolve problems;
- make decisions;
- comply with procedures;
- ensure involvement;
- give and receive support.

When planned well, meetings will not merely share information but will also improve morale and commitment. There could also be a regulatory angle, with a formal need to make policy or comply with procedures, or a social consideration with the need to promote greater cohesiveness within a group.

Planning a meeting will make it more likely that many of the potential problems highlighted above can be avoided. If the meeting is well structured and the reasons for holding it are clear, negative attitudes are more likely to be kept to a minimum.

Some of the issues to consider when planning a meeting are:

- What are my objectives?
- Why is a meeting necessary?
- Who will need to be involved? (primary interest)
- Who might like to be present or be kept informed? (secondary interest)

There are clear advantages in preparing an agenda (see Figure 9.4). For regular departmental meetings this could be a standing agenda. It should ensure that attendees are properly prepared and are therefore more likely to plan points and arguments in advance.

A device which can be invaluable in keeping the bureaucracy associated with meetings to a minimum can be the 'chairperson's agenda', in which notes are divided into three columns, thereby creating a shorthand note of what has been decided (see Figure 9.5).

Chairing meetings

The chair for a meeting has responsibility for ensuring reasonable progress on all issues under discussion. There is a fine line between pushing things through, and therefore restricting discussion, and enabling people to feel that they have had their say. It is also the chairperson's responsibility to maintain a positive tone to the meeting, even if some healthy disagreement is aired.

Departmental meeting

Agenda for April meeting

1. Matters arising from last meeting
2. March billing
3. Marketing update
4. Training
5. HOD points

Figure 9.4   *Departmental meeting agenda*

140

Item	Reminders	Agreed
1. Matters arising from last meeting		
2. March billing		
3. Marketing update		
4. Training		
5. HOD points		

Figure 9.5   *Chairperson's agenda*

Most basic of all, it is a general principle of meetings that only one person should talk at a time, and the person to decide who it should be is the chair. It is a good idea always to start regular meetings on time. If people adjust to the idea that they can have five minutes grace it will become 10, then 15 and so on. There are firms where it seems to be part of the established culture to turn up late on principle, but this simply results in more wasted time. The best response if chairing a meeting is always to start meetings on time.

Before the meeting some thought should be given to stage management. Is the room large enough, warm enough, free of interruptions, etc.? At the start of the meeting the chairperson should try to generate some enthusiasm for it. Certain question techniques can be useful to get discussion going: perhaps the overhead question which is a general theme for the meeting or rhetorical questions which pose the issues to be confronted. It is also advisable to lay down rules about messages and mobile phones. Thought should also be given to finish times and what clients and other callers will be told about what is going on and when it will be possible to speak to the participants.

The real skill of the chair is to get others to suggest the 'right' outcome even if they had thought of it already. The chair should encourage others and try to tease out discussion. Likewise, the chair should try to refrain from giving out opinions too freely and try to remain neutral for as long as possible in each discussion.

The more general the involvement, the better, and it is wise to make a mental note of who has contributed and who has not. If someone is trying to get into the discussion and cannot they should be acknowledged. Specific contributions can be asked from the less forthcoming.

As groups move to agreement or decision it is important to be wary of the 'Abilene' effect – the tendency for a group to agree the compromise solution which satisfies everyone, but nobody thinks makes sense. In extreme cases a group will make a decision that all know to be nonsensical simply to achieve compromise. Agreement is fine, but not at the expense of common sense.

A final issue is the question of a record of discussions. In too many firms formal minutes become a good opportunity to avoid action. The participants wait for formal minutes to be typed and distributed, by which time all momentum from the meeting has been lost. An effective alternative can be for the chair to complete an action sheet, as in Figure 9.6, and copy it for all attendees at the end of the meeting.

Acceptable meetings behaviour

- Politeness: be punctual or apologise if you are late; greet and handshake (external meetings); do not gloat if winning a point.
- Empathy: try to listen to and understand issues; be open to people as people.
- Helpful: give help without its being requested; deliver on commitments.
- Trust: show genuine liking, gratitude, sympathy, etc.; reciprocate – quid pro quo; criticise constructively and confront early.
- You should:
  - stick to the rules;
  - stick to the structure;
  - get your facts right;
  - make your contribution helpful and intelligible;
  - make your contribution attractive;
  - have a positive attitude.
- After the meeting consider:
  - do we need minutes, or will they hinder activity?
  - as an alternative, try an action sheet (see Figure 9.6).

Item	Agreed	Action	By whom	By when

Figure 9.6   *Action sheet*

Main points

- Teams need to be formed for various purposes and their effectiveness will have a major bearing on the success of the practice.
- Attention needs to be given as to who will co-ordinate teams most effectively: this will not necessarily be the person who knows the most about the subject in hand.
- All meetings should be well organised and conducted to gain the best contribution from all present

References to Lexcel

D6 Communication
D7 Supervision

Notes

1 Hunter, S-A. (1988) *Axiom*, Issue 6, June, p. 318.
2 Belbin, R. Meredith (1981) *Management Teams – Why They Succeed or Fail*, Butterworth-Heinemann.
3 Owen, H. (1996) *Creating Top Flight Teams*, Kogan.
4 Belbin, R. Meredith (1981), *op. cit.*
5 Mayhew, J. (1998) *Axiom*: Issue 6, June, p. 516.
6 Maslow, A.H. (1954) *Motivation and Personality*, Harper.
7 Herzberg, F. (1959) *The Motivation to Work*, Wiley & Sons.
8 Sturges, J., (1999) 'What it means to succeed', *British Journal of Management*, vol. 10, pp. 239–52.
9 Institute of Personnel and Development (1996) 'CIPD Report of compensation forum' .
10 Armstrong, M. and Baron, A. (1998) 'Performance Management – the

New Realities', *Institute of Personnel and Development*, 1998, p. 243.
11   Belbin, R. Meredith, (1997) *People Management*, 20 November, p. 36.
12   Belbin, (1997) *op. cit.*

Delegation and coaching

- Implications of poor delegation
- Delegation patterns
- Coaching
- The manager's involvement
- Mentoring

Few in the law would disagree on the importance of effective delegation within the office, of both fee earning and administrative work. Unfortunately delegation seems to be a technique that is difficult for many lawyers and is commonly regarded as a weakness. In his book *Managing the Professional Service Firm* Maister titles his chapter on delegation as 'Solving the Under-delegation Problem'.[1] Numerous articles admonish the profession for reluctance to delegate and provide checklists on how better to do so.

A simple definition of delegation is 'committing powers to another to represent or act for that person'. There is more to it than this, however.

> Delegation is not simply dumping unwanted tasks on someone else and letting them get on with it; delegation is giving someone (usually a subordinate) a task to achieve, together with the authority necessary to get that task done.[2]

The two stages of the delegation process each seem to cause difficulties for lawyers. First is prising away tasks from fee-earners in the first place, and second is bestowing authority on the delegatee to do the task in hand. The whole process depends on trust, which appears to be the greatest difficulty:

> Professional people tend to be poor delegators; either they do it themselves to ensure it's done properly (too insecure to trust others) or they abdicate responsibility and leave it to someone else to do it (too insecure to accept responsibility if it is out of their hands).[3]

There are various factors which contribute to this lack of trust.

Fear of mistakes

The law is unforgiving of mistakes and those that are responsible for them. The perfect lawyer has probably not yet been born, however. Avoiding errors of oversight or omission is a constant concern for the professional, increasingly so in ever more litigious times. The risks are all too obvious: the word 'not' seems insignificant enough, but its presence or absence from a document could have potentially dramatic effects. Luck, of course, plays a major role in this. All will make errors over the course of a career in the law, it is the detection and consequences of such errors that stand to make or stymie any individual's career. Small wonder, then, that many hesitate to accept the consequences of the errors of others when they have more than enough worries on their own account.

There was an interesting observation on the risk of errors in a retirement feature on Henry King, an unusually entrepreneurial lawyer who became senior partner of Denton Hall, as they then were:

> In business, if you have a group that is right 70% to 75% of the time, that's a pretty good record. Translate that to the law and say that my lawyers are right 75% of the time and you would have second thoughts about using them. When taking business decisions, you are prepared to take more risks.[4]

What Mr King might have gone on to say is that the route to commercial success is often dependent on risk-taking, which assumes the occasional mistake. The law is more risk-averse, with prudence the better part of valour. This tends to be true in the external dealings of the firm with clients: small wonder, then, that internal risks are similarly avoided by many.

Clinging to the familiar

Many of the difficulties arising from the fear of mistakes are tied up with the prevailing culture of the firm and, to a degree, the culture of the profession as a whole. A similar observation can be made in relation to the preferred work patterns of many lawyers. Preferring to do what we do best, rather than risk less familiar activities may be another element of fear of mistakes.

In management the encouragement to partners and other seniors is to delegate in order to free up time for practice development and other such activities that only seniors can undertake. There is no point, it will be agreed, in undertaking work which is uneconomic at partner level while management is neglected. It is, however, precisely this type of fee-earning work that enabled the individual to attain that position and it can hardly be surprising if there is a preference to continue to do this while other less familiar tasks beckon.

Time pressures

There is an unfortunate paradox in relation to delegation. One of the principal attractions of delegation is that time will be saved through passing work to another. Often, however, it will take time to delegate. In cases where the task is complex, and either the delegatee is junior or is unfamiliar with the matter, it may take longer to delegate the task than to do it oneself. It can easily seem to be the case that there is simply not enough time today or this afternoon to pass the work on. The alternative is to stay late and deal with it personally. Only if this vicious circle can be broken will systematic delegation stand a chance.

Measurement and reward

Our actions are shaped by the incentives and rewards on offer. These could be direct financial rewards or they could be the approval of our colleagues. One of the most common disincentives to delegation is that it does little to assist the individual lawyer in most firms, and might even count against them. If the firm encourages delegation on the one hand, but measures and evaluates data confined to the individual's chargeable time recorded and bills personally delivered on the other, the true message may easily be seen to be that delegation does not pay. It follows that the firm that is keen to improve working patterns should change, if needs be, the assessment of performance from the norm. Many firms have switched in recent years away from the assessment of personal billing data in favour of team performance targets to overcome the problem.

In one major firm the heads of department would meet monthly and review print-out data on every fee-earner, categorised by department. This encouraged:

- lack of focus on the overall departmental performance;
- 'individualism', as it is termed by Charles Handy: – the tendency to reduce complex problems to the perceived fault of one or more scapegoats;[5]
- the heads of department to make sure that their own figures were the best, or clearly amongst the best.

It was difficult to see how this reporting set-up encouraged team-working or delegation. The change recommended was that the personal data on each fee-earner should be available only to the head of department concerned and the managing partner. Monthly reporting could then be confined to overall departmental business performance.

Not all agree with this change and it might not be right in every circumstance. Team reporting, it can be argued, allows 'passengers' to hide behind the general figures. This should be seen as the challenge for team leaders, however. Theirs is the responsibility to coach under-performers and deal with problems in their team.

Implications of poor delegation

Various problems arise when delegation is neglected or avoided. Some are quite clear to detect; others are more indirect and need to be assessed within any given firm so far as it is possible to do so.

Profitability

In circumstances where fixed fees become the norm, and where the true ceiling on fees becomes more a matter of commercialism than regulation, the cost-efficient conduct of work becomes essential. This requires constant attention to the appropriate level of personnel for the task in hand. Few would quibble with Maister's suggestion that some 50 per cent or more of a senior lawyer's work should be undertaken by a subordinate: few could also doubt the impact this must have on profits.[6] Turning good intentions to reality, however, requires recognition that what is appropriate may vary over time. The development in most areas of work should be to 'productise' as much as possible. The senior should develop the new services and documentation: the job can then be passed down the line, at least in part. Supervision, over a period of time, should develop in place of processing.

The exercise shown in Figure 10.1 can produce useful ideas on better delegation. The skill is to examine in greater detail what should be capable of being delegated, something that will vary considerably by work type. Litigators and conveyancers commonly identify telephone calls as a task for delegation, but this is less likely to apply to commercial lawyers for whom calls are less frequent and more important to the immediate progress of their work.

As with all such tests, the value is not in the wish list that it is likely to produce, but rather the action which then develops. Who can be

Aspects of my job	% time spent on them	Could be delegated?	Reasons for non-delegation

Figure 10.1   *Better delegation*

promoted to absorb the work that should be passed on if there is no resource at present? What changes will be required for this to occur?

One general practice decided to deal with the volume of unimportant telephone interruptions that fee-earners complained of by designating the senior secretary in each department as the 'departmental administrator' and setting out details of her role in their client care correspondence. It was explained that she would take the call and would be able to answer most queries. Where she could answer the point, which was the case in most calls received, no further action was needed by the fee-earner. If necessary, she would pass a message to the fee earner concerned. The volume of unimportant calls by fee-earners was reduced.

While on the point of profitability it is interesting to see how many more firms now apply a lower hourly rate to administrators and charge for their time. In this way a call actioned by a member of the 'support staff' will not necessarily be a lost charging opportunity.

Personal development

Formal education plays a part in the development of our skills, but for the most part lecture-based activities provide us with the opportunity to learn and not the finished skill-set that we need in practice. It is only as we gain experience on real tasks that we can apply theory to practice and become as accomplished as we wish. In a very real sense, delegation is how we learn. When the supply stops, so does learning, and we stagnate, or run the risk of doing so.

Systematic delegation of work, including always a measured supply of new tasks where possible, enables growth to occur. Only if this is the case will the firm stand any chance of being a 'learning organisation': only then will the firm be adapting to new demands or a new, increased level of demand. If individuals are developing, the firm is increasing its potential and a virtuous circle will be in place.

Clearly there are related risks in failing to create this state of affairs. The reason for most avoidable and unwanted departures of staff elsewhere seem seldom to be primarily financial. The experience at 'exit interviews' will generally be of a new challenge or opportunity which, it is perceived, the current firm cannot or will not provide. Encouraging personal growth can therefore be seen to encourage staff retention (increasingly, partner retention also) and so also contribute to morale and professional standing. How do we assess the firm locally that is going from strength to strength? In part, no doubt, it is the firm that seems to recruit with ease and retain the talent that is already in place. Better delegation should be understood to be a part of any personnel retention policy.

Delegation patterns

Examples of poor delegation are easy to elicit for any group of solicitors, particularly the more inexperienced. Most examples feature lack of proper instructions, usually compounded by the inexperience of the delegatee making the situation all the more difficult. Lack, or the absence of, feedback is also commonly quoted.

> An e.mail flashed up on my screen that a deal was going badly at one of our offices in mainland Europe. 'Please go and help.' When I approached the partner for more background he treated me as something of a nuisance. So far as he was concerned, the matter was sorted.

> As a newly admitted solicitor I was passed a large file on a long-running matter with a request that I took it over. When I went back to the partner concerned to ask for more background he reacted with irritation. 'If you can't be bothered, give it back.' That was not what I was saying at all.

> As a trainee I was asked to prepare a particular document for a partner. I spent a long time doing so and felt that I had done quite a thorough job. A few months later the file crossed my desk again, and I was upset to find that my draft had not been used at all. To this day I still have no idea why.

There is a great deal of emphasis on delegation not being off-loading, but if delegation is defined as securing the involvement of another in tasks that need to be performed it is one model which might occur. What is needed is a view of delegation that can show when, if at all, off-loading may be appropriate, and how work should be distributed in any given situation.

The most helpful distinction is as between 'hard' and 'soft' delegation. Hard delegation is any situation where the delegatee has the necessary skills and experience to do the work. In cases of soft delegation this will not be the case. This distinction is helpful with one of the perennial problems of when to delegate: there is often the realisation that by the time instructions have been given, particularly to a trainee, the work received back, corrected, explained and then re-worked, more time will be taken by the delegator than if he or she were simply to do the work themself. It is helpful to be clear on the benefits to the delegator for passing work on. In cases of hard delegation the benefit should be immediate, and so readily apparent. The work is done at a more cost-effective level and the quality of the job, in terms of both technical and service level, is not compromised. In soft delegation, however, the benefits are longer term. In the short term it will take longer for the delegator, but this is necessary if they are to develop the future resource to be able to assist on the task in question. In soft delegation the emphasis is on training and development rather than merely resourcing the work.

There may be instances of one extreme or the other, but often there will be shades of both. A model for delegation should allow for a phased development, particularly with more complex work (see Figure 10.2). We may need several attempts before we can regard ourselves as competent, and in the meantime will continue to need a safety net in the supervision of another. Clarity of role and responsibility is needed, or there is the risk that one party or the other may be relying on checking that the other had not intended. Where there is confusion on such issues, instances of professional negligence or poor client service are more likely.

Finally, delegation is usually a process from a senior (delegator) to a junior (delegatee), but this need not be the case. If I receive work directly from a client and choose to refer it on I could either do so to a peer or to a superior. I may then have no involvement at all, or some input for a variety of reasons. The model should therefore cope with upwards, as well as downwards, delegation.

Which shade of delegation should be chosen depends on various factors. These will include:

- the current skills of the delegatee;
- the future planned patterns of work;
- the career aspirations of the delegatee;
- the proven ability and future potential of the delegatee.

As a general rule, the more capable the work is of being 'productised', the more it will lend itself to vertical delegation. Developing legal aid work in this way has been a major challenge for many firms in recent years. The LAFQAS standard introduced more stringent requirements for supervisors, probably because it was envisaged that more legal aid work would need to be delegated in a systematic nature for it to be cost-effective.

The problems are the greatest where delegation is seen as an all or nothing activity. Either the file is with one person, or another. If that other is a relatively junior fee-earner, perhaps lacking in formal qualifications, the auditor would understandably expect to see more frequent file reviews. If there is a team of such people in any given area of the work the ability of the supervisor to undertake their own work would inevitably be limited. The better for such situations is clearly vertical delegation, in which the senior person is designated as the person dealing. The review of the contribution of the junior would occur within the process, while the need to supervise a senior person is stated to be much less.

There is little radically new in such ideas, especially in the field of

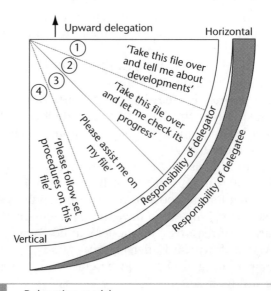

| Figure 10.2 | *Delegation model* |

legal aid work. In his book Jamie Dirks set out models of the flow charts of different elements of litigation work.[7] Many are not convinced, however, and others react with greater distaste for such 'unbundling' of a professional service. Countering such resistance, however, lies the basic business view of quality, that quality is providing a technically competent service in a manner appropriate to the work and the circumstances of the client. The stark reality is that in areas of work going well beyond legal aid, the client or funder will no longer pay for the level of service involved in having a senior lawyer undertake all work from start to finish. Some degree of vertical delegation is needed in order to achieve profitability.

Clarity is also needed in such arrangements. This might go as far as varying the job descriptions of those concerned. It is possible to take this as far as assessing the stages of process that the jobholder might undertake, based on an examination of the process in question.

Pursue a petition for divorce:

- initial interview with client and advise (senior lawyer);
- fact find: take full instructions (paralegal);
- draft petition and paperwork (paralegal);
- check all paperwork with client (senior lawyer);
- submit to court (paralegal);
- apply for decree nisi (paralegal).

The job description in the *Lexcel Office Procedures Manual* envisages having specific duties contained in it along the lines of the above example.[8] Such arrangements are also key to managing a profitable conveyancing practice, save where the firm has the luxury of dealing with less cost-conscious, higher value private clients.

Greater structure might be needed for vertical delegation. In any situation, however, full and clear instructions are invaluable, and avoid the wasted time of repeating instructions or having to re-direct inappropriate work. A checklist should include the following:

- What needs doing. This may be obvious to the delegator, but will not necessarily be so to the delegatee. In all cases the 'please deal' which is so commonly quoted is likely to prove inadequate.
- Why the work needs doing. This is useful for context and may make the task more of a valid learning exercise for the delegatee, but it will also make it more likely that the right slant is taken. Knowing why a piece of research is needed, and why it is important to that client, should ensure that re-working is less likely to be needed.

- When the work should be completed. There is a tendency to regard everything as urgent, but where there are competing demands this is unfair and inefficient. A timescale should always be quoted and enforced.
- Time to be, or not to be, expended. In cases of hard delegation this might be a factor. In cases of progressive soft delegation it may well be appropriate to encourage the delegatee to spend as long as they wish on the task if it is a valid learning activity. Whether the client should be charged for this is another matter, however, and a view will need to be taken when billing as to which element of the time recorded should be charged to the client. The remainder will need to be written off, or transferred to a training budget where it is measured.
- Know-how and other materials. Back-up materials, be they drafts, precedents or even similar files, should be referred to.
- Reporting back. The delegator should establish what needs to be reported back, if anything, especially problems in the activity.

In one firm's very thorough quality system a checklist based on the above appeared as a quality procedure. Whenever a trainee was asked to undertake work a copy would be completed in hand and put onto the file clip. This was felt to be well worthwhile. Adding a minute or two to the instruction stage was likely to save more time later, especially in respect of trainees coming back for a repeat of the earlier brief. Even without such a formal procedure, the simple task of getting the trainee to repeat the instructions just taken ensures less wasted time.

The final ingredient of delegation is feedback. Where work is done well it is important to say so. Where it not done well it is also important to say so, but with an explanation as to why the work needs to be done differently and how it should be done next time. Training always works best where there is a contemporaneous opportunity to put the message into practice, so the better trainer would look for a further opportunity as soon as possible. If several attempts fail to produce the desired improvement, the work may be beyond this delegatee and re-assignment may be needed. Whilst delegation to that individual may not work, it will no doubt for others. The rather pessimistic view often encountered – 'delegation doesn't work' – has to be proved false if the firm is both serious about its own development and that of its key people.

Coaching

The process of coaching emerges from and is an integral element of better delegation. Good coaches delegate work in an effective manner.

Their own time is wisely deployed and those around them are better developed than they would otherwise be. Good coaching is a positive experience for all concerned.

There are various definitions of better coaching. In their book *Performance Management: the New Realities* Armstrong and Baron define coaching as: 'a person to person technique designed to develop individual knowledge, skills and attitudes'.[9] They also stress that it works best where it takes place informally and as part of the normal process of management or team leadership. The key element is guidance. Coaching involves guiding people to improvements in such a way that their involvement is retained. It can therefore be contrasted to the giving of simple instructions or with a lack of contact and consultation.

It is tempting to treat coaching as a set of skills which can be made the subject of a checklist. Although this is no doubt helpful, coaching starts with an attitude rather than a skill-set. The aspect that is most striking about those held up in their firms as the best supervisors is their sustained positive manner, leading them to regard difficulties and mistakes as learning opportunities rather than semi-disciplinary issues. Dealing consistently with colleagues in this way builds over time a quality of relationship which encourages trust, learning and the development of collective expertise.

Looked at this way it is possible to analyse the conditions that need to be in place for an effective coaching environment.

- Teamwork: even if the team is simply two people, rapport and trust has to exist. Coaching requires openness and self-criticism, which in turn requires a supportive environment.
- Awareness: the coach needs awareness of his or her own strengths and weaknesses, and of those around them. A knowledge of one's own limitations is particularly important: good coaches are more likely to understate their knowledge and will seldom be judged to be 'know-it-alls' within the office.
- Respect: the effective coach retains the memory that he or she did not always know what they now do. Consequently those around them who lack experience are not 'stupid' and do not get treated as such. What we know may be obvious to us, but it will not be so to others. Respect is needed for the inexperience of others and also the different skills, knowledge and talent which they possess.
- Organisation: coaching requires time and the better coaches will be able to make time to discuss issues and the action that they might require. Constant backlogs and stressed work patterns do not sit easily with the time needed to coach others.

As with the subject of teamwork, of which coaching could be seen to be a part, the sports analogy is worth examination. Even the best sports performers keep coaches: at the top level they often regard them as being all the more important. Perhaps it is fair to say that everyone is capable of being coached. What is also remarkable is how often the best coaches were not necessarily the best players, if they were players at all. Getting the best out of others, and encouraging them to perform to their best level, does not seem to require a similar skill level on the part of the coach. The qualities that seem to be more important are the focus on issues, the drive to improve where possible, and the communication expertise to make the points which make the crucial difference. Where we coach those with greater talent, simply showing them what to do is not an option. So too in coaching legal work: providing a precedent which can be followed line by line is a poor substitute for guidance on how to do better.

The stages of coaching

Coaching should be a continual state of affairs as opposed to a set-piece occasional activity, but is worth looking at the circumstances that can trigger the coaching meeting and how the discussion should then be handled.

(1) The opportunity

Coaching could be initiated by the day-to-day discussions or as part of a more formal supervisory system. For those on a steep learning curve – trainees recently into the department or newly appointed inexperienced staff – a regular review is advisable. Once a week the supervisor clears a space of time to review work and problems in a more structured way than might otherwise be possible.

The situation may be anything other than relaxed, however. If a time limit has just been missed, if the client is making discontent very clear or if any other urgent corrective action is needed, the first priority is to put things right if at all possible. It is a good principle to involve the coachee as much as possible if this is the case, but if relationships have broken down a more active intervention may be needed.

(2) Questions to build the picture

Good coaches are more inclined to ask than tell. Whatever the situation they will build a picture of the situation by eliciting the coachee's views. Open questions prompt the necessary information and explanation:

'Tell me the situation . . .'
'What do you know about this . . .'
'What experience do you have to draw upon . . .'
'What do you suggest we do next . . .'
'What help do you need from me . . .'

As in counselling, the process works best where the coachee can be prompted to think things through for themselves, rather than be spoon-fed with an instant response. This may take longer, but the commitment gained is worthwhile for ensuring that the recipient learns from the experience.

(3) Agree an action plan

The coach needs to ensure that there is understanding on:

- what needs to be done;
- the significance of the situation and any sensitivity;
- why it needs doing;
- who will do what and the levels of authority;
- what problems should be referred back;
- the timescale.

The list of considerations is very like the delegation checklist (see Figure 10.1).

(4) Review

Implementation of the agreed plan of action is not the end of the story. It may be necessary to check that all occurred as it should have done, particularly if the coachee is inexperienced or has been unreliable in the past, and then reflection can be encouraged. The good coach will encourage the individual to reflect for themselves on what they have learned from the situation and how they would do it differently next time. This learning may be cemented by asking for a note on this, if time permits. A further opportunity to consolidate experience, or to address the limitations of performance first time around, is also ideal. It is wise to provide opportunities to repeat the challenge, provided as contemporaneously as possible, thereby enhancing the prospects of completing the learning cycle.

The manager's involvement

It is worth mentioning in passing the emphasis placed on coaching in the Investors in People standard. A number of the indicators make it clear how important the manager's continuing involvement is in achieving the business improvement described in the strategy.

> managers are effective in supporting the development of people (Indicator 8)

> managers can demonstrate their commitment by describing specific actions that they have taken and are currently taking to support the development of people (evidence statement to Indicator 1).

The most significant change that most firms could make along these lines is in relation to the manager's attitude to training. In firms where training is left to the individuals it is often a case of booking onto any necessary courses and attending them. The greatest interest by the partners may simply be in cost control – why do you need to go on this course and how many hours of continuing professional development (CPD) will you gain? In other firms the monitoring which should occur, both before and after the course, may be seen to be an administrative tasks for the personnel or training department. In firms which are truly focused on quality there will be the recognition that the investment in training only makes sense if the line manager within the department discusses the learning objectives in advance, discusses the reaction to the course afterwards and then looks for opportunities to exploit the improved know-how or skills which should have been gained. The Lexcel standard includes the advice that a person trained should be encouraged to impart their knowledge soon afterwards. This does not just make sense in terms of making training cost-effective, it also prompts much better understanding or 'internalisation' by the speaker. As many will know, nothing confronts the gaps in knowledge more starkly than having to train others in the subject.

Mentoring

Mentoring has received a great deal of management attention in recent years, and has to be considered in relation to coaching and development. Mentoring is the process whereby a guide, or mentor, is designated from within the organisation to show particular interest in a particular colleague. The thinking goes that by opening up an avenue of review and enquiry other than through formal line management reporting the individual will be able to seek help more readily and explore issues that they might hesitate to raise with supervisors. The most obvious reasons for this reluctance would be fear that it would show unexpected inexperience or incompetence, or that it might involve sensitive issues of personality or acceptable behaviour.

There are instances of formal mentoring programmes having been judged to be highly successful, but there are also authorities who hesitate on the issue. These seem to be of the view that mentoring is likely to be a good thing, but that formalising it can stifle the natural guidance which should occur in any event. When Shell introduced a scheme for graduate employees they modified the first programme to allow those concerned to find their own mentors within the company a process of 'natural selection' was seen as important. External research into the programme suggested that training of the mentors was important, particularly if the issues raised were outside their control or influence. A wider understanding of the process was also recognised to be necessary to prevent embarrassment and misunderstanding. In its worst manifestation mentoring has been described as a charter for sexual harassment.

Neil Blunt of De Montford University has argued that many of us can look back with affection and respect for those who took us 'under their wing' and provided the counselling that we could now term 'mentoring'.[10] Formalising this process, however, might destroy the chemistry of the relationship.

This seems to be apt advice for most law firms. Encouraging informal mentoring as part of a coaching environment is likely to be the best course of action for most firms, but greater formality could be a response to any situation where the culture does not seem to produce the desired dialogue more naturally. The size of the organisation will also be an issue. It is probably no coincidence that most of the reported schemes apply in major international corporations. The smaller the firm, the greater should probably be the informality.

Main Points

- Delegation is an important skill in legal work and is crucial if work is to be performed cost-effectively.
- Common barriers to delegation are lack of trust and clinging to familiar duties, but these must be overcome if the firm and the people in it are to develop.
- Delegation is one of the prime means by which we learn. Proper instructions and constructive feedback are essential.

References to Lexcel

D6 Communication
D7 Supervision

Notes

1 Maister, D.H. (1997) *Managing the Professional Service Firm*, The Free Press (Simon & Schuster).
2 McLaren, F. (1992) *Practice Marketing*, April, p. 22.
3 Temporal, D. (1993/4), *International Law Firm Management*, December 1993/January 1994, p. 115.
4 [1996] *Gazette*, 27 November, p. 14.
5 Handy, C. (1976) *Understanding Organisations*, Penguin.
6 Maister, D.H. (1997) *op. cit.*
7 Dirks, J.J.R. (1990) *Centralized Litigation Practice Management*, Waterlow.
8 Moore, M. and Dodd, M. (2001) *Lexcel Office Procedures Manual*, Law Society Publishing.
9 Armstrong, M. and Baron, A. (1998) *Performance Management: the New Realities*, Institute of Personnel and Development, p. 243.
10 Blunt, N. (1995) 'Learning from the wisdom of others' *People Management*, 31 May, p. 38.

11

Personnel systems

- Personnel plan
- Recruitment
- Person specification
- Recruitment procedures
- Selection
- Psychometric testing
- Induction process
- Disciplinary procedures

In any organisation there will need to be arrangements in place relating to personnel resourcing – ensuring that the right complement of people are in place to undertake the tasks needing attention within the firm. Most of these requirements revolve around the process of recruitment, a function which has a very obvious bearing on the quality of service provided to clients. If the firm can know that it is consistently selecting the best candidates possible and doing all in its power to avoid unsuitable appointments it will inevitably be making a considerable contribution to its eventual success.

Personnel plan

Many organisations make the preparation of a personnel plan the basis of their activities in this area. The preparation of the plan is not difficult and can be a useful basis for decisions then to be made, but it is not a compulsory requirement of any of the quality standards. The only direct reference in any of the standards appears in Lexcel in the guidance notes to D1:

> Practices may prepare a personnel plan to help ensure that skills, knowledge and experience within the practice are developed to meet needs indicated in the forward planning documents.

Most firms that undertake personnel planning do so as part of other exercises, departmental plans in larger firms or strategic plans in smaller ones. Personnel issues may feature in long term strategies in general terms, especially if growth is planned, but are more likely to be detailed at the level of 12 month action plans. There is some logic in dealing with personnel resourcing alongside issues such as the budget and marketing as part of an all embracing management plan of action for the year ahead, but large firms would be more likely to have separate documentation.

The benefits of personnel planning are that the recruitment process can be performed in a very much more controlled manner. Issues of temporary cover can be predicted to a greater degree which should mean that the panic which is often associated with unexpected resignations can be lessened. As with any plan the aim is to predict developments and so not move from one crisis decision to another. At the essence of a personnel plan, or the personnel section of another more general plan, is a calculation of resource needs. This can be simply expressed as:

Recruitment needs = projected needs − adjusted staff figures

There are two major components to the exercise: assessing current resources and matching them with likely needs. It is probably easiest to start the exercise with what is essentially a stock-take of existing personnel. The profile should include seniority and age. The firm will then consider likely changes over the period of the plan, starting with probable retirements and resignations. Retirements are fairly easy to predict and will be known about some time in advance, but resignations can be more difficult. The larger the firm the more predictable the pattern of resignations from past data. There are values in measuring this so-called 'attrition' rate. This is generally calculated as a percentage as follows:

$$\frac{\text{Leavers}}{\text{Average number of staff during the year}} \times 100$$

The reduction of the percentage in many firms makes a worthwhile management objective. Any firm will want a good degree of stability in its operations, as will clients of the firm. A frequent concern expressed by clients of commercial firms is the apparent lack of continuity in relation to advisers working on deals or disputes. Continual changes are unsettling and are bound to create fears that fees escalate through duplication of perusal time on the file. Worryingly high attrition rates as high as 40 per cent are reported in some firms, suggesting major cultural issues which should be addressed. In smaller practices the difficulties caused by any one resignation are likely to be proportionately greater, but staff turnover will seldom be so pronounced.

The organisation is unlikely to be static and planned development will also need to be taken into account. There are likely to be plans for growth but there could be planned contractions also. If the firm has decided to rationalise its operation and close a branch office there will be an obvious need to consider the personnel at that location. Can they be re-deployed and are they likely to want to move to another office? Do they have skills which will still be important to the firm, could they be usefully retrained or are they redundant? Dealing with such issues will be a major challenge for management who will want to ensure not only fairness in dealing with the personnel concerned but also the reaction of the workforce generally to the treatment of their colleagues.

By subtracting current resources from planned needs the firm will have a calculation of its likely recruitment needs. The immediate value of this will be to provide data on the size of the task, perhaps prompting a review of the adequacy of support services for the function. Is a personnel manager now needed to prevent busy partners becoming too embroiled in the administrative arrangements of recruitment or is further help needed?

Attention can now turn to the central issue: how will the needs of the firm be met? The external recruitment of new personnel may seem to be an obvious starting point but perhaps internal promotion and development should be considered instead. Any appointment constitutes a risk, but existing personnel who already know the firm and its procedures and who are familiar with many of the firm's clients are often more likely to settle into the role than newcomers. This will probably throw more emphasis onto training and development than will be the case in most firms.

Recruitment

When a member of staff resigns the temptation is to replace like with like as soon as possible but a more thorough approach may pay greater dividends. Many organisations treat a staff departure as an opportunity to review operations to see if improvements could be made to systems of work. Where improvements can be found a further contribution to quality will be possible.

This process of review is known as job analysis. It consists of collating views from a number of sources on the position to be filled in order to achieve an objective statement of who and what is required. Emerging from this a job description will be developed, as required by various of the quality standards. This job description will form the basis for the selection of the eventual appointee and for subsequent appraisal interviews.

The best starting point in the job analysis exercise will be the 'exit interview' with any departing member of the firm. Interviewed skilfully they may be forthcoming with various insights on the position and how it could be improved. The reasons for leaving one job to go to another usually comprise a combination of perceived shortcomings in the present position and hoped for improvements elsewhere. Many interviewees may wish to emphasise the future opportunities that they have identified but it is as well to probe current frustrations, with questions such as 'what would have made this job more interesting for you?' or 'what advice would you give to your successor?'.

The views expressed will not be completely objective in many cases since the departing member of staff is likely to 'post-rationalise' their decision, but in most cases the interview will be revealing and as such is an opportunity not to be missed. Discussions might then be broadened to encompass any other individual who would have a bearing on the position in question, most obviously the head of team or department, but perhaps other peers also. Whoever is responsible for the process now has the wherewithal to prepare a job description.

The job description sets out as objectively as possible what is required of the role being discussed. The requirements for job descriptions in Lexcel are found at section D1 which provides that:

> Practices will document the skills, knowledge and experience required of fee earners and other staff, the tasks they are required to perform, usually in the form of a written job description; but employment contracts may preserve job flexibility.

In Lexcel these requirements do not necessarily extend to partners but there seems little point in excluding them from any exercise to develop or review the job descriptions in use. The requirement in Lexcel in effect embraces a person specification as well as the conventional job description since it extends to skills and experiences which are more personal elements of the paperwork. The wording makes it clear that as long as the necessary elements are covered they need not necessarily be in the format of a job description. The most likely alternative would be the provision of greater details than would be normal to be included in job offers or contracts of employment.

There is no standard format for job descriptions, nor is there any standard view on the amount of detail which needs to be included. It is usual practice however to set out the main details of the position at the top showing the jobholder's place in the organisation and then describe the main purpose or purposes of the job, followed by a list of key duties.

There are differing views as to whether there should be a 'sweep-up' clause at the end providing that the jobholder will also: 'perform any other duties as requested'. This may well provide the flexibility in the job that most firms will hope for, but such clauses also tend to devalue any other list of more specific duties. Indeed, with the renewed emphasis on flexibility and teamwork in the workplace, many industrial organisations are dispensing with job descriptions altogether.

The *Lexcel Office Procedures Manual* contains two main formats, one shorter than the other.[1] The amount of detail is a matter of style and preference and there are advantages in either format. The shorter format allows for more flexibility in the role which might be helpful to the firm, especially in times of rapid development. On the other hand a more specific list of duties could mean that there is less scope for misunderstanding as to what is expected of the role.

Many firms have added details to their job descriptions in recent years by developing statements of competences for different roles and levels. In technical terms there is a difference here between a competence and a competency.

A **competence** describes what someone will need to do in order to perform a designated role successfully. Examples for a litigation solicitor might include:

- interview clients to take instructions;
- organise files and maintain satisfactory records of matters;
- apply legal principles to problems;
- advocate in designated courts.

A **competency** is more concerned with effect than effort – output as opposed to input. From the above example equivalent competencies might involve:

- interview in a manner to inspire client confidence and comprehensively in relation to pertinent legal issues;
- maintain files so as to minimise wasted time in the office and to optimise chargeable time;
- regularly achieve a favourable outcome relative to the client's case and its strengths;
- advocate so as to maximise the client's prospects of success and to enhance client approval.

Armed with a job description which provides for such specific examples there would be far greater prospects of a job-related discussion in the appraisal interview. It might then be possible to provide examples of what would be favourable and unfavourable indicators of, for example, exercising legal judgment:

Positive indicators
- Alternative course of action are weighed up before action is taken.
- Decisions are based on sound research and careful consideration of all the client's circumstances and instructions.
- Decisions made are usually easily implemented.

Negative indicators
- Fails to take account of some key factors in situations.
- Fails to think through the likely practical or legal implications of decisions.
- Frequently comes to an ill-advised conclusion as a result of careless analysis, flawed assumptions, or ignorance of law or procedure.

Many firms will feel that this level of detail would enable them to work a greater degree of objectivity into the recruitment process and then into subsequent appraisal interviews.

Person specification

The person specification supplements the job description when it is being employed as a device for selection by setting out the characteristics and abilities that an applicant should have in order to fill that role. There are various methods of undertaking this exercise: one is to 'profile' current attributes, but this option might preserve stereotypes and perpetuate an inefficient method of working. It is better to evaluate the attributes along the lines of something like Alec Rodger's seven point plan.[2]

- **Physical make-up**: health and abilities, in which the firm will be careful not to discriminate unfairly against the disabled. Is it truly necessary, for example, for the adviser to be able to drive, which will exclude the blind or poorly sighted?
- **Attainments**: these will usually relate to educational and training achievements. A member of the criminal department may be required to advocate, in which case status as a solicitor would be important. Others might be involved in the preparation of Crown Court trials, in which case it would not. What of police station representatives? Must they already hold the appropriate qualifications or will the firm be willing to train the right calibre of applicant?

- **Displayed intelligence:** this is usually an assessment of the impact made by the individual at interview, dealing with their general projection. Issues will include whether they are able to articulate their views well and thus make a favourable impression.
- **Special aptitudes:** increasingly, computer skills could be worked into this heading, but the particular job might create a whole range of other desirable abilities. Languages would be one example, especially if the firm has a high multi-ethnic client base.
- **Interests:** various interests could be important for particular positions. One could be familiarity with the farming community for an adviser who will work with a predominantly agricultural client base. Many commercial firms expect trainees to show at least an interest in the business world, while media or sports law firms will probably expect enthusiasts for their specialist line of legal work.
- **Disposition:** personal traits might be listed here, such as the ubiquitous 'must work well under pressure' or good application to tasks. Asking candidates to have a sense of humour might lead them to wonder quite what they are letting themselves in for, often justifiably.
- **Circumstances:** these will generally relate to the personal circumstances of the candidate, perhaps their current location and ability to move to the area where the job is located.

The risks of inadvertently allowing discriminatory barriers into person specifications should be borne in mind. These might extend to the whole range of prejudices that the firm will be committed to avoiding. One additional area to consider, however, is age discrimination. The Chartered Institute of Personnel and Development ran a campaign a few years ago against the setting of unnecessary age restrictions into jobs and would not carry advertisements in their journal which offended these principles. It is important to think why an applicant for a position should be 'under 40' since many above that age may not only possess the desired qualities of energy and enthusiasm hoped for, but greater experience also. At this stage of the recruitment process, the wider the net of appropriately qualified potential applicants, the better are the prospects of securing a successful appointment.

Recruitment procedures

Apart from responsibility for preparing the job description and person specification, a number of other issues will need to be dealt with in relation to recruitment procedures. These will include the promotion of the vacancy, who then interviews, whether any other testing will be undertaken and the firm's position on medicals and references. The purpose of recruitment procedures is clear within the Lexcel standard which provides at D2 that applicants should be assessed for their suitability for posts in the practice and their integrity and suitability. The firm should aspire to make the best appointment possible and deal fairly and decently with all applicants.

It is common for different people to have responsibility for recruitment within the firm. There may, for example, be a separate trainee solicitor recruitment partner. Secretarial recruitment might fall to a supervisor or to the office manager, while fee-earner recruitment is usually the responsibility of the department in larger firms or the partnership as a whole in others. The office manual needs to state who is responsible for what.

Positions can be promoted through various means. These could include:

- advertisement;
- agents;
- personal contacts;
- former staff;
- previous applicants.

Advertisements need careful checking, not least since they are a public statement about the firm. One firm unwittingly found itself subject to proceedings from the Equal Opportunities Commission when advertising for secretaries by including 'A Secretary's Prayer: "Let her be willing to listen to her master's voice on eternal tapes and to provide him with endless cups of coffee"'. The attempted humour led to a finding against the firm. How specific the wording should be on the responsibilities of the position and the rate of pay will depend on the particular circumstances of the job.

Recruitment is often principally achieved through a grapevine effect in which everyone in the firm is notified of the vacancy in case they should know of people who might be interested. In many cases this helps to foster the 'family' feel that the partners prefer. There may be not just friends working together but siblings and offspring also. This method of recruitment is potentially illegal, however, especially in larger firms. There have been various findings against large scale employers that this practice is discriminatory if the ethnic balance of that organisation differs to the general balance in that location.

Former staff and former applicants are less obvious sources of candidates but it is possible that both can be usefully exploited by the firm. Changing jobs is one of the more stressful life events that we face and many will conclude that they have made a mistake. An approach from the previous employer might reassure an individual that they would be welcome back into the organisation. Former applicants who were unsuccessful or who were unsure about the change of position beforehand might also be contacted. In this regard it is good practice that recruitment papers are maintained for at least 12 months beyond the date of interview.

Most firms will establish working relationships with agencies that they feel comfortable with. There will be an expectation of professionalism which is not always forthcoming. There should be an assurance that any agent working with the firm will not contact individuals within the firm in order to entice them elsewhere. An agency simply links applicant to position, whereas consultants offer a more personalised advice service. Most will claim to be consultancies and firms need to check credentials on this carefully.

Selection

Having recruited a suitable list of candidates the selection of the most appropriate person can now follow. There may be a shortlisting exercise following which interviews will occur. The firm needs to think through who interviews and whether there is one stage to the interview process only or a number of stages. The general rule is to have no more than two interviewers to prevent creating too imposing an environment.

The quest of most personnel practice is to make processes as objective as possible, but where individuals meet to assess each other it will always be largely subjective. The job description and person specification should improve the objectivity of the occasion and will also help to deter the notorious 'halo' or 'horns' effects, where those with the right or wrong allegiances, to schools, university, football teams or other, are either judged favourably throughout or seen as poor applicants whatever they say. Recruitment interviews benefit from being organised into a number of distinct phases:

- preparation;
- introduction;
- information gathering;

- information exchange;
- conclusion and follow-up.

As with any meeting, good preparation helps to improve the occasion. Application papers should be read and considered. Joint interviewers should agree who will deal with which elements of the meeting in order that they can develop lines of questions to probe for the true worth of the candidate. There should be agreement on what follow-up will occur. For better candidates the meeting soon changes from the applicant trying to persuade the firm to take them on to the firm trying to persuade them to join. The more professional the process, therefore, the more likely it is that the better candidate will accept an ensuing offer.

The style of the meeting should be friendly but challenging. There are those who interview in an aggressive manner to ascertain whether or not the candidate can cope with pressure. The difficulty with this is that the rather false environment of the interview will bear little resemblance to the actual pressures of work and will therefore simply risk portraying the firm as an unattractive environment. This is not to say, however, that the interview should not stretch the applicant and questions should provide the better candidates with an opportunity to show their true worth.

Many of the rules on question types and the accompanying 'non-verbal behaviour' are much the same as for performance appraisal interviews which are dealt with later. The main rules are to ask open questions which cannot be answered with a simple 'yes' or 'no' and then probe for further details. Encouraging the answers will enable applicants to show their true potential and experience.

Avoiding discrimination during the interview will again be vital, as will be the taking of detailed notes of the process in case of later complaints. It is advisable to ask a question only if it is of clear relevance and always to ask the same questions of both men and women. Asking women applicants only about child care provisions, for example, would show a clear discrimination in relation to the circumstances of female candidates. A blunt question on child care would in any event probably be better avoided altogether and the applicant might be asked instead if evening work or occasional weekend work would be problematic for them.

The interview should start with an opportunity to settle. Innocuous questions about the journey to the office or comments about the weather are helpful for letting all parties adjust to the environment. The interviewers should introduce themselves and explain who will deal with what. Given the tension that might accompany the interview it is often appreciated if a reminder of names is provided: the practice of providing a business card at the start of every meeting is helpful in this regard. The interviewers should then make it clear how long the meeting will take and what ground they wish to cover. The interview proper can then commence.

The first main phase of the interview is information gathering, in which the interviewers question the applicant for more details on the information that they will already have provided, whether by CV, application form or both. Clarification should be sought on any aspects which are unclear and examples requested of skills or abilities which the applicant claims to possess. Asking the candidate to provide examples is key at this stage.

Once the interviewers have satisfied themselves that they have the information that they require to make a decision the emphasis changes to the applicant. What questions do they have for the interviewers? Many may rehearse these, especially applicants for training contracts, but the better candidates will often show their potential through their choice of questions.

The interview is then concluded and the applicant is told what will follow. When might they hear from the firm? What is the position on any medical checks and references – may the firm take these up yet or will this have to wait until later? It is important to maintain professionalism over these important phases of the process.

Evaluation of the candidates should be against the criteria worked out in advance. Fellow interviewers should avoid any general reaction until they have worked through the job description and person specification. Firms need to question whether they do commission any medical checks, especially if there were concerns on repetitive strain injuries or there were frequent absences in the last position. References need to be understood to be either part of the decision-making process, as they tend to be in the public sector, or a substantiation of a decision already made.

Psychometric testing

Given that interviews are essentially subjective and that many of us are not as good a judge of character as we would like to imagine, there has been increasing use of testing as a supplement to the interview in recent years. The term 'psychometric' embraces tests of ability as well as personality. Both have their problems: ability tests have fallen foul of discrimination provisions since different abilities, such as linguistic ones, may discriminate against certain sections of society. Personality tests may have difficulties with gender discrimination given evidence that men and women tend to provide materially different answers on areas such as dominance and social responsibility, especially in the over-30s age group.

Firms wishing to test need to know what it is that they are looking for. The validity of the test is measured by how well it assesses what is being sought. The reliability of the test is shown by whether the test could produce similar results from different people under the same conditions. The effectiveness of the test looks at its previous track record and its record of past use.

In recent years there has been growing concern about the cultural context of tests. Research prepared by Robert McHenry for a conference of the British Psychological Society in 1997, for example, highlighted a statement 'I very much like hunting' which was answered 'yes' by 70 per cent of American males as opposed to only 10 per cent of British men. The values system of the questions is bound to shape who scores well or poorly on such exercises.

Those firms that do use tests tend to do so for senior appointments where the costs of a mistake are that much higher. On balance they should be seen to add objectivity to the recruitment process but they need careful management. Many tests encounter interviewee resistance and the British Psychological Society has strict guidelines as to the responsibilities of the testers in relation to such issues as sharing the data with the subject. If the firm is sure that it knows what it wants to test for it might be a worthwhile option to investigate.

Induction process

Any firm should have two reasons for managing an effective induction process. First, as a responsible employer it will wish to minimise the stress which will usually accompany starting a new position. Second, it will want to have the new employee working as effectively as possible as soon as possible. The key is to make sure that somebody has clear responsibility. An office manual also helps considerably and might be edited down into an induction pack.

Induction should be a two way process in which the firm discusses the issues facing new members of staff, or those new to a position within the firm. This should cover in its fullest format the position, the environment and the people. A reminder of the job description is always a good starting point in this connection. This will have been provided to the applicant at interview or beforehand, but that might be several weeks or even months ago. This will also be the best way to pick up on any initial training needs which need to be discussed. The larger the firm or office the less likely it is that a full tour of the building will be helpful; many may find a sea of new faces and the complex layout of the buildings overwhelming, in which case it would be better to spread the task over the first few days. So far as people are concerned it is advisable to concentrate primarily on immediate colleagues.

Many organisations have introduced mentoring schemes to overcome the difficulties of welcoming new employees effectively into the firm. An experienced person is asked to maintain a helpful relationship with the new joiner. Some of these schemes work well but others have caused difficulties, especially where the intentions of the parties have become the subject of gossip and innuendo. Many firms have therefore concluded that it is as well to keep such schemes as informal as possible, save that training in counselling and training skills for those who mentor can add professionalism to the process.

The requirement in Lexcel under staff induction is simply for 'documented arrangements' which are likely to be informal in smaller firms. It recommends that the various policies are emphasised and that induction needs to occur when insiders change position also, although their induction training content may be more selective. It is good practice for the induction process to include an initial assessment of training needs. The Investors in People standard includes a reference under Indicator 9 that 'People learn and develop effectively' that 'people new to the organisation, and those new to a job, confirm that they have had an effective induction'. The evidence of this is bound to be through interview in part but the completion of standardised checklists, as found in the *Lexcel Office Procedures Manual*, will also be helpful.[3]

Disciplinary procedures

The quality standards tend not to require disciplinary procedures to be in place but they will be important as a matter of general law. There are clear guidelines from ACAS which all organisation should strive to follow. The main aims should be objectivity and consistency, both of which are more likely if there are systems and procedures in place which are followed as a matter of course when a problem does arise.

Most procedures will be based on an ascending level of warnings, each of which might be by-passed in the event of serious circumstances. These are generally a preliminary 'counselling' interview to try to head off the problem before it develops, but then possibly followed by the first verbal warning, the first written warning, a final written warning and then dismissal.

ACAS produced new guidelines on disciplinary procedures which took effect in September 2000 to give effect to the provisions of the Employment Relations Act 1999. The principal change is the right of workers to be accompanied in disciplinary and grievance procedures, other than at preliminary counselling interviews where warnings are not envisaged. The new code provides that disciplinary rules should be in writing and that employers should be specific on what might constitute gross misconduct for which they might dismiss, such as 'serious incapability brought on by alcohol or illegal drugs'. The code also suggests that there should be a right of appeal in relation to disciplinary procedures which might include claims about the fairness of process. On grievance a three stage process is recommended but it is recognised that this will not be feasible in smaller organisations.

The impact of how well these difficult situations are managed on those who remain within the firm should not be under-estimated. Good employers will follow good procedures and will probably find it easier to gain and keep the services of key personnel.

Main points

- There needs to be fair procedures in place for recruitment and selection.
- All personnel should have a job description.
- The firm has responsibilities to act fairly and with confidentiality to all applicants for positions.
- An effective induction process ensures that the person joining the firm will be as effective as possible as early as possible.
- Disciplinary procedures need to follow established guidelines.

References to Lexcel

D1 Job descriptions
D2 Recruitment
D3 Induction

Notes

1 Moore, M. and Dodd, M. (2001) *Lexcel Office Procedures Manual*, Law Society Publishing.
2 Alec Rodgers quoted from (1988) *Gower Book of Management*, Gower Publishing, p.965.
3 Moore, M. and Dodd, M. *op. cit.*

12

Performance management: appraisals and training

- Objectives of appraisals
- Designing the system
- Partner review schemes
- Conducting the interview
- Training

The term 'performance management' has a distinct technical meaning in the personnel world. It describes a management philosophy of how to get the best out of people and the organisation that they belong to. Fletcher described this in 1992 as:

> an approach to creating a shared vision of the purpose and aims of the organisation, helping each employee understand and recognise their part in contributing to them, and, in so doing, manage and enhance the performance of both individuals and the organisation.[1]

There is therefore more to performance management than simply being 'nice people to work for' – there is a business edge to it also. In a service sector such as the law, where so much depends upon the skills and knowledge of everyone within the firm, it is vital to business success. Performance management is generally regarded as having four phases: see Figure 12.1.

The link to the Investors in People award will be immediately apparent to those familiar with it. Performance management has become the orthodoxy of the personnel world in recent years and IIP largely enforces the regime through its provisions. The organisation's

Determine performance expectations

Review and appraise

Support performance

Manage standards

Figure 12.1 *Performance management*

175

appraisal system, whether annual or more frequent, becomes critical. Most of the writing in the field of performance management examines how performance appraisals can be improved: most of the research shows that performance appraisals generally fail to provide the value that should be expected from them.

In line with the development of performance management in recent years, appraisal schemes have become fairly standard practice. Quality standards certainly seem to treat appraisal schemes as an essential element of personnel management to greater or lesser degrees. Although most of the requirements in this area concentrate on the operations of the performance appraisal scheme there are three elements involved, each of which appear in the Lexcel initiative. These are:

- the setting of objectives;
- the conduct of an appraisal process;
- the management of an effective training system.

Firms could link these three areas to differing degrees but they can obviously be merged through the appraisal process. At the interview there will be a review as to whether previous objectives have been met and, if not, whether these should be carried forward for the next period under question. New objectives might otherwise need to be agreed. Training also follows on logically from the appraisal process. Given the objectives agreed during the process what training and development will be helpful to enable the appraisee to meet the goals agreed upon?

Appraisals are one of the mainstays of Investors in People. They are also a compulsory requirement of CLSQM and the Lexcel initiative. According to CLSQM the arrangements in legal aid firms must extend to:

> all personnel that are directly or indirectly concerned with the provision of LSC funded services, including partners who supervise or undertake work in LSC funded cases. (J1.4)

There are possible exceptions within CLSQM for sole principals who can agree with their auditors that they should be exempt from the process. The provisions of D4b in Lexcel are that practices should 'evaluate performance of staff at least annually against their responsibilities and objectives', so partner appraisals are not compulsory. Investors in People does not draw the distinction of hierarchies within the firm, but requires instead a number of policies to be in place for 'people' within the firm. The most significant requirements are under Indicator 6 which forms part of the section on planning: 'The development of people is in line with the organisation's aims and objectives'.

I have encountered one practice accredited to IIP where the partners did not have an appraisal scheme but the general view would be that partners must also be under review.

Although performance appraisal schemes are standard practice so far as the quality standards are concerned it would be a mistake to regard them as being completely accepted by the authorities on this area of management. The detractors can be grouped into two camps: those who think them a good thing that do not work in practice and those that think them a bad thing that do not work in practice. Deming remained implacably opposed to appraisals throughout his long and illustrious career.[2] Even the more ardent supporters will generally concede that the weight of available evidence is that these schemes generally work badly and risk appraisee disillusionment from being handled ineptly.

Common failings include:

- the discussion focuses too much on traits or personality issues;
- the appraiser is too wary of raising unfavourable points;
- the appraiser does not have the skills needed to do the job properly;
- the appraiser sees it a waste of time;
- the organisation does not take it seriously.

The effective appraisal interview requires an open, honest, positive, two-way communication between the parties and will call upon the leadership qualities of the appraiser. Appraisals are a more difficult device to master than many other elements of management, in which respect there are two recurring contradictions which tend to arise:

- although there is general support for appraisal schemes in the personnel world, they seldom become popular with either appraisers or appraisees;
- although ACAS can make recommendations for fair disciplinary procedures and there are relatively standard devices for job descriptions there is no such thing as a standard appraisal scheme; the system has to be right for the organisation and may differ greatly from other systems elsewhere.

There is helpful guidance in the various standards on the design of appraisal systems. According to CLSQM, organisations should ensure that the appraisal scheme is:

- appropriate for the type of firm: too formal in a small firm, or too informal in a large firm, will lead to difficulties;

- able to relate the performance of the individual to the needs of the business;
- a two way communication process, ensuring that the objectives are clear on both sides, with ample time being allowed for discussion;
- documented and agreed at the end of the meeting, with both appraiser and employee understanding clearly what has been agreed;
- able to identify training needs as well as set objectives.

Similar guidance can be found in Lexcel under D4b that:

> the appraisal will review past performance against previously established criteria and set objectives for the future. The appraisal process need not be elaborate. However a written record of the appraisal is mandatory.

Finally, although partner appraisals are not compulsory under Lexcel, the requirement under D4a for the setting of performance objectives does specifically extend to 'each partner, principal and member of staff in the practice'. This will mean that there will need to be at very least some form of discussion, probably on an annual basis, where these can be agreed. In smaller firms this might be achieved as part of the agenda at an annual strategic meeting.

Objectives of appraisals

The good appraisal scheme will achieve a number of aims, most of which share the objective of aligning the performance of each individual within the practice to the overall aims of the organisation. This is most evident in Investors in People, as one of the explanatory statements under the planning section emphasises: 'People have clear expectations of what their development activities should achieve, both for them and the organisation'.

In similar vein, Lexcel talks of everyone within the firm being able to 'describe the aims and objectives of the organisation at a level appropriate to their role' (D4a). Where this can be achieved the net effect should be a more embracing culture than is otherwise likely and greater focus throughout the organisation on its strategic priorities.

Performance appraisal schemes should also seek to motivate the appraisee. Even where negative points have to be made the meeting should serve to improve motivation and morale. Appraisers are encouraged to raise points for improvement rather than criticisms of performance. Dealing with criticism in a constructive manner can retain a sense of motivation in the meeting and should avoid demoralisation. The two-way nature of the process often means that the appraiser will be provided with insights on the team and perhaps themselves. The interview should always extend beyond the performance of the appraisee to the circumstances of their position and the supervision that they are subject to.

In most firms the development of any training policy or plan for the year ahead will be shaped by the data collected at appraisal meetings. The discussions should shape the general needs of the firm and so plan any in-house provision. This is an advantage of conducting all appraisals in a batch within a month or two as opposed to spreading them over the year, as some firms do, usually to coincide with the anniversary of the person joining the firm.

In some ways the whole of personnel management can be seen as a quest to make processes as objective as possible. As long as people are involved in the process, however, this can only be partially possible. Any interview, be it for selection, promotion, disciplinary or appraisal always has the interpersonal dynamic to it.

One way to make the performance appraisal interview as objective as possible is to use the job description in the interview more than most firms do at present. The more specific the job description, the more focused is the appraisal interview likely to be. If the firm develops a competency framework, as discussed in Chapter 11, and accompanying positive and negative indicators, it will be in a better position to have very much more specific discussions about performance issues.

Designing the system

The requirements in appraisal schemes were described by two researchers as:

> A good performance appraisal scheme must be job related, reliable, valid for the purposes for which it is being used, standardised in its procedures, practical in its administration and suited to the organisation's culture.

First, the assessments must be relevant to the job and not simply personality based. A common failing of how appraisal interviews are conducted will be that the interview does not concentrate adequately on the conduct by the appraisee of their job role. In its place there occurs instead a general assessment by the appraiser of whether the appraisee is helpful and a good team member. This is considerably less than should be expected by all concerned.

Other requirements are that the paperwork should actually test what is regarded as important and be capable of producing consistent results with everyone who undergoes the process. Part of the reason that appraisal schemes often struggle to become popular is that they inevitably attract a certain amount of bureaucracy. The requirement in Lexcel in D4c is that:

> Practices will have documented procedures to record in writing the performance appraisal, the record to be kept confidential to the practice and the post holder (D4c).

Without the agenda of points to cover that will be found in the appraisal report many difficult points will not be covered and the formal record will be deficient. The objective should be to ensure comprehensive cover of relevant issues with the least possible burden to those involved.

Most systems simply rely upon the appraiser collecting views from the appraisee and then adding their own observations at the interview. There is an obvious limitation to this process in that the interview is limited to the perceptions of the two parties involved. There will be a lack of objective data on issues that are likely to be key, such as the standard of client service provided or the supervisory skills shown by the jobholder. For this reason many firms in recent years have introduced more elaborate systems. The simplest addition will be the introduction of some peer assessments, as occurs in various partner appraisal schemes. All members of the firm are invited or required to comment on the contribution of all others. Whoever then conducts the appraisal meeting is properly mandated to raise any points since they will be genuinely collective views. A further source of data will come from inviting direct reports to the supervisor to comment in confidence on how well they feel that they are supervised. These so-called 'upward appraisal' schemes are becoming more common in the more forward-thinking firms and are in line with developments elsewhere in business.

The widest collection of pre-appraisal data will occur in '360 degree appraisals' which have become standard in most areas of commerce (see Figure 12.2). These schemes widen the sources to include clients with the result that the information is properly rounded in advance of the meeting and therefore less likely to be disputed, adding therefore to the validity of the discussions.

For the sake of completeness it should be added that there are also in business '540 degree appraisals' where the circle of participants is extended to include other 'stakeholders', such as professional contacts.

| Figure 12.2 | *360 degree appraisals* |

The general advice on appraisals and pay is to keep the two separate from each other. The rationale for this is that:

- the appraisal interview should be a reflective meeting to discuss improvements and should involve some self criticism by the appraisee: this is less likely if a salary negotiation is being conducted;
- pay levels depend on many more factors than just performance, most obviously going rates locally, the overall performance of the firm, etc.

In many firms there will be widespread cynicism as to whether there is a link and, if so, how it works. Frequent reminders on the role of the appraisal interview are important. If pay has been distanced from appraisal there should be another opportunity at a different time of year to discuss targets for fee earning, along with pay where strict bands do not apply.

Most of the first appraisal schemes in law firms relied upon a ratings systems, where marks were awarded against the various criteria covered, either A to E or various numbering scorecards. Many firms have abandoned such schemes in recent years. The general view in the personnel world is increasingly that ratings in schemes are unhelpful for the following reasons:

(a) inconsistency: in most firms there will be those partners who will never give a grade A on principle, but others will give it as a matter of course. Apart from the unfairness of such differentials there is also a considerable risk of demotivation. If a secretary is quite clearly functioning in a way where no improvement could reasonably be suggested why not admit that her contribution to the firm is excellent? If she knows this to be the case what is the impact of telling her that this is not so?

(b) middle banding: the tendency will always be to use just Bs and Cs in the majority of cases. It could be argued that if performance is unsatisfactory (E) the issue should have been dealt with other than at appraisal. There are comments only and ratings-based appraisal systems in the *Lexcel Office Procedures Manual*.[4] The rating-based schemes are based on four categories rather than an even number to force a decision on whether the appraisee is above or below the median level of performance.

(c) avoidance of real discussion: the reluctant appraiser can show compliance with the requirements of the system simply by ticking a number of letters: genuine discussion is not necessarily encouraged.

In favour of ratings is that there will be a harder edge to discussions. Appraisees are more likely to know where they stand. If there is a performance-related pay scheme in operation the ratings will be helpful to determine who should be in which band of award. As to who should appraise some firms prefer to limit the task to supervisors while others ask anyone in a line management position to do so. This will be determined by practical considerations for the most part, including the personalities concerned.

Generally it will be necessary to provide appraisees in advance with:

(a) a pre-appraisal questionnaire;
(b) a copy of their job description;
(c) copy of last year's report.

One format, which can be effective, is for like forms to be completed by appraiser and appraisee in advance of the meeting. These will be exchanged and compared, with the discussion then focusing on points of perceived difference. This type of system will usually be ratings-based, but could be limited to comments. The dangers of this system, however, are that:

- the whole system depends on paperwork being completed and exchanged to a fixed timetable: in the event of delay, which is always a possibility in the professional service environment, the meeting might have to be postponed; this could be demo-tivating and should be avoided where possible;

- all is fine if the appraisee reads in advance of favourable or expected ratings, but if the first they know of a perceived prob-lem is a cold comment or mark on the form it might cause resentment.

Partner review schemes

In many ways partner appraisals might be more helpful for firms than staff schemes. In most firms the partners will feel comfortable to call in a member of staff on any point of concern in order to discuss it – effective supervision suggests that they should not hesitate to do so. Where there are issues with partners, however, there may be greater sensitivity. This makes the holding of a formal conversation where the contribution of that person can be discussed and misunderstandings resolved all the more important.

It would be naive to under-estimate the difficulties with partner appraisals, however. In some firms there may be positive dangers in forcing issues which do not really need to be addressed and which have the potential to damage working relationships. There may some-times be long-standing difficulties which might not benefit from being brought to the surface. The design of the system should take such factors into account. By and large the paperwork for staff schemes will be inappropriate and the firm should always consider the different criteria by which the partners should be assessed. The partners in most firms will have to be more than simply a reliable fee-earner, so the qualities of supervision and their participation in mar-keting activities assume greater importance. Finance is also a probable difference. Whereas the advice in staff schemes is to keep finance out of the discussions it will probably weigh heavily in any partner meet-ing. In an attempt to encourage greater teamwork and more effective supervision the forms in the *Lexcel Office Procedures Manual* list not just the partner's billing but their own profitability and the profitabil-ity of any team that they supervise.

One of the likely differences between partner and staff schemes is therefore the issue of timing. If pay awards for staff are not to be an issue there is logic in distancing the discussions as much as possible away from the pay reviews which are likely around the end of the business year. Assuming a March or April year end, the autumn emerges as the best time for staff schemes. Partners, however, should have a clearer focus on financial issues in their reviews and the spring seems to be the obvious time for them to occur. By the end of the business year there will be a shrewd idea of the current year's performance and the plans for next will be taking shape. If an overall target of a 10 per cent increase in billings is going to be in next year's plans, what help will the partner need with his or her contribution? How do the general targets impact on their area of practice and what training might they need to enable them to achieve their personal objectives? A discussion on these lines will make the achievement of the next year's objectives very much more likely and should serve to increase the contribution from partners not directly concerned with management.

A further common difference with partner schemes is the number of appraisers. In most staff schemes there will be one appraiser only, perhaps accompanied by the staff partner, office manager or personnel manager who will usually act more as an observer and ensure consistency of approach in all interviews. In most partnerships there will be undercurrents of relationships which mean that two appraisers will be preferable. A panel of reviewers is a common arrangement with any two from the panel being able to conduct the discussions. This will mean that their fellow committee members will be able to cover their own personal reviews.

Upward appraisal schemes are particularly appropriate for partner schemes. Supervision will almost always be discussed and some views from the direct reports of the appraisee will add objectivity to the discussions. This is an issue which must be introduced with great care, however, as the culture of the firm will have to be quite open for the data to be offered without fear of recrimination in the first place and to be acceptable by the partners. Maister recommends all partners rating their peers into one of four bands of partners' performance levels, but this reflects the more competitive nature of the commercial firm in America and would be too divisive in most firms in the UK.[5] Where firms are concerned that the partners should have a proper focus on quality some measure of upward assessment, perhaps coupled to some client feedback, should be quite sufficient.

Conducting the interview

However well designed the appraisal paperwork may be the interview will need to be handled professionally. A badly conducted interview could achieve more harm than good and the responsibility of conducting interviews needs to be taken seriously. This suggests that all appraisers should be trained in appropriate techniques and there should be discussions between all involved before a round of appraisals in order to try to agree a common approach and style.

In many firms the appraiser will have a pre-appraisal form to complete themselves but it is more common for the paperwork at this stage to be confined to the appraisee. In any event the appraiser should consider in advance of the meeting:

- how well the appraisee has done in achieving objectives set last year;
- to what extent personal development plans have been implemented;
- feedback that is intended and evidence of it;
- factors affecting performance;
- possible career progression and objectives for the appraisee.

Practical points also need consideration. It is advisable to try to avoid sitting behind a desk in the way that the supervisor generally does. A meeting room will be more away from distractions and a round table creates more of a sense of equals. Above all, the interview needs to be treated as being at least as important as any client meeting. Interruptions should therefore be avoided and phones must be diverted.

At the meeting a likely agenda of points will be:

- introduction and agreement of objectives;
- review of job description and key activities of the appraisee;
- review of points on appraisee form;
- discussion (and completion) of appraisal report form.

There are three broad strategies that can be adopted in the interview itself.

- Tell and sell: in this approach the appraisee is told how the appraiser sees the issues and 'sells' to them the course of action which is felt to be appropriate. This can be suitable for junior members of staff but should be used with great care with more senior personnel.
- Tell and listen: in this the appraiser again 'tells' to start the process, but has an open mind as to what should be done as a result of the process.
- Joint problem solving: this is the most democratic of the styles of interviewing in which the aim is to define and then deal with any problems identified; this is the style certainly to be adopted with senior personnel or in partner appraisals.

The good appraisal meeting is one where the appraisee does most of the talking. Appraisees are in the best position to comment on how the work is performed and how it might be improved. The issue of questioning techniques is clearly important. For the advocate it will be necessary to reverse court questioning skills. It is necessary to ask open questions, not knowing what the answer will be. Questions should be as open ended as possible and should give the appraisee the opportunity to pick up on any concerns or suggestions that they might wish to raise. Good questions to prompt discussion would include:

How do you think things are going?

What can we learn from that?

It is often a good idea to preface the question with 'tell me':

Tell me, why do you think that happened?

The appraiser should follow up general answers to open questions with 'probe' or 'reflective' questions:

So how well should the computer program be working now?

And I suppose we would have to change departmental arrangements for that to be possible?

Closed questions are fine at the end of the sequence to confirm the final details:

So would you like to go to training on that?

In her book *Effective Interviewing*, Helena Twist encourages a view of personnel interviews along these lines as a funnel (see Figure 12.3).[6]

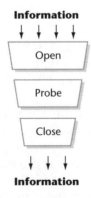

| Figure 12.3 | *The funnel* |

A technique of particular value is 'self-appraisal' in which the appraisee is asked to volunteer views on the issues themselves. General rules of interpersonal behaviour also need to be borne in mind. It seems to be generally accepted that we read more through the non-verbal channels than the verbal. Does the appraiser look interested or do they continually glance at their watch to check the time? The staging of the process and the attitudes on show are at least as important as the design of the paperwork in ensuring that the meeting produces the benefits intended from it.

Many appraisees may be reticent and appear to lack any desire to involve themselves in the interview as they should. The atmosphere of the meeting is crucial here, as is praise and encouragement. Open and probing questions are needed to ensure the involvement needed. Perhaps more difficult are the situations where the appraisee does have problems in their performance levels. Theory might tell us that the meeting should be positive and motivating, but this may be very difficult in such situations. The key here is to lay the groundwork for the interview. At its simplest, if criticisms are to be part of the discussion, examples are needed. Lack of preparation will create the danger of loss of control. The main recommendations are that appraisers should always criticise performance, not personality. The use of positive language – putting areas of difficulty as areas for improvement – is helpful. If problems are extreme it is advisable to keep all issues of a disciplinary nature away from the appraisal interview, or word may spread that the interviews are to be much more intimidating than people are being led to expect.

Whatever the situation some follow-up is advisable. If the scheme is annual it is a good idea to have a six month review of what is being done on training or other developmental activities. This can help to ensure that momentum is maintained and that the next year's meeting avoids the danger of repeating much of the previous year's discussion because very little has happened in the intervening time, which seems to be all too frequent an occurrence in many firms. It is difficult to imagine anything more likely to harm morale and devalue the appraisal system. All parties concerned, the appraiser and appraisee, as well as the partners or managers in control of the system, share the responsibility to ensure that this is avoided.

Training

If quality is concerned in any way with the improvement of performance then there must clearly be arrangements in place for training. It is therefore no surprise that there are provisions on training in all the quality systems, ISO 9000 included. The appraisal process is the obvious way in which training should be addressed, a process which is envisaged at D5b:

> Practices will have documented arrangements to ensure that training and development needs are assessed for each person against the objectives of the practice and are reviewed at least annually.

The objectives for the jobholder will be discussed and agreed and it will then be logical to consider if the person has the necessary skills to achieve these goals. The setting of personal objectives and the choice of training activities should therefore be seen as essential accompaniments to each other.

It should be remembered that although partner appraisals may not be compulsory under Lexcel, the setting of objectives applies to all personnel. The general advice is that objectives should be as specific as possible and stated in a way that can be judged at a later stage. Technical examples could spell out the level of matter and responsibility which might be expected. Take an associate who is hoping to be considered for partnership in two years' time. In relation to technical development the following is agreed: 'to undertake own advocacy in at least eight county court trials this year'. Wider management objectives are also considered. Rather than simply, for example: 'get more involved in marketing' the discussion could agree what form this will take: 'get more involved in marketing, to include meeting with one existing or potential client per month and organising a seminar during the year as part of the firm's programme'.

The associate in the above example could have training needs to make their objectives a reality. Advocacy training or further training in evidence could be important in the first example, whereas presentation skills or more general marketing and selling skills could be appropriate in the second. A good personal training plan should arise without too much difficulty from the discussions in the meeting.

Compulsory post-qualification training was first introduced in 1985. Initially it was limited to solicitors in their first three years post-admission, but the requirements have been extended in various tranches so that the whole profession is now covered. The general rule is 16 hours per year, but this is expressed as 48 hours in each three-year period for most. There is less opposition to compulsory training than seemed to be the case a few years ago, though many feel that they have difficulty in finding the right type of course for them. The problem is in part that solicitors are not sufficiently flexible in relation to the other options for undertaking the necessary activity. Alternatives to attending training sessions include the following.

- Preparing and delivering any session which counts for Continuing Professional Development (CPD) (e.g. an approved in-house course within the firm), or for non-CPD courses (e.g. a talk to be given to an outside organisation) if it is 'of particular relevance and benefit to your work'. Any such talk has to be at least 30 minutes in duration and can be counted as twice the delivery time to include preparation.
- Writing law books or articles in legal journals, for which the actual time spent doing so can be claimed.
- Legal research: the actual time can be counted if it is of use 'beyond the particular case and results in the production of a precedent, practice note or other form of written guidance'. Any such note should be retained for future reference. This could be relevant if the fee-earner were to talk at a departmental meeting which did not count as an in-house training session because it was too short to count as such.

Compliance with CPD requirements is a consideration within the programme, but should not be the prime reason for it. Training should be undertaken primarily to improve the expertise and level of service provided, and not to satisfy the requirements of the Law Society or the Institute of Legal Executives.

As to the content of the training there is a requirement in Lexcel in D5c that the:

> skills and knowledge required for the management and organisation of the practice (as well as for legal practice) are provided for in training and development.

Other law societies are more prescriptive: the Law Society of Scotland has a requirement that at least a quarter of the annual requirement should involve practice management or other such skills.

It is possible to observe different levels of commitment to training in different firms. The larger firms are more likely to have their own in-house programmes as their numbers will permit them to do so more cost-effectively. Whether through internal or external provision, however, the three levels of training commitment are as illustrated in Figure 12.4.

The leading edge firms will take a view of themselves that they are in a knowledge management concern where training is part of the mainstream activity of the firm. This may also mean that providing

> (3) Training as a core activity;
> (2) Training to improve the organisation;
> (1) Simple CPD compliance: hours collecting.

Figure 12.4   *Three levels of training commitment*

training becomes part of its services to clients and the constraints of providing advice only on a one-to-one basis are discarded. This is close to the concepts of the learning organisation which provide that there need to be strong links between the experience of the firm and the improvement of its expertise and performance. Many firms will recognise this as part of the management challenge with know-how: CLSQM requires 'cascading' of knowledge by supervisors and there are other provisions in the legal quality standards for sharing of know-how and legal information. There is exciting potential for firms with this more ambitious outlook through the latest developments with information technology.

Main points

- Appraisal schemes should be part of a performance management system.
- All personnel, including partners, need to have personal objectives which will usually emerge from the appraisal process.
- How well the interview is conducted will have a critical effect on its effectiveness.
- There is no such thing as a standard appraisal scheme and the systems will have to be appropriate to the firm in question.
- Partner appraisal schemes are not a requirement of Lexcel but are increasingly regarded as good practice.
- The appraisal process should align the appraisee's objectives to the overall objectives of the practice.
- Training should go beyond CPD compliance and should be seen as one of the prime means by which the firm will improve.

References to Lexcel

D4a   Setting objectives
D4b–c   Appraising staff
D5   Training

Notes

1 Fletcher, C. and Williams, R. (1992) *Organisational Experience*, quoted by Armstrong, M. and Baron, A. (1998) *Performance Management: the New Realities*, Institute of Personnel and Development, p. 9.
2 Deming, W. E. (1986) *Out of Crisis*, Massachusetts Institute of Technology/Cambridge University Press.
3 Lazer, R. I., and Wilkstrom, W.S. (1997) *Appraising Management Performance – Current Practices and New Directions*, New York – the Conference Board.
4 Moore, M. and Dodd, M. (2001) *Lexcel Office Procedures Manual*, Law Society Publishing.
5 Maister, D. (1997) Managing the Professional Firm, Free Press, part 5.
6 Twist, H. (1992) *Effective Interviewing*, Blackstone Press, p. 30.

13

Financial management

- Responsibility and reports
- Cash management
- Time recording
- A new financial outlook

As with most elements of the Practice Management Standards, satisfying the requirements of section C on financial management will not be unduly onerous for most firms. Managing financial performance as well as firms should, however, may not follow quite as easily. It may well be that improving financial management skills is one of the prime challenges facing partners in their management development over the next few years. Newer methods of planning and monitoring performance may soon be needed to cope with changing expectations from clients and funding organisations.

Responsibility and reports

The first requirement of section C in Lexcel is that there should be clear responsibility for financial matters. In years gone by this would probably have been the senior partner who would retain the bank statements and ensure that performance remained satisfactory. It seems remarkable now to think back to a time when many firms would have little idea of their true profit performance for any given year until the end of year accounts arrived from the accountants, but these times are not too distant. Greater sophistication of monitoring is now the norm and it should be clearly understood as to who is responsible for what. In many firms this may still be the senior partner, but many more have a managing partner, or perhaps even a designated finance partner. The standards recognise that there will probably be an employed finance manager in larger firms, but even here it might be advisable that the manager has a clear line of responsibility to a designated partner.

The finance function in any organisation consists essentially of reporting, predicting and monitoring. The combination of these three functions informs the management of the firm of the changes and interventions that are needed. The distinction is made between financial reporting, which is concerned with the production of reports such as the annual profit and loss account and balance sheet, and management accounting, which is the budgeting of income and expenditure and the subsequent monitoring of performance. Both are found in the standards at C2.

Whereas financial reporting is a function that will necessarily involve outside expertise through the firm's auditors, management accounting is a function which can be undertaken purely within the firm and should at least be understood by any partner who is actively involved in the management of the firm or any department within it. The main requirements are for an annual budget, an annual cash flow forecast and quarterly variance analysis at least from them.

The production of a budget need not be an onerous task and cannot be precise. The budget is simply one form of plan to guide the performance of the organisation and so to ensure optimum or required success. Essentially pragmatic in nature, it is necessary to look back at past performance to project forward to the required levels for both income and expenditure. The main steps are as follows:

(1) Analyse figures to date and determine if they are satisfactory. In an increasing number of firms performance for the last 12 months can be produced as a report at any stage, but in others an analysis of the first nine months of the year with three still to go is a good starting point.

(2) Vary the base figures produced in this way if there have been unusual factors over the period: a department may have billed considerably more than usual through having completed a long-running and highly lucrative matter, or perhaps an exceptional deal has been processed in the commercial group. Likewise there may be items of expenditure which will distort the figures and which will therefore require an adjustment.

(3) Project forward the desired figures for next year, allowing for profit growth and inflation. Adjustments will then be needed for developments which can be envisaged at this stage, perhaps changes to personnel with new staff joining the firm. It is important to consider any elements of the business plan for the period in question. Plans to increase the volume of work in one area or to reduce another are bound to have an effect on the figures under consideration.

(4) Check the figures with all concerned, which in most firms will

involve discussion of the figures at a partners' meeting. It is particularly important to check if there are any other developments which should be taken into account and which will affect the figures. Ideally, later changes to the budgets should be minimal and the figures presented to the meeting should be seen as realistic by all concerned.

(5) Once the income and expenditure budgets are agreed the assessment of likely profit will also be calculable. The partners will need to determine if this is satisfactory. If it is not, the process of reviewing the figures will have to commence: where can more be earned or expenditure saved? Eventually, agreement should be achieved.

As with any plan, the budgets should be living documents and not regarded as a once and for all effort. It is wise to maintain details of how the figures were calculated in case of later uncertainty. A revision of the process might be necessary in the event of major developments, perhaps the unexpected defection of a team from one of the departments or an opportunity to 'bolt on' a team from elsewhere. In normal circumstances, however, review can simply take the form of variance analysis of the figures. The system will produce a projection of what the figures should be and a comparison with where the figures are. Clearly such programmes vary considerably in their complexity. Most will be based on 'equalised' figures for the 12 months of the annual plan, but this might be varied in the case of one-off payments which are only made on an annual basis. All that really matters is that management have figures to guide their performance and alert them to dangers.

Cash management

There is a requirement in C2 in Lexcel that firms should produce an annual cash flow forecast and quarterly variance at least of cash flow. The whole area of cash management is one of the principal concerns in running a legal practice. Many work areas consist of long-running matters where the client will feel that they have acquired little true benefit until the end of the matter. There may nowadays be greater acceptance of cash on account, especially for disbursements which will have to be met, and interim billing, but cash flow is likely to remain a concern for most practices.

The measurement of the capital which is locked up within the practice is relatively simple. The balance sheet figures for work in progress and unpaid bills can be converted to periods of days as shown in Figure 13.1.

It is very difficult to say what these figures should be. As always, much depends on the type of firm and its particular profile of work. Total lock-up periods of just over 100 days are currently being achieved by certain City practices, whereas a survey conducted by Andrew Otterburn in 1998 of general practices showed that over a half of the firms surveyed billed within two weeks of the end of the matter, but 32 per cent of firms in London and 15 per cent of firms in the provinces then waited a further 2–3 months for payment. The average value of work in progress was not measured in this report but was calculated elsewhere as being between 4–7 months for many firms.[1] This would suggest 300 days as a high level of lock-up.

Various developments in practice have inevitably impacted upon these figures. Conditional fee agreements have increased the volume of work in progress. Block contracting of legal aid work is designed to smooth out the pattern by making steady monthly payments with occasional adjustments for variations from the projected pattern of work.

Although external comparisons can be difficult, internal comparisons are always possible and relevant. The partners will want to feel that the performance never deteriorates from its level without due cause. Where improvements are possible they should be worked for. The benefits of better cash collection should also be calculated. Figure 13.2 shows the value of each day's turnover for smaller firms. Each day that the lock-up period can be reduced by that amount means less borrowing on overdraft and its consequential saving of interest, or investment to produce a return.

As an example of the possible savings, a firm with a turnover of £5 million which manages to improve its lock-up by five days will save 13,700 x 5 = £68,500. Either this could be taken from any borrowing which could save, assuming 10 per cent interest charges, £6,850 per year, or it could be invested by the firm or the partners and make slightly less than that figure by way of an investment. Clearly, the

$$\frac{\text{Work in progress}}{\text{Turnover}} \times 365 \qquad \frac{\text{Debts outstanding}}{\text{Turnover}} \times 365$$

Figure 13.1   *Measurement of capital*

Turnover £ millions	Daily value £
one	2,740
two	5,480
three	8,220
four	10,960
five	13,700
eight	21,920
ten	27,400

Figure 13.2   *Value of daily turnover*

higher the prevailing interest rates, the more important this exercise would become.

In most firms cash flow would be a computer-generated program, but an understanding of the exercise is always useful, as is an ability to perform a quick, simple assessment in any particular situation.

Cash in

There may be a considerable difference between bills delivered and cash collected in any given month. First, the percentage of cash collected to bills delivered will seldom be 100 per cent, though the nearer it can be to this ideal figure, the better. Comparison of this percentage between departments or even fee-earners can be a telling report from time to time. Furthermore, there will be seasonal variations, according to busy and quiet times of the year. The curve of anticipated cash receipts will therefore be unlikely to be a straight line (see Figure 13.3):

> Cash in is calculated most easily as the percentage of cash which tends to be collected against the previous month's figures. In many firms a more complex calculation would be needed.
>
> Cash in will be added to the opening office account balance for cash flow calculations.

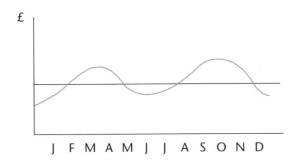

£

J F M A M J J A S O N D

Figure 13.3 *Anticipated cash receipts*

Cash out

Partners' drawings and salaries are the major outgoing and will tend to be a flat and predictable figure throughout the year. In relation to other outgoings the expenditure budget should provide reasonably easy figures to work from, but it will be necessary to edit these or add to the figures for unusual or exceptional items

The calculation of cash flow is therefore: opening balance on office account plus anticipated cash receipts, less anticipated cash out.

An example is given in Figure 13.4, which shows the cash flow statement for a firm with a 30-day cash collection period where, on average, 90 per cent of the previous month's bills are collected. Exceptional items are a six-monthly instalment of partners' tax at £150,000 in January and a brochure printing bill of £20,000 which will need to be paid in March.

Summary reports will generally illustrate trends more effectively than great volumes of print-outs. By and large reporting has improved in most firms in recent years.

Time recording

Finally within section C is a requirement for a 'documented system' to ensure that 'time spent on casework can be properly recorded and attributed'. In all but the smallest of practices this will now be under-taken through computerised time recording, which itself becomes more sophisticated with time. Many firms have moved beyond the practice which has been standard for many years of fee-earners mark-ing up in hand an analysis of time to be recorded to then be passed to the accounts department for inputting by another operator. Newer

	Jan £000	Feb £000	Mar £000
Bills delivered	450	500	550
Cash in (90% of previous month)	360	405	450
Less drawings and salaries	250	250	250
Other expenditure	100	100	100
Exceptional items	150	–	20
Cash outflow	500	350	370
Summary			
Opening balance	100	(40)	15
Cash in	360	405	450
	460	365	465
Cash out	(500)	(350)	(370)
Anticipated balance	(40)	15	95

Figure 13.4   *Cash flow statement*

systems allow or require the fee-earner to enter the data themselves, perhaps by use of a light pen to computer codes. The advantages of direct entry of data are:

- better time capture: less is forgotten by the fee-earner as they struggle later in the day, or perhaps even several days later, to remember what they did when for whom;
- reduction of delay in recording and avoidance of backlogs, so reducing the irritation of time coming to hand after a final bill has been sent out;
- costs efficiency: less personnel are needed in the accounts department or their time can be more usefully deployed, as on credit control, which remains neglected in many firms.

More firms now require personnel to record all time and not simply chargeable. This makes for more complete analysis of the costs of management activities and can form a record of who is taking more or less holiday than they should. It is always important, however, to guard against the notion than chargeable time is good and non-chargeable bad. A partner undertaking chargeable work which should have been delegated and which will not justify partner charge-out rates should never be allowed to be seen to be preferable to another partner undertaking marketing activity in line with plans that the firm have agreed upon. The other frequent over-simplification in the analysis of time recording data is the easy conclusion that a partner with a charge-out rate of £150 per hour who has spent three hours at a training session has 'lost' £450. This would only be the case if three hours of work were turned away as a result of attending the course. What tends to be the case with most partnership management activities is that the fee earning work is done as well – time tends to be regained rather than lost. It should also be remembered that the common targets of 1,100 to 1,500 chargeable hours per year allow for some non-chargeable activity. A 40-hour week over 45 weeks equates to 1,800 hours, the more commonly worked 45 hours per week to 2,025.

The practice management standards do not require analyses of profitability, but these will be important calculations for firms and departments within them. There are two headline profitability measures: profit per partner and percentage profitability. For a firm of 10 partners generating £1,950,000 of turnover, where staff costs and other expenses account for £1,350,000, the figures would read thus:

Profit:

$$£1,950,000 - 1,350,000 = 600,000$$

Profit per partner:

$$\frac{600,000}{10} = £60,000$$

Percentage profitability from turnover:

$$\frac{600,000}{1,950,000} = 30\%$$

These simple calculations will allow the partners to see how they could improve performance. Either they could increase fee income from the same resources, economise on expenditure, perhaps through efficiency gains, or seek to maintain income from fewer personnel. Which will be appropriate will depend on the firm's particular circumstances.

Less commonly undertaken is a profitability analysis of the various departments within the practice. This is a very helpful comparative report and is undertaken as follows.

(1) Decide on the costs centres: departments, services, etc.
(2) Determine fee income for last year for these centres.
(3) Prepare a list of all personnel and their total cost to the firm,

allowing for notional salary against equity partners; include salary and NI; total this list.

(4) Prepare details of all overheads, premises, insurance, etc.

(5) Using time records identify how much of each fee-earner's time has been spent on each cost centre (i.e. department or service); an approximation may be necessary.

(6) Now allocate to each cost centre the personnel costs that it bears and a proportional part of the general overhead. Bases of proportion are most obviously numbers of people per service, but they might alternatively be floor space occupied. It might be necessary to work in more detail, e.g. if cars are provided to some personnel and not others, in which case the expense should be allocated where it falls and not generally. This sum will be the running costs of the department or unit chosen.

(7) The calculation is now to deduct the running costs figure from total income for that unit. The difference is profit (or loss!).

(8) To calculate profitability do the simple sum of:

$$\frac{\text{annual fee income}}{\text{running costs for department}}$$

and express as a ratio for comparisons. This gives you the result of how much profit each £1 spent provides for the firm, e.g.

$$\frac{£120,000}{£100,000} = 1.2$$

(i.e. each £1 spent on the department earns £1:20).

As legal practice becomes ever more competitive it may well be that this type of information needs to become more a part of the appraisal process and is envisaged in the partner appraisal paperwork in the *Lexcel Office Procedures Manual*.[2] Few will argue that partnership carries greater management responsibility for performance and is no longer simply a licence to pursue an agreeable and worthwhile practice without regard to business performance. In a world where society no longer owes its professionals a living, harsher commercial measurements become all the more important.

A new financial outlook

The cost of time calculation has remained the mainstay of solicitor finance management for many years. It involves the calculation of hourly rates on an assessment of the hours that are likely to be billed as chargeable. Although this has been standard practice for many years in most firms, under-recording of time remains one of the most stubborn of practice management problems. Fee-earners clearly work long hours and seldom waste time, yet struggle to break through five hours of chargeable work per day, an annual total of 1,125 on our 45 week year. The problem could be poor discipline in entering time, but the more common problem is fee-earner rounding down of data. There is an intriguing analysis on time loss to be done in most firms concerning the under-recording of fee-earner time as a letter or draft makes its way through the various stages of its production. Analysis in a couple of firms produced a flowchart of production: see Figure 13.5.

The cost of secretarial time will be absorbed as part of the general overhead in most firms and will be part of the hourly rates of fee-earners, but should not be dismissed, with secretarial rates of pay in certain commercial firms outstripping the earnings of many junior lawyers. The main factor observed is that fee-earners tend, at best, to round down the time actually spent on the later stages. Either they feel that they should edit fairness into their client's charges or they feel that they will be criticised for working inefficiently if too much time is written off before billing. Many fee-earners have commented

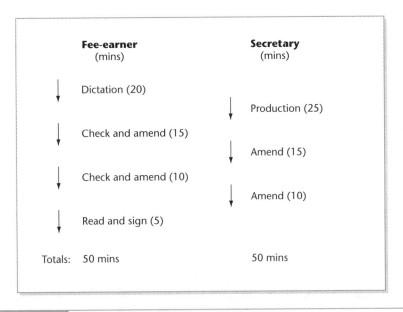

Figure 13.5   Flowchart of production of letter of advice

to me that they will learn to record about the amount that will be capable of being billed. Better, they conclude, to be short of a couple of hundred hours at the end of the year on what should have been recorded than systematically to write off time which was correctly recorded.

The approach to this issue of time recording is one of the principal differences in American firms now making headway in Europe. The partners seem much more relaxed about writing time off if the bill will simply not stand it. In so doing they seem to be more aligned to principles of market-based pricing. The traditional approach to costing legal services has been based on the expense of time calculation, under which:

- the firm first totals its desired turnover;
- it then adds the total chargeable hours available;
- it then allocates the number of hours at the appropriate rate to all fee-earners.

This 'cost-based' approach to pricing is reinforced through taxing procedures. The appropriate costs of services are determined by the costs of running the practice and the fair profit expectations of the partners. The increasing commercial reality, however, is that there will be rate for the job, be it a one-off commercial deal, a standard conveyancing transaction or a set of instructions under a block contract from the Legal Services Commission.

How firms now need to adapt their thinking is to see time recording much more as management data than billing data. The emphasis needs to shift from accurate billing – information for external billing purposes – to better internal management data. If we are offered a £30,000 deal fee should we welcome it with open arms or turn it away as a liability? Without true data on the time actually spent by our fee-earners we will not be able to make correctly informed decisions.

If we do see a continuing drift towards market-based pricing, inspired in part by the increasing commodification of the law, firms may have to re-visit the validity of the expense of time calculation as the prime means of planning for future performance. In its place we may see instead marginal costing. Under marginal costing the assessment begins with costs that can be predicted, which will either be fixed or variable. Salaries are fixed and generally the major item for most firms: likewise most professional and premises costs are known in advance. Unlike manufacturing, raw materials or variable costs do not truly feature: items such as stationery, telephone calls and the like which will increase if the firm is busy are unlikely to be significant.

The result is a total costs line for the practice which is not too different from its fairly flat fixed costs line.

Next projected income is added, varying as we saw in the cash flow statement according the time of year. This encourages a 'break even' analysis. At what stage will we go beyond costs and start to make a profit return for the partners? An issue for firms to determine is whether they wish to add notional salary to the costs lines, thus showing 'true' profit through the chart.

Marginal costing and break even charts may become very much more relevant to firms in years to come as we move away progressively from being paid for effort and input (hourly rates billing) to being paid for volume and turnaround.

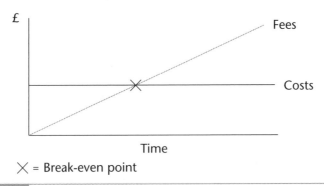

X = Break-even point

Figure 13.6   *Break-even chart*

Main points

- There needs to be clear responsibility for financial management.
- Firms need management accounting as well as financial accounting.
- Performance needs to be monitored against budgetary figures.
- Time recording should be complete, with decisions on billing being based more on market factors than cost.

References to Lexcel

C Finance management

Notes

1 Otterburn, A. (1998) *Cashflow and Improved Financial Management*, Law Society.
2 Moore, M. and Dodd, M. (2001) *Lexcel Office Procedures Manual*, Law Society Publishing.

14

Information technology

- Communication
- Job roles
- Place of work
- Other uses
- The future
- On-line delivery

The legal process is essentially one of information management. Information is obtained from various sources: the client, other advisers and the opponent or other parties most obviously. There will then be critical analysis of that information. Facts will be tested against precedents and the various legal sources which apply. In this way advice is developed and a service is provided to clients.

Within this context the relevance of ever-improving information technology resources should be readily apparent. Computers store and manage data. As these facilities increase in processing power and sophistication, the IT revolution stands to revolutionise our most basic of understandings about the delivery of legal services.

A question asked less often now is whether it is possible to run a practice without computerisation. Recent revisions to various quality standards have made this more unlikely. There are frequent references to computerised records throughout Lexcel, though it falls short of ever stating that there must be a computerised system in place for any of the functions described. CLSQM, however, does not leave open the option to run a practice without computerisation. In relation to the requirement at N1.1 that organisations must be able to produce separate lists of all open and closed Legal Services Commission funded files by franchise categories it states that as of 1 August 2000 'appropriate technology' had to be in place to satisfy this requirement. This caused difficulties for only the smallest and most informal of firms. For the great majority the issue is more how sophisticated their computer facilities should be and not whether they should exist at all.

There are firms that have been quick to embrace the potential opened up to provide legal services in new ways and to promote themselves more effectively, but most reports tend to be damning of the slow take-up of new technology by most firms. A report prepared for the British and Irish Association of Law Librarians (BIALL) in 1999 found that law firms were 'lagging behind other law professionals in their use of IT'.[1] The report suggested that much of the resistance to on-line databases was on grounds that 'people stick to what they know'. The advantages of researching through electronic means were listed as:

- the increased capabilities of research undertaken;
- the amount of information that can be accessed;
- ease of updating;
- multiple users.

The Legal IT Interfirm comparison of 2000 found that there was clear evidence of the efficiency gains in investment in IT. However, most firms were failing to capitalise on the benefits through poor implementation planning and a lack of proper training policies. The gains to firms were more likely where there had been effective investment in training. There is also a cautionary finding that most firms had no policies in place in relation to e.mail use and permitted use of the Internet, adding to concerns about the risk profile of practices in the post-Solicitors Indemnity Fund era.

The need to invest in computer facilities is sometimes mentioned as one of the factors behind the increasing numbers of practice mergers. Firms now face greater capital investment requirements than before and there are clear economies of scale in larger units. The costs of designing a computer network for 50 users are unlikely to be substantially greater than for twice that number and the additional hardware costs will be absorbed more readily in a larger organisation. Efficiencies, however, can be elusive. Most firms will need either fairly senior IT managers or expensive maintenance contracts, or both. The issue for management is cost-effectiveness: how to maximise the use and possible efficiencies of the system that they have invested in. This is best considered in terms of the likely uses of systems in any given practice.

Communication

Perhaps the most striking development in recent years has been the explosion of e.mail facilities in firms, both internal and external, and their ever-increasing take-up by so many more individuals and businesses. The subject of appropriate e.mail use did not arise as an issue when I co-wrote the Law Society's *Office Procedures Manual* in 1997; now, however, there is little doubt on the matter, as evidenced by the recent Grant Thornton report and recent guidance from the Law Society.[2]

Electronic communication has its enthusiasts and doubters. E.mails certainly provide greater freedom for many advisers: the ability to send off a quick message without waiting for the laborious process of inputting words, formatting, checking, amending (often) and then signing. On the debit side, the expectations of clients and other correspondents have also increased. Given near-instant access the time honoured excuse of 'there's a letter in the post' no longer applies. Faster communication cuts both ways. It is possible to communicate with others more quickly, but those same correspondents can now also contact the adviser with little interruption or delay. The problem of ever-increasing expectations for instant turn-around are widely recognised. It is a factor behind the increasing stress levels to which numerous reports testify.

Beyond the pressure for instant replies most of the challenges faced by increasing use of e.mail facilities stem from the essentially transient nature of the device. The e.mail is an instant communication which can be sent with minimal effort, but the law generally requires complete records of all communications, carefully compiled and maintained. In relation to external e.mails sent and received the dangers can be listed as:

(1) unwittingly sending the message to an unintended recipient, a risk all the more likely if an e.mail network has been established during a particular deal or series of negotiations;
(2) failing to keep a proper record of all advice given;
(3) confidential information being received by unintended recipients through transmission technology difficulties;
(4) the by-passing of normal post supervision checks in relation to post in and out.

In its guidance note to firms the Law Society recommends that e.mail templates should always be developed. Currently there are requirements that the name of the firm and its status as a solicitors' practice should be identified in some way, also that the address is included and details of where a list of partners can be inspected if the list does not appear on the stationery itself. It follows that personal e.mails, to the extent that they are allowed within the practice, should be distinguished by not using this template, or by using an alternative format. On the difficult issue of confidentiality it is advisable to include a confidentiality notice as most firms already tend to with fax messages. The specimen provided is:

> Information in this message is confidential and may be legally privileged. It is intended solely for the person to whom it is addressed. If you are not the intended recipient, please notify the sender and please delete the message from your system immediately.

It would be naive to rely on this wording in place of the greatest care when sending a message. Whatever the niceties of the legal position, an adviser inadvertently sending an attached advice from counsel which is damning to the client's case will be bound to feel that the client's position has been prejudiced. The encrypting of messages is a sensible precaution which more firms are now employing.

Provisions also need to extend to continuity of service to clients, through the monitoring of e.mail messages while a person is absent from the office, and computer back-up of messages exchanged. In most organisations the 'delete' button of the user will not necessarily eradicate the message from the system – a point to remind people within the firm in relation to the more personal messages which tend to be exchanged by various individuals within any organisation. Within this feature may lie the solution to the post-opening problem. It should be possible for a supervisor to check messages received and sent for any given period of time through the systems controller printing out all messages sent and received. The office manual should make clear to everyone what is likely to be seen in order to minimise possible embarrassment and resentment.

The safe course of action in most firms will be for a hard copy of any messages to be stored on the paper file, but this will be less appropriate in the case of more progressive firms where the file may be in electronic format only. Here the back-up for future reference will be through the computer back-up systems.

Other concerns are the validity of undertakings by e.mail, given that it might later be claimed that they were not sent by the alleged party in question. Accepting undertakings through conventional means only is a step taken in various firms. The issue of data protection also needs to be considered and increasingly is a standard term dealt with on the Rule 15 client care confirmation of terms of acting. At the time of writing the legal position on checking employee e.mails is still unclear.

It is as well to be aware of possible liabilities through e.mails. Copyright could be infringed if certain files attached to transmissions are opened and the potential for 'cyber-liability' through inappropriate material being introduced to the system has been widely discussed. In a recent action brought against Norwich Union the insurer was required to pay out close to half a million pounds in compensation and costs to a rival concern following the circulation of untrue allegations on the internal system as to that company's trading position. In another case Asda Supermarkets responded to a complaint from a police officer about faulty goods by alerting other stores to what they alleged to be a fraud. Legal action ensued.

Numerous cases from the USA show the potential hazards of harassment and discrimination by e.mail. A number of major corporations have faced damaging and expensive suits for permitting the circulation of allegedly offensive material over the internal system. The passing of pornographic material and sexist jokes have also led to major pay-outs: one oil company was sued for harassment by a woman who found an item 'Why beer is better than women' on the company's system. In another action a national bank was alleged to have subjected black employees to 'a pervasively abusive, racially hostile work environment' where messages between white employees were regarded as racially hostile.

The Practice Management Standards contain a cautionary note in relation to lists of counsel and experts and the combined effects of the rights of data subjects and the law of defamation and discrimination (at F8c): this should be read to cover potentially damaging internal e.mail messages also. Any organisation, law firms included, would have to treat the potential PR disaster of such an action as being as real a threat as any payment of potentially substantial damages.

The difficulties of internal e.mail facilities are mostly to do with the time that can easily be wasted by dealing with inappropriate messages. Irritation can stem from a free flow of personal messages over the system. In larger offices it may be prudent to place restrictions on this type of message, particularly if the system immediately alerts users to the fact that an e.mail has been received. The disturbance to the flow of concentration to find that someone wishes to sell a bike or buy some theatre tickets is worth taking seriously.

Those responsible for the design and implementation of e.mail systems need to be alert to these dangers. There are facilities which can minimise inefficiencies. Missing files or deeds, or untraceable items of correspondence, lend themselves to the general message to all personnel asking for help, but they can often be set to self-delete after a period of a day or two. Experience shows that missing items usually materialise relatively soon after they go missing, and if not, more extreme measures may be needed.

As new systems bed in it is also important to remind all personnel that it is one form of communication only, and is not necessarily the only or even the best method. More urgent messages might still be better by phone, while the value of colleagues communicating in person often needs to be re-asserted. A short conversation can easily cover the same ground, but more conclusively and sooner, than several e.mail messages.

Most systems also offer day-to-day diaries and it can be worthwhile to insist that these are maintained. The ease of co-ordination of meetings is a major gain from any system, but will only be obtained if everyone uses the facility. Any fee-earner can maintain some degree of control over their routine by ruling out blocks of time that are important to them, e.g. 4.00 p.m. to 5.00 p.m. each day for post signing.

All firms should issue clear guidance on what may be regarded as acceptable and unacceptable messages. Communication which could stray beyond the boundaries of legal professional privilege must not be allowed to be defamatory in nature. Policies against sexual and racial discrimination are a requirement of Lexcel and it should be made explicit that these principles extend to e.mails in addition to all other aspects of office life. Although absolute protection for the firm from potential liability probably cannot be guaranteed, enforcement of these provisions in relation to any disciplinary code will be likely to diminish prospects of vicarious liability for at least the more offensive material.

Job roles

Another consequence of increasing computerisation of legal process is a blurring of the traditional distinction between fee-earner and support staff. There are many who, perhaps quite rightly, object to the use of both terms. 'Fee-earner', they will say, is a little too stark for use with clients, while 'support staff' could easily be interpreted in a pejorative manner. Whatever the terminology, however, the traditional pattern of legal work has been based on a division of functions which is very clearly changing in many firms. We have fee-earners who are able to output their own e.mails and other communications and who draft on screen, whether from precedent or from scratch. On the other hand secretaries can now be freed from the endless volume of copy-typing and are therefore better able to contribute more productively to the fee-earning output of the practice.

The transition to new job roles is often poorly managed in law firms. At its most crass, partners will eulogise about the changing staff ratios within earshot of their secretaries. What is needed in many firms is a clear policy, starting with the aims of the practice. Broadly speaking there are two options, to reduce costs relative to turnover or to increase turnover relative to costs. This can be represented as 'plan A' or 'plan B': see Figure 14.1.

The appropriate policy may vary for different departments within the same firm. Where the plan is to reduce support services, developments tend to take a while to achieve and redundancies can usually therefore be avoided. This need to be stated publicly or the staff concerned may well understandably fear the worst. If paralegal work is to increase a re-grading exercise will be needed, resulting in new job descriptions for the different grades of jobs that will develop. The difference between the copy-typist and the paralegal must be reflected in the job documentation and the benefits package.

As to whether it will be preferable to reduce costs or re-deploy better secretaries, much will depend on the work in question. The more 'commodified' the service, the greater is the potential for paralegal input. The most obvious paralegals for areas of litigation, be it debt recovery or other, or the more routine elements of conveyancing work or company secretarial tasks, will be the secretaries who know the firm, its procedures and the clients. This will require greater emphasis on support staff training than has been standard to date and more skills for the supervisor. For those wishing to develop in this way the predictions are of an increasing role in practice for the paralegal and the eventual demise of the copy-typist, though it would be unwise to write off the role before further improvements to voice technology become commonplace.

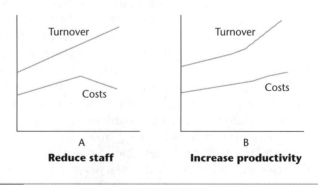

A	B
Reduce staff	**Increase productivity**

Figure 14.1   *Changing job roles*

Place of work

Computerisation of legal process creates another possible revolution in our way of thinking about the work of lawyers and its organisation. This is the assumption that work is essentially an office-based activity and that each member of the firm will need their bespoke space within the facilities available.

The justification for the traditional reliance on offices has been that files were always bulky, heavy items. Furthermore, for many lawyers, there would be so many files that might need attention on any given day the only sensible course of action was to centralise them in an office where anyone could deal with them if and when they needed to do so. Likewise for the information sources that are needed for research. Legal books are legend for their detail, while brevity is not a quality associated with the better law reports. Since colleagues might also need the same report at the same time an office-based routine will be needed.

This reliance on an office will soon seem odd to more of the workforce, however. A Henley Management College survey in the mid-1990s found that some 70 per cent of large and medium sized businesses were planning to introduce teleworking practices, while a conference held as part of 'European Teleworking Week' (one wonders who authorised this) heard that a third of work would be based at home by 2020.

The circumstances enabling legal personnel to work from home are increasingly in place. As files are computerised they can be accessed and worked upon by anyone able to access them from wherever their computer terminal or laptop happens to be based. Furthermore, the law reports are likely soon to be available in electronic data format only, whether CD or other. The two great justifications for office life will be removed, to the extent that they have not been already. What will then need to change will be the management attitudes that work is an activity which needs supervision. McGregor's theory of motivation tells us that there are theory X managers and theory Y managers. The first believe that employees are inherently lazy and uncommitted to the firm, whereas the others will trust their workers to work responsibly to their own agenda. Theory X managers are bound to want their employees to be based in an office so that their efforts can be monitored. Theory Y managers may be more relaxed and prepared to analyse the productivity data which will be available. Study after study has shown that the right sort of work is performed more efficiently away from the office, but resistance remains. There will be those who resent being expected to set aside part of their home as an office extension, a point often made by unions where larger organisations have undergone this process. The clear boundary between work and home will be removed, which many would regret, though the reality for more and more lawyers is that this is happening in any event. Most of all, the sense of camaraderie gained from colleagues around us will be reduced, or at least put at severe risk.

The opportunity presented to firms is to reduce expenditure on their premises budget. 'Hot-desking' has already been introduced by many of the larger accountancy offices as well as numerous other service organisations. It will be difficult to argue that lawyers are not capable of making the same transition. There may well be differences between the commercial lawyer, however, who is required to draft documentation with precise care, see clients seldom and communicate frequently by e.mail, and the high street lawyer who sees a number of clients per day, writes and receives a great deal of letters and is required to churn through a large volume of matters. As always, generalisations about the whole range of legal services are dangerous. Each firm and department needs to analyse its appropriate strategy on a case-by-case basis.

Other uses

Other obvious uses of the computer system are for improved management data, whether financial or marketing. Here the problem for many firms is restricting the data produced to manageable proportions. Information overload is a factor recognised by an increasing number of organisations. If there is insufficient time to read, analyse and then act upon data there is little point in generating it.

Much is made of the power of current facilities to research both client information and legal sources. Gone are the days when legal research could safely be confined to the latest published reports. There is access now to a wealth of unreported materials, both primary and secondary. Meanwhile the activities of clients can be researched in greater detail, especially for firms undergoing competitive presentations for work.

The future

A whole new area of management writing examines future work and life patterns. The most celebrated 'futurologist' of the legal world is Richard Susskind whose book *The Future of Law* has received such widespread acclaim.[3] There are those who argue with his conclusions, but few can doubt the observations and analysis of the trends that we will experience.

Central to Susskind's arguments is the steady development of legal information sources and so-called expert systems. The Internet is an information free-for-all that stands to put out of business any traditional intermediary who cannot or will not adjust. Currently travel agents and estate agents are grappling with the by-passing of their services by websites that provide information to which they previously held privileged access. What is moot is the extent to which lawyers too are 'gatekeepers' of information that others will choose to access for themselves. If this is the case lawyers too may find themselves by-passed by process and having to adapt. Traditionally, for example, a client had to consult a lawyer for advice on employment issues since they alone could access the law which was relevant. The alternative was to resource the personnel department with expensive journals and well trained personnel. The same client can now peruse the sources for little or no cost and can consult a plethora of other consultancies that are alternatives to traditional legal advice.

Where will this leave the law firm? In the preface to his second edition Susskind concedes that there are heavily service-based areas of law, such as matrimonial advice, which stand much less risk of being by-passed in this way. It is not so much knowing what the law says on divorce as the precise implications in any given situation and the interpersonal support from the adviser that the client is always likely to want to achieve. On the other hand the more factually-based commercial lawyer, used to dealing with in-house counsel as a client, may need to add something more distinctive to his or her current offering. This is the quest for 'value added service', according to Susskind. Others doubt the extent of the threat – most notably Michael Chambers in a well argued editorial in *Commercial Lawyer* entitled 'Law on line – is it doomed to fail?'.[4] Give me the information on flights and hotels and I might book my own hotel, it is argued, but confront me with complex provisions from case law, primary or secondary legislation and I will still need a higher service element to meet my legal needs.

So far as expert systems are concerned there is a telling analysis of the difference between computers and the human mind which shapes our current uses:

- Computers are: Immediate; Reliable; Stupid.
- People are: Slow; Unreliable; Brilliant.

This may be true at present, but what of the development of expert systems? What do we make of a computer program that can give better legal advice than any lawyer in that field, a scenario which is tantalisingly painted by Susskind? How the profession and society at large will cope with such developments are issues for the longer term development of the law and its place in society as well as those who practise in it.

On-line delivery

As with every development in business there are threats as well as opportunities in relation to the development of on-line legal services. On the upside there are opportunities now to provide advice and services to a far wider geographical spread of clients than ever before. The more information-based is my service, the less is the need for me to be physically accessible to my clients. I can therefore run an on-line advice service on, for example, educational or employment law from literally wherever I choose, within the jurisdiction or without. It is when I add service that matters become more complex. 'Negligence Alert over Law Firms' Websites' announced the headline in the *Gazette* in May 2000.[5] The Law Society e-commerce group warned of competition between providers increasing risks of misinformed customers and more complaints to the Office for the Supervision of Solicitors. It may be little comfort that the worst offending sites were non-solicitor enterprises. Risks that were present in many included failure to give proper advice on do-it-yourself divorce websites on the risk of loss of pension rights, future financial rights and arrangements for children. Wills could be written without due checking of fraud or undue influence. Clearly on-line delivery of service is not without its difficulties.

The enthusiasts are unlikely to treat current concerns as much more than teething problems. Furthermore, the next stage of communications technology developments may, ironically, take us back to former patterns of work. We will soon expect instant face-to-face access to our advisers, suggests Susskind, while the enormity of the payments for the next stage of technology rights suggests that radical changes to our practices of dealing with each other are bound to occur. What if I expect a client situated in another part of the country to consult with me screen to screen via mobile technology as part of my 'know the client' requirements? This may push forward on-line delivery into new areas.

Going hand in hand with the development of on-line advice is the enhanced potential of promotion through electronic means. The Grant Thornton IT Interfirm comparison[6] found that most firms were missing the business opportunities of the Internet through not having a website or through it being little more than a static brochure site. The first challenge for firms is to develop a site that is more interesting than mere flat text. The next challenge is to ensure that people know about the site so that they are likely to hit on it. Many firms have found in recent times that it is one thing to have a website, but quite another to have the interest and awareness of it to justify the time and expenditure on its development and maintenance. As with all elements of computerisation, the benefits are real, but only for those who apply imagination, industry and investment to the task in hand.

Main points

- Increased use of information technology stands to change many of the traditional working practices of law firms.
- Efficiency gains have to be planned for.
- Internal e.mails need management policies and external e.mails give rise to issues of confidentiality, both of which need attention.

Notes

1 British and Irish Association of Law Librarians, 1999, quoted in [1999] *Gazette*, 17 December, p. 18.
2 Grant Thornton (2000) 'Legal Interfirm Comparison', reported by Kendrick, R. [2000] *Solicitors Journal*, 28 April.
3 Susskind, R. (1998) *The Future of Law*, Oxford University Press.
4 Chambers, M. (1999) *Commercial Lawyer*, Issue 33, June, p. 46.
5 [2000] *Gazette*, 5 May, p. 1.
6 Thornton, G. (2000), *op. cit.*

15

Marketing

- Definitions and basics
- The marketing mix
- Branding
- Strategic marketing
- The marketing plan
- Promotional options
- Marketing databases
- Likely developments

Traditionally the professions did not market themselves. Work was acquired through very much more discreet means – word of mouth and local reputation. Most professional bodies will have had at some stage prohibitions of varying severity on 'touting', while most retain to this day restrictions on what may and may not be included in advertisements and promotional literature. The Law Society of England and Wales is no exception, with the current Publicity Code ruling out of order mentions of success rates, comparisons to any other identifiable firm or practitioner and any other publicity which could be said to be 'in bad taste'.

The legacy of this traditional rejection of marketing is part linguistic. Although 'marketing' is a term in increasing use with solicitors there is still a marked preference by many to talk instead of 'practice development'. The sole reason for preferring this phrase seems still to be to distance solicitors from a process which they consider to be beneath them.

The first reforms to the prohibition of most marketing techniques were passed by Council in 1984, with further changes being sanctioned two years later. The original Practice Management Standards which were passed in 1991 included a provision that firms should have an 'approach to marketing'. Within less than a decade the Law Society had moved from prohibiting active marketing to recommending its adoption. Small wonder that many practitioners still feel ill at ease with techniques that were traditionally the exclusive domain of the commercial world and from which they thought they would always be exempt. Marketing is the area which best illustrates the abandonment of the traditional professional regime in favour of a more overtly commercial view of practice.

There is contradictory evidence on the take-up of promotional marketing activity by firms depending on the type of firm in question. A report from 1997 produced by researchers McCallum Layton and commissioned by marketing consultants Wheeler Associates concluded that law firms were spending on average £3,000 per fee-earner on marketing, in contrast to a mere £1,700 per fee-earner for accountants.[1] Some law firms were reputedly spending as much as £7,000 per fee-earner, a quite remarkable figure. Going with this state of affairs is a new breed of senior in-house marketer able to command serious six figure salaries, with a trend in recent years at the top end of the employment market of these people moving away from accountants to law firms. This research was based, however, on a 50 per cent response rate from the largest 50 firms. The picture in general practice is very different, with budgets of just a few hundreds of pounds per fee-earner being more the norm in most practices. Just as common is the pattern of the marketing budget not being spent through a shortage of activities during the period in question.

The current quality regime for lawyers contains requirements on marketing in both Lexcel and the CLSQM. This is not to say that all firms have to promote themselves in an attempt to gain new sources of work – indeed, one of the guidance notes in Lexcel provides that firms may wish to use marketing techniques to restrict the supply of work. What is required is that firms document their range of services and describe how they will be delivered; they must also have an approach on the subject and ensure that this too is documented.

The requirements of Lexcel, found at B1, will best be met by developing a marketing plan which is kept under regular review. The plan will describe the range of services and their method of delivery and then describe the promotion that is planned to gain any change in the supply of work that is desired. The Lexcel standard, as did former editions of the legal aid franchise standards, draws a distinction between marketing or the 'services' plans and the main strategic or business plan. This is no longer the case in the latest version of CLSQM which deals with marketing requirements under H1 on 'future business planning'. Normal practice is to distinguish the longer term strategic plans from the operational plans for the business year ahead. Whether separate plans are felt to be beneficial is a matter of choice for each firm: as the Practice Management Standards provide: 'practices may choose the format and level of detail of such documentation that suits them best'.

To gain true benefit from the process, an understanding of what is meant by marketing is important and a grasp of its application in the professional environment. Most of the published works on marketing relate to manufacturing and retailing and the specific circumstances of the professions do vary standard practice somewhat.

Definitions and basics

The formal Chartered Institute of Marketing definition is that marketing is:

> the management process of anticipating, identifying and satisfying customer requirements profitably.

Most explanations of what is meant by 'marketing' in the professional sector concentrate on the balancing of what the organisation provides with the demands and preferences of its clients or customers. In his book *Professional Services Marketing* Neil Morgan suggests that:

> Marketing is the management skill of matching the firm's personnel, resources and expertise with client needs in such a way that the firm achieves its long term goals and the client receives continued satisfaction.[2]

My own preferred working definition is that marketing is simply the 'management by the firm of the relationship with its clients, present and intended'. The point to be stressed is that there is very much more to marketing than simply promotion. Promotion forms one key element of the marketing process, but should not occur in isolation to the planning which should precede it. Promotion without a sense of strategy or priorities is likely to be wasteful and is the source of one of the most commonly quoted disappointments with marketing in firms.

Throughout the business world the 'marketing concept' is the philosophy which underpins the subject. It provides that in the provision of any service or the manufacture of any product, clients or customers should be the starting point in any planning exercise. Recently the trend by outstanding marketers seems, if anything, to be to get closer to the marketing concept. Tesco's first 'clubcard' manager was reported as saying that:

marketing is moving away from trying to change consumers' behaviour to understanding it and giving them what they want. This means that future competition will revolve around who knows their clients best.

In the context of the law firm the marketing concept suggests that rather than determine which services the firm will provide and then find the clients second, the process should be reversed. Jeremy Knott of Clifford Chance explains marketing as being: 'about talking to the client and the market and to deliver what the market wants'.[3]

This is also an approach hinted at in guidance notes in both Lexcel and CLSQM. The Legal Services Commission provides that organisations: 'should have procedures to review their future plans . . . alongside the Commission's published regional strategies' (at H1), while Lexcel provides under B1b that 'how the practice provides services will depend upon its clients and services'. The firm that is in tune with its market and which provides the right range of services in an appropriate manner could be said to have good market positioning. This remains one of the main challenges for firms in any strategic or marketing review: given who and where we are, what should be the range of services that we should provide to what depth and in what volume? A firm that enjoys good market positioning does not struggle for a supply of work and will often have to be selective as to what it takes on and what it turns away. Managing the firm becomes very much easier when this state of affairs is achieved.

The marketing mix

Marketing practitioners will base much of their activities around the marketing mix, also commonly known as the 'four Ps' theory. The general view is that the main factors are:

- product;
- place;
- price;
- promotion.

Product

The starting point for any successful marketing campaign should always be a good product. Many of the differences between product and service marketing stem from the fact that there is no physical product to display when promoting services. The solicitor offers instead an intangible 'product' which is an amalgam of their expertise, experience and service level.

In his book *Practice Development for Professional Firms* Aubrey Wilson shows how legal services, along with management consultancy, are one of the most highly intangible services of all.[4] Getting clients to perceive value where there is so little that they can physically evaluate remains one of the core challenges of legal marketing. This is a theme taken further by Berry and Parasuraman in their book *Marketing for Services: Competing through Quality*.[5] Word of mouth recommendation tends to be limited for goods but high for services. Marketing plays a large part in customer need identification with goods whereas services are generally sold before they are produced. These key differences make various standard marketing techniques more difficult to apply to the professional service sector, a point not always appreciated by marketing experts from other sectors who aspire to work within the law.

In recent years many firms have benefited from shifting the focus of their marketing from the range of technical services provided to the range of client types served. Combining a description of these in promotional leaflets which show sectoral knowledge can clearly create a legal 'product' which will be very attractive. This strategy is generally known as 'segmentation' and has proved highly successful for many practices. Although the term 'product' is based more on retailing or manufacturing it is helpful when planning services in this way. Distinct groups of clients – be they small businesses, high value individuals, haulage carriers or other – will have a need for a distinct range of services with many attributes of a legal 'product'.

Place

For retailers the relevance of 'place' in the marketing mix is largely an issue of whether their products are available when and where needed. Marketing in this context has been described as ensuring that the 'right product is on the right shelf at the right time'. Issues here would include the geographical location of offices and the advantages that opening arrangements offer to certain clients. Issues for commercial firms include whether it is still viable to offer a commercial service from one location only or whether merger with firms from other locations is now necessary.

Price

The current tension in practice is between costs-based and market-based pricing. Traditionally lawyers have been paid for effort as will be the case if fees are based on chargeable time recorded only. There is growing pressure for this to change with advisers being forced much more into providing 'added value' for clients and concentrating more on results. Increasingly firms are confronted with a choice of performing work on terms which favour the client or turning it away. The traditional costing of services on a straight expense of time calculation, turning to mark-up factors to 'uplift' the bill seem increasingly anachronistic. For many within the profession the traditional embarrassment of talking about money remains. As the law becomes more of a commodity so it will increasingly attract prices for the various services provided by firms. The decline of hourly rates for billing seems likely.

Promotion

Promotion is part of the marketing effort and not the whole. Attention should always be given first to the other 'P' factors to see what should be promoted how, where and when. Promotion without the 'product' to back it up will lead to problems. Promoting services in such a manner that demand is over-stimulated will also cause difficulties: the firm will have to turn work away, or its personnel will struggle to cope, or the quality of work done will suffer, or perhaps all three. In services marketing generally the balance of supply and demand needs careful attention and management. Promotion which generates mismatches can lead to counter-productive results.

To gain a fuller picture of the marketing mix in professional services a number of further factors need to be considered. These stem from the fact that solicitors do not provide physical products and are constrained by professional rules.

These might be listed as:

- personality;
- presentation;
- professionalism;
- process.

Of all the additional factors personality is probably the most important. The choice of professional adviser is often a personal one, and is seldom subject to scientific analysis of experience or expertise. It seems clear that much of the client's confidence in the advice received will hinge upon their confidence in the adviser that they are dealing with. Empathy skills are important for any adviser and, when combined with expertise, create client confidence.

Presentation is likely to have a number of facets, mostly to do with the office and all personnel that the client encounters. Given the relative inability of most clients to assess the expertise of services provided, attention can easily turn to the physical environment. Issues such as how clean and well decorated the reception area is and whether the exterior of the building is well cared for will be easily assessed. The physical presentation of how the various individuals within the firm present themselves will also take on greater significance in this regard.

Professionalism is an important barrier. The professional advises the client how much of his or her services it should commission. This responsibility has to be respected by providing advice which is truly in the client's interests. The adviser who puts his or her own personal interests above the client's best interests will be guilty of one of the most basic of all betrayals of professionalism.

Process forms the final component and seems to be the most common failing. Process simply consists of ensuring that the participators do what they set out to. Good ideas for promotion are easily generated but often not then acted upon. A limited amount of sustained marketing activity is the best option for most firms, as opposed to good intentions which are not acted upon or occasional sporadic initiatives. To overcome the problem of poor follow-up a device much used in commercial departments is that of the moving 'target list'. This will carry the 10 current main targets, be they potential clients, existing clients or referrers of work. The list is reviewed by the team each month. Progress is discussed (or lack of it) and changes are made to the list for next month. The marketing partner can attend the meeting or be informed of progress on the list.

Branding

There has developed, especially in the larger City and international practices in recent years, something of a 'holy grail' attitude to firm-wide branding. A brand consists of established customer recognition and loyalty and can be measured as the degree of preference in the eyes of the buying public for that provider as opposed to a substitute. A former Heinz senior executive described it as whether a shopper, finding that the store that they were in did not stock their make, would leave that store and find the product elsewhere.

Berry and Parasuraman see the quality of services provided as being the sole long term differentiation between service providers. They are great enthusiasts for branding, distinguishing the brand message put out by the provider from the 'brand meaning' perceived by the client. The core of the brand should be distinctiveness, relevance, memorability and flexibility, they advise. They recommend as practical steps for establishing the brand to:

- start with client research: what matters to clients?
- select the right medicine (do not seek miracles);
- build on what exists;
- internalise the brand: make sure there is full commitment to it from within.

They also recommend that the firm should 'tangibilise' the service as much as possible since there can be better controls over printed items and other physical devices. There are those who argue that branding is not possible with professional services. Certainly, it will be difficult to achieve and may occasionally have its disadvantages. The essence of the problem is that professional advisers are in business not to represent themselves, but clients. They do not therefore act directly on their own behalves and have always to take into account how their clients would wish matters to proceed. Take a firm famed for its aggressive style of litigation, for example. How does it cope with instructions where the client is in defensive mode and wishes simply to proceed on a damage limitation basis. What of the Woolf regime and its emphasis on 'proportionality'? Is it viable to maintain the brand image for tough talking when the particular instructions or external framework for dispute resolution are at odds with this style? There could easily be circumstances where aggressive tactics could prolong a losing case, in which case brand image might be said to contradict the duty to do the best for one's clients. The issue of whether the preferences of service providers can ever be allowed to prevail over the particular preferences and needs of clients could be seen as a barrier to the effective development of a brand image in terms of lawyer style.

Aside from potential professional difficulties what would be involved in developing a brand image if a firm wished to do so? Clearly this will be very much more difficult than would be the case with the manufacturer of products. The car manufacturer, for example, can choose designs, colours and images which suit their desired place in the market in question. Are they safety-first family-friendly or sporty and slightly racy? It is not unknown for candidates for certain positions to be asked 'if you were a car, which would you be?' – proof surely of the strength of brand image for particular models and their manufacturers.

Given that, in the absence of physical product, personality and presentation become the prime elements in the client's perception of services, branding is clearly more difficult in the law firm. There are those who have enthused about their office building being core to brand value, especially with the largest City and international practices. Take, for example, the following quote from Linklaters' managing partner:

> We've got a great new look; and now we've got a wonderful new building with all the facilities that we need to deliver a service that's second to none.[6]

The building was also included in the brand image by their rivals Clifford Chance, whose marketing director was quoted in a recent *Gazette* as saying that branding was: 'the way people act and behave and it's also about the building and the environment'.[7]

The argument would be: you know about us and our expertise: our building reflects the values we aspire to and achieve and is reassurance to you on the quality of firm that you are dealing with.

What of personality, however? Here branding gets into very real difficulties. Do we expect the lawyer from our firm to stand out in a legal crowd? If so, how? Various firms have tried to differentiate their advisers in different ways, mostly around the theme of added value, with descriptions such as the lawyers with 'more commercial sense' or who will go 'the extra mile', but making this a reality in the largest firms with literally thousands of advisers in different jurisdictions is an enormous challenge. Internalisation is the key: unless the partners in particular buy into the image and are willing to conform to it, a perceivable gap will develop or remain between the public message and the client's experience. Given word of mouth assessments of the firm in what might be closed markets, the initiative will soon be devalued. A branding exercise need not set out to make everyone a clone of a leading figure in the firm, but it will require every person within the practice to subscribe to the values described and do all in their power to make these a reality. Given the traditional autonomy of advisers and the frustration of managing partners who spend their time 'herding cats', as it has been described, the development of coherent brand images will be a tall order in most firms.

Strategic marketing

In the firm that plans growth some consideration will be needed for the strategy behind its marketing plan. Growth may come from organic means or mergers, but either way should be planned and should feature in any strategic or marketing plans.

The precise line between strategic business planning and marketing is difficult to draw. Various corporations have made marketing more of a main board responsibility than it used to be. Take, for example, the views of Sir Clive Thompson who left Cadbury Schweppes to manage a surge in the fortunes of Rentokil:

> I am more and more convinced that corporate and marketing strategy are the same thing. The chief executive has to be the chief marketer. If you delegate that responsibility you're not doing your job.[8]

On the more micro scale of the law firm this suggests that there has to be at the very least a clear and close link between any managing partner and marketing partner or other employees in these positions. The situation found in some firms where the marketing partner does not sit on the main executive could be questioned for these reasons.

One of the most commonly quoted strategic marketing analyses is that of the Boston Consulting Group matrix (see Figure 15.1) which divides the goods or services into four groupings according to their growth potential and the share enjoyed in the marketplace.

The main conclusions from this analysis are that income generated from cash cows should be used to support the development of question marks and to nurture emerging stars; question marks with the most uncertain long term prospects should be divested. The firm will need to review any area of activities which might be identified as a 'dog', though there may sometimes be policy considerations which suggest that a presence must be retained.

Stars	**Question marks**
High share High growth	Low share High growth
Cash cows	**Dogs**
High share Low growth	Low share Low growth

Figure 15.1   *Boston Consulting Group matrix*

This analysis can also be useful in evaluating merger or lateral hire prospects. Most firms will want a complementary profile from any new teams, but smaller firms may simply be looking for 'more of the same' to generate economies of scale and critical mass.

The matrix suggested by Ansoff in 1965 (see Figure 15.2) provides one of the most focused ways to examine routes to development in terms of client groups and services provided.[9]

This can be adapted to a highly practical analysis for law firms as shown in Figure 15.3.

The general advice would be to stay as low as possible in the plans of the firm. For many firms better cross-selling of services – i.e. better selling its existing range of services to its existing range of clients – would be all that is required for the growth it plans. Others may have to plan on new services or new sources of work, but level three marketing will be speculative and will take the firm into uncharted territories, and so should generally be avoided.

In analysing the current client base, the 'Pareto principle' is often helpful. It is likely that 20 per cent of clients will account for something like 80 per cent of instructions. Who are these 20 per cent and what more could be done for them? Does the description identify a type of firm that the firm or office should target?

Existing services Existing clients	New services Existing clients
New clients Existing services	New clients New services

Figure 15.2   *Ansoff's Matrix*

Level 3	New services	New clients
Level 2	New services Existing clients	Existing services New clients
Level 1	Existing services	Existing clients

Figure 15.3   *Marketing analysis for law firms*

Market research may be invaluable at this stage of the strategy, or might have been conducted earlier as part of the strategic planning activity. The aim of research is either to quantify the 'gap' which will usually exist between the standard of service that the firm aspires to and the standard of service as it is perceived by the recipients, or to gain new ideas in relation to new services. As Kim Tasso, the former marketing director now turned consultant, has observed:

> the only way to find out what clients think is to ask them. Sometimes the very act of asking someone for their views generates good-will and gives the right messages about a firm's willingness to listen and improve.[10]

Research can be described as being qualitative, where questions are more detailed and are addressed to fewer respondents, or quantitative, where the value lies in the volume of responses collected. Both have a role to play with solicitors, but the quantitative might be more appropriate where client satisfaction is being investigated: qualitative where marketing direction is being considered. Where the firm has a predominantly commercial base qualitative research tends to be the more frequently adopted strategy, unlike general practice where simpler quantitative client questionnaires will probably be preferable.

The marketing plan

As already mentioned, the marketing plan might take various forms. It could be a departmental action plan or it could be a separate firm-wide plan. There is guidance on the likely contents of the marketing plan in the guidance note to Lexcel B1.7:

- the services to be provided;
- the client groups to be served;
- how services will be delivered;
- the client care policy;
- a description of resources available including skill and knowledge;
- the objectives to be pursued;
- development needed in the structure of the firm;
- a timetable and a budget;
- responsibility and monitoring.

Although the precise format of the documentation may vary between firms it is important that the plan should concentrate on action rather than words. It can be helpful to deal with the sections as:

- list of services and internal controls over them, such as the roles of a marketing committee and/or the departments or offices;
- the objectives for the year which should be 'specific, measurable and achievable';
- the activity that will be needed for the objectives to be attained, most obviously the promotion to be undertaken over the period of the plan and any internal management developments, such as the recruitment of a marketing manager or assistant;
- a budget, which should be set once the firm knows what it wants to do and not before. It is recommended not to set a figure in advance and then determine how it should be spent, for fear of incurring expenditure without good cause.

There is considerable emphasis on measurement in the marketing profession. Measurement can be difficult for law firms. A common exercise is to try to cost particular initiatives, such as a client seminar. The costs of mounting the event are totalled and may be substantial, but they will almost certainly be dwarfed if lost fee-earner time is taken into account. A month on, the question may be asked, 'what work have we gained as a direct result of that seminar?', to which the answer may be very often, 'not much at all'. The limitations of this approach are that client-buying behaviour with law firms can be very long term. It may take clients several years to decide to leave current advisers and transfer elsewhere. What of the client that was thinking of going elsewhere but who is wooed back by the presentation? They will be listed as 'existing client' in any analysis, but should be seen as successes of the event. What of those who were pleased to be invited but who could not attend? Further, there are only true costs of lost fee earning time if work is turned away or dealt with in less detail than would otherwise have been the case and fees are thus reduced. More often than not the seminar comes from the fee-earner's own time or from an allowance already made in target figures for practice promotion activities.

This suggests that long term measurement will be more appropriate for most firms. The easiest starting point is to take the objectives set for the year ahead. If the firm meets these, the sum total of the promotion undertaken can be judged to have succeeded, if not, then it has failed. Which initiatives the firm or department would wish to repeat can be decided upon as details.

Promotional options

It is useful to distinguish the promotional options as being personal to the advisers in question, or non-personal: see Figure 15.4.

Meetings and entertaining

A continual programme of client networking and entertainment will be the mainstay of many firms' promotional programmes. There should be sustained efforts to nurture contacts with potential clients and other referrers of work, while important clients must not be taken for granted.

Most firms will have experimented with occasional client lunches and receptions. Events such as these can often be very time-consuming, but need to be balanced against the cost of not maintaining an appropriate level of such activity. For those firms that find regular in-house entertaining too much of an imposition, an occasional larger reception might be preferable. These can work well if themed in some way, perhaps a viewing at an art gallery. There are also advantages in the occasional sports or arts event in bringing people together in circumstances where there are more obvious topics of conversation than just work. As to the value of such events, it seems to be common experience that most invitees take any reasonable opportunity to return the favour of their having been invited. The consolidation of client loyalty, given the importance of existing clients in relation to new work, is always a worthwhile objective.

Client seminars

The occasional seminar, or even series of them, will be an effective way to represent the firm as having good expertise and a helpful

Personal	Non-personal
Meetings	Brochures and leaflets
Entertaining	Mailshots
Seminars and other public speaking	Newsletters
Training	Articles and features
Sponsorship and exhibitions	Advertising, including directories
	Press quotes and coverage
	Internet

Figure 15.4   *Promotional options*

attitude towards its clients. In the largest of firms a continual programme of seminars might be a mainstay of the promotional activity undertaken.

There has been a change in style of seminars over the years. There is much greater concentration now on quality by many firms at the expense of numbers of invitees. There may be occasional developments where a large audience might be appropriate, but most practitioners would take the view that more value is likely to come from working more closely with a smaller number of attendees. This enables seminars to be repeated for different client groups. New product liability provisions can then be offered to manufacturers, bankers and then retailers, tailoring the notes and materials each time to be as relevant as possible to each distinct audience. Many firms have started to charge a modest payment for a place which seems to make attendance by those who accept more likely and may increase the perceived value of the contents.

If seminars are to be regarded as a personal method of promoting the firm it should follow that smaller audience numbers are to be preferred. It should also follow that there should be a fair number of representatives from the firm present to mingle with attendees during the more informal parts of the event. Standards of presentation are important and training in these skills has become standard practice in many larger firms. The 'performers' should not be just the presenters but should include all members of the team from the firm. One effective way to do this is to assign guests to particular members of the firm in advance and to 'de-brief' afterwards to see if any interest was expressed by anyone in taking the areas described, or any others, further.

Public speaking

Performing on other people's platforms has the potential advantage of exposing the representative of the firm to a greater proportion of potential clients and is an activity that many enjoy. It is fairly easy to put word around that the solicitor is a willing speaker. Those who perform well usually get more invitations from the normal word of mouth recommendations. Chambers of Commerce or other such trade organisations provide speaking opportunities which cost little, if anything, but which can be invaluable in raising profile and client awareness. Public speaking is an interesting option for divorce departments where more common methods of promoting the firm can be difficult to apply. Offering to talk to guidance and counselling services on legal developments is one effective option used to good effect by many.

Client training

The final personal method of promoting the firm is one that is too often overlooked. Client training might be little more than offering a seminar in-house to an important client. It might also involve taking a wider view of the role of the fee-earner. Having revised terms and conditions of trade for a major commercial client how better to cement relationships throughout the concern than by offering to talk to the sales staff who will have to apply them? The time spent doing this will seem invaluable if it helps to retain that client and makes recommendations more likely. A comment frequently found in research on commercial firms is that they are too aloof from the business operations that they advise. Client training can be an effective way to counter this.

Brochures and leaflets

Most firms will have or will have had a general brochure at some time. There are clear advantages in having a single authoritative statement by the firm of its values and range of services. On the other hand if there are distinct client groups there is likely to be greater value in having a range of complementary leaflets which allow the firm to 'mix and match' according to the interests of the planned recipient.

Brochures can assist with cross-selling of services and will enable all personnel within the firm to do so more effectively. Perhaps the main conclusion is that it can count against a firm not to have a brochure, whereas having it will not necessarily advance its cause with potential clients to any real degree. This certainly seems to the case at competitive 'pitches' for work where a brochure will usually be one of the standard pre-presentation requirements. The brochure in itself is highly unlikely to sell the firm, but it might open doors which otherwise would not be open.

The prevailing styles of brochures have also developed over the years since they were first permitted. If the first wave of brochures were epitomised by breathtaking photo-calls, more recent productions have concentrated on quality of text and layout. Water-colours have often replaced photograph library materials. In the earlier years a whole series of 'picture cliches' developed: the litigation lawyer outside the Royal Courts of Justice, the property partner with plans laid out on a building site, the earnest handshake. The problem that many firms recognised with this style which is still favoured by many, is that legal work is seldom very photogenic. The posed photograph of a group of lawyers huddled around one end of the boardroom table, supposedly working together on the random document, might have frightening cost implications for any client gullible enough to suppose that this was true to life. Worse still, where people shown in the brochure have left to join opposing firms: should the firm continue to use the print run or abandon it at considerable expense?

In recent years there has been a move towards annual reviews rather than brochures. Annual reviews have many advantages: it is possible to include genuine news on the firm, both legal and personalities. They are also stated to be for one year so avoid the dating problem of changing personnel and fashions.

In addition to, or sometimes as an alternative to, the general brochure most firms might benefit from an additional range of leaflets or guides to the work of particular departments or for certain groups of clients. The marketing partner or committee should ensure that there is consistency of appearance between these devices. Lengths may vary but the general appearance should not.

Client newsletters

The client newsletter is an excellent way to maintain contact with existing clients and might also be useful to maintain links with those potential clients who indicate that they might instruct the firm in the future. The usual advice is not to be over-optimistic at the outset of the project. Filling subsequent editions will almost certainly be more difficult than the first issue. It is also advisable to keep the length and complexity of contributions to proportions that will be manageable for most clients. More firms are now producing their newsletters using desk-top publishing applications which can be to the best of professional standards as the technology improves.

Public relations and the media

Public relations can be defined as the management of the firm's profile by all means other than advertising. In the current context it is useful to concentrate on press relations in particular.

Dealing with radio and television is an increasingly important skill for the profession. This might be seen as being more an aspect of representing the client effectively than promoting the firm, but the two will often be difficult to separate. Training is again advisable for anyone who might find themselves involved in media interviews.

Part of the skill of promoting the firm is to capitalise on any effort made and to get maximum value from it. If a seminar has been arranged, it will usually be possible to convert the text into an article for the press, or a contribution to a newsletter. Efficiency of effort by re-cycling the input of fee-earners is clearly advisable.

In the more outward-looking firms there should be procedures for sending out press releases on which there are clear general guidelines. Headed paper should be used with text double spaced below. There should be a simple headline and the story should be condensed into the first, short, paragraph. Named quotes should be included where possible. A press release should be no longer than two sides in length and should give details of who should be approached at the end of the text. Home telephone numbers are advisable in addition to the office number. Press releases are more likely to succeed in getting into print if they contain some interesting story which will be relevant to the journal in question.

Articles and features

Articles on legal topics are always an effective way to promote the firm. Placing them, however, is something that few firms do well and is a service that PR agencies might be worth considering for. The firm that does want to place an article in a less obvious publication might be well advised to invest in one of the press guides available which will, on an annual basis, list all publications and name editors. Preliminary telephone contact should establish whether there is interest in a proposed article.

Advertising

Of all the promotional options which have opened up to law firms in recent years advertising remains the most contentious. Advertising can be defined as 'conveying a message in the media through purchased space'. Advertising is most obviously relevant where the pool of potential clients for a service is very wide and cannot sensibly be approached directly. The firm that seeks more claimant personal injury work, for example, could not identify and then approach those potential clients direct, unlike most commercial departments. This is not to say that advertising is for private clients only. There are occasional advertisements by specialist teams within commercial firms in trade journals and specialist features. A new computer group, for example, would be hard pressed to approach all potential clients in the firm's region. An advertisement, preferably coupled to an article, in a suitable computer journal might produce a good rate of response.

Sponsorship

Sponsorship is a promotional option that might be personal or non-personal. Since personality is so important a factor in promoting legal services personal methods should be preferred where possible. Sponsorship can be an effective supplement to the networking of partners and staff. Advertisements in magazines of church, social or sporting groups naming the person who has placed it are more commonplace now and would be unlikely to offend in the way that they might have done just a few years ago.

Internet

The Internet stands to revolutionise some of the ideas on legal marketing that have developed over the last decade. The medium goes beyond mere promotion with more firms now providing a whole range of services on the Internet, though with frequent teething problems in relation to professional standards according to advice given by the Law Society.

The creation of a webpage is an attractive option but involves just as great a commitment to manage the facility as in compiling any newsletter. It can offer up-to-date information and should be changed monthly. If browsers identify themselves, follow-up is possible in a more targeted way than before but there will be an expectation of a fairly prompt response. This is a development for the better resourced, therefore, and a flat information-only website will be of very limited value.

The other problem experienced by many firms is that having the website is one thing, but people knowing about it and therefore seeking it out is another. Efforts will have to be made to educate the potential market about the website, perhaps through the other means listed above.

In conclusion there is no set 'right and wrong' in the choice of promotional methods: they have to be determined according to the nature of the service, the client and the message to be conveyed. Given the importance of personality in the 'marketing mix' the personal methods will be more likely to be how instructions are actually developed, but the non-personal methods are useful in creating the opportunities for such discussions to occur. This orthodoxy will be increasingly challenged if the move to e.commerce continues to grow at it current exponential rate, however.

Any promotion which is useful to the client is more likely to succeed: brochures should include the type of information which clients will want to know, for example, and industry specific newsletters or information services might be particularly well received. Training and seminars are always an effective opportunity to develop profile. General advertising, in isolation, can easily become a waste of money, but linked to other initiatives or set alongside articles by the firm it will probably be useful. Claims about distribution and readership by publishers of directories should always be treated with caution.

It is important not to fall into the trap of believing that simply because promotion is being well conducted, further work is bound to follow. Many solicitors' firms are now also working on selling skills. Selling is usually badly done since lawyers are reluctant to involve themselves in it, usually through long-standing reticence about being seen to be 'touting' for work. The main principles of better selling can be summarised as 'listen first, talk second'. A 'hard sell' style should always be avoided. If the representative of the firm can deduce what it is that the client wishes to buy and whether they might be interested in the firm, selling becomes the simple act of matching needs which have been described to services and expertise which are available. It can therefore be seen as one application of the marketing concept.

Marketing databases

Most firms have agonised over client databases in recent years. The main problem with databases is the cost efficiency issue: is it worth the costs, particularly the personnel costs in maintaining the data? To produce reliable up-to-date data on all clients will usually involve greater fee-earner discipline than is the norm in most firms at the point of taking instructions and then considerable investment for inputting the data so collected. The second of these difficulties at least will diminish as fee-earners start to record instructions directly onto screen themselves, as already happens in most doctors' surgeries. The first may be more of a long term problem.

If difficulties over systems cannot be overcome there will remain great dangers in relying on partially complete databases. The nightmare scenario for many firms is the mailshot letter to private clients where the firm is already acting on a probate, a situation that I have been told of on more than one occasion. For most firms the impact of computerisation and marketing will have to remain 'walk before you run' for some time to come. Elsewhere, the integration of accounts and marketing databases has provided significant improvements to marketing effectiveness.

Likely developments

The most significant developments in marketing practice are bound to be driven by IT improvements in the years ahead. There are those who argue that the orthodoxy of marketing – that the management of marketing is mostly to do with fine-tuning of the marketing mix – is fast being overhauled. New computer facilities will enable us to individualise services as never before, enabling us to build unique profiles on clients and communicate to them in this way. The leading authority on strategy and marketing, Philip Kotler, has talked about mass marketing through the marketing mix giving way to segment marketing, then niche marketing and then eventually customer specific marketing.[11] Others doubt the viability of what is in effect being described as 'a segment of one', but this may depend on the significance of each individual client and their potential billings to the practice.

In more advanced firms, marketing will take the management of the relationship between firm and clients to new heights. Traditional marketing is 'transactional', in which the various 'P' factors are managed for the benefit of firm and client. Beyond this we are seeing already the development of 'relationship' marketing within firms, creating secure extranets for use by the client in question. Promotional messages will be more consistently up to date, while increasing use of websites will mean that the traditional problems of obsolete print runs will lessen.

Computerisation can also improve the marketing effort through much better internal communication. A weekly e.mail which lists:

- absences next week
- important meetings to be attended
- events in the office
- notable new instructions received
- recommendations and referrals received
- requests for help

can result in a more focused effort and greater cohesion within the firm.

Main points

- Marketing needs to be planned and is more than simply promotion.
- Marketing plans should be drawn up in line with the overall business or 'forward' plan.
- The boundary between strategy and marketing will often be difficult to draw.
- Marketing effectiveness is improved through having a number of clear objectives.
- In choosing promotional options the firm needs to consider a variety of factors, including the client groups to be influenced.
- Lack of systematic approach to the management of marketing is the most common weakness in most firms so far as marketing is concerned.

References to Lexcel

B1(b)–(d) Services and forward planning

Notes

1 [1997] *Gazette*, 19 November, p. 20; the report on marketing, commissioned by Wheeler Associates and performed by McCallum Layton.
2 Morgan, N. (1991) *Professional Services Marketing*, Butterworth-Heinemann.
3 [2000] *Gazette*, 15 June, p. 28.
4 Wilson, A. (1984) *Practice Development for Professional Firms*, McGraw-Hill.
5 Berry, L. and Parasuraman, A. (1991) *Marketing for Services: Competing through Quality*, The Free Press.
6 [1997] *Gazette*, 19 November, p. 20.
7 [2000] *Gazette*, 15 June, p. 30.
8 Thompson, Sir Clive (1997) *Marketing Business*, October, p. 27.
9 Ansoff, H. I. (1965) *Corporate Strategy*, Penguin.
10 [1997] *Gazette*, 5 March, p. 28.
11 Kotler, P. (1997) *Marketing Business*, February, p. 26.

16

Supervision and risk management

- Risk management
- Practical risk management steps
- Vetting of new work
- Conflicts of interest
- Key dates
- Undertakings
- Supervision
- Supervisory practice
- Miscellaneous techniques

In days gone by the law was mostly an autonomous pursuit. If fee-earners had the necessary qualifications to undertake the work assigned to them they would be left pretty much to their own devices. Supervision more often than not occurred at the prompting of someone needing help rather than at the instigation of the supervisor. Many partners and other senior staff would resent the time requested, taking the view that trial and error was probably the best way to learn the law and that there was therefore nothing wrong with a 'sink or swim' philosophy. Assistants equally resisted the imposition of time recording on the grounds that it was clearly an underhand device by the partners, to check up on them.

These attitudes are still prevalent in many firms but are now under attack as never before. The advent in September 2000 of a commercial indemnity insurance market for solicitors gave prominence to the whole area of supervision and risk management. The days of the 'sole practitioner mentality' in firms, where different fee-earners run practices which are, to all intents and purposes, isolated from their partners and colleagues, are in hasty retreat.

The impact of the changes to the indemnity insurance market cannot be overstated. In many respects the developments in the market reflect the development of the profession over recent years. In 1973 some 21 per cent of firms did not carry any form of indemnity insurance cover. Clients simply did not sue if things went wrong. If they tried to do so they would probably have struggled to find a firm willing to take their instructions. The prevailing view was that professional advisers, like everyone else, should be allowed to make the odd mistake. Although this might impact on the reputation and the prospects of repeat work it would have been sharp practice for a client to have the audacity to sue for compensation.

The advent of consumerism throughout the latter years of the twentieth century brought an end to such a benign regime from the solicitor's point of view. The value of deals got greater, the rules on time limits more punitive and clients generally became more litigious. Professional negligence became a growth area in many firms, whether claimant or defendant, or both. Worst of all, from the profession's point of view, the lending institutions took to frequently dubious claims in relation to domestic conveyancing in an attempt to recoup some of their losses from the negative equity market of the early 1990s. Given the general level of dissatisfaction with the insurance market in the 1980s the Law Society had instituted the Solicitors' Indemnity Fund (SIF) in 1987. All firms would have their first £500,000 of losses (later £1,000,000) covered by the scheme. The mutual fund calculated contributions mostly through partnership size.

At the outset of the scheme few could have foreseen the enormity of the business that would eventually need to be handled. During the 13 years of its operations the SIF managed some 200,000 actual or reported claims with a total outlay of some £2.5 billion. By the mid-1990s the system was in crisis, with a shortfall approaching £500 million. Pressure started to grow for firms to be allowed to opt out of the mutual arrangements. The more profitable firms with a good claims record would quite evidently benefit from the ending of the scheme: others would not be so fortunate. As with so many developments in commerce generally, the large and successful would do disproportionately well from the changes. The lucrative end of the market from the insurers' point of view is the 'top-up' market for cover in excess of £1,000,000. The total number of claims against this cover for the two years preceding the eventual demise of the SIF were 11 and 15 respectively. The potential for substantial claims always existed but statistically they were very unlikely. Firms covering for substantial losses would generally gain from the change in the market whereas smaller firms would often end up paying more.

It should be noted that the total solicitors' market would always have to pay more for going to the commercial market. SIF did not charge brokerage commission nor did it have profit expectations. It did not have to cover marketing costs and would cover a shortfall by a levy rather than higher commission. It retained its investment income for the benefit of members and did not pay insurance premium tax because of its mutual status. Ironically the good news for the fund came after its demise. The much hyped millennium liability risks which were provided for did not materialise while progress was made in successfully defending a number of other claims, the value of the provision therefore falling sharply.

As most firms have discovered in recent months, risk profile is now a significant factor in this potentially substantial partnership expense. The surge of interest in quality accreditation is attributable in no small measure to strengthening the firm's position in discussions over premiums. Even if not externally audited, all firms should have clear supervisory and risk management arrangements in place. Most general practices will have a number of systems in place if they have run their legal aid work under the Legal Services Commission's franchising regime, but this may not extend to private paying litigation or to non-contentious work. The challenge in those firms is to level up their system to make it of general application. Many will be relieved to gain some benefit from their management time and expenditure in developing franchise systems other than the increasingly dubious privilege of being able to provide legally aided services.

Risk management

In the summer of 2000 the Solicitors' Indemnity Fund distributed to all firms in private practice a self-assessment questionnaire. It is more than simply a checklist, it is a practical guide to the errors and problems that led to the claims levels against the fund being much higher than ever should have been expected. The guide has been widely used and has generally received justifiable praise.

Risk management is a concept that needs explanation in order that firms can determine their approach to it. First, the risks to be guarded against are of professional negligence first and foremost but also complaints of poor service and harm to the reputation of the firm. Risk management therefore impacts not just on the financial health of the practice but also issues such as client care and marketing. The questionnaire makes a helpful distinction between a number of levels of risk:

- strategic risks, such as whether to open a branch office or merge with another practice;
- operational risk, arising from the day-to-day activities of the firm;

- disaster risks, from criminal acts or road collisions;
- conditional fee risks, which are seen as strategic risks;
- financial risks, such as a client who cannot pay fees which are due; and
- environmental risks, perhaps arising from the premises of the firm or their previous use.

Various levels of risk are dealt with elsewhere, most obviously in the areas of strategic risk discussed in Chapter 4. The Lexcel requirement that there should be clear responsibility for the management of finance of the practice (C1) would be helpful in relation to the area of financial risk. For risks in most of the other areas contingency planning would seem advisable, depending upon the magnitude of the risk and/or the damage that might result. At very least a back-up plan for the failure of the firm's computer is advisable, as any who have experienced this trauma will certify.

It is the area of operational risks, however, that will concern us here. For the most part this will be addressed through the various provisions which can be found in the sections dealing with case and file management in the Practice Management Standards. These are also the areas highlighted by the questionnaire. The contents of the *Lexcel Office Procedures Manual*[1] are intended to provide samples of the types of procedures that would be required to address the suggestions of the questionnaire. One individual should accept responsibility for overall risk management at this level. Who this individual should be will depend on all the usual factors which are particular to each firm but in many cases it will be the managing partner. Other firms have one partner, perhaps the senior partner, who manages the relationship with the external insurers. A further alternative might be the quality partner, since so many of the risk management procedures will be under his or her control.

The job description for the overall risk manager can be found in the seven key principles in the questionnaire. They need to have a thorough understanding of the business and the risks that it is exposed to. They also need to be proactive in alerting the firm to dangers, reporting on developments and instituting measures to reduce undue exposure. The size of any additional risk management structure will vary according to the size of the firm but it is important that risk management remains 'an integral part of management of the firm'. In some firms a risk committee might be established with a remit to review and manage risk throughout the practice. Such a committee could comprise the heads of department or even a quality committee in those firms that have established them. It is important, however, that the philosophy and procedures associated with the programme need to be absorbed at all levels of the firm, so it is clear that a quality programme with its eventual audit will have a great deal to offer since it may well extend to the parts of the firm that other management initiatives do not reach.

The main provisions of the Lexcel standard start with the provisions of F1f that there should be 'proper risk management procedures in place', including the appointment of an overall risk manager for the practice. The firm should maintain lists of the types of matters that it will and will not accept according to whether they are at acceptable or unacceptable risk levels. There might also be a list of instructions that might be accepted in certain circumstances only. An annual review of risk is also required.

The concept in ISO 9000 of the annual management review is perhaps the most helpful way to address the need for an annual report. Ideally this report should not appear in isolation and it would be helpful to make it part of a more general review of the firm's development. The requirement for an annual management report in ISO 9000 is now linked to the suggestion that there should be a 'quality plan' setting out how the firm's quality systems should develop in order to maintain progress to continuous improvement. Often considered by an annual strategic meeting, a typical agenda for such a report could read as:

- introduction: developments in the quality system;
- relationships with external bodies: record from external audits;
- summary of data from:
  - internal audit data (probably in ISO 9000 firms only);
  - file reviews;
  - client complaints;
- quality improvements and initiatives recommended;
- review of quality documentation and recommended revisions;
- report of risks partner and recommendations;
- objectives for year ahead.

Practical risk management steps

Unfortunately the SIF questionnaire went to print shortly before the Law Society Council approved the revisions to the Lexcel standard. This means that some of the more disparaging comments about the value of quality standards in terms of risk management are no longer true of the Practice Management Standards. The questionnaire states, for example, that the standards 'pay no more than superficial attention to operational risk management' (11.1 of Introduction). Likewise the comment that they do not 'require any one individual to accept ultimate accountability for risk management within a firm' (12.1 Introduction) is not true of the revised Lexcel standard. The questionnaire does recognise, however, the 'excellent recommendations or requirements for good systems and procedures' in the main legal quality standards.

Vetting of new work

One of the most effective ways to manage the risks posed by certain files is never to take them on in the first place. Firms should consider in advance which categories of work they will and will not take on and those marginal cases where a view will be taken. Vetting should also extend to clients and decisions as to who the firm wishes to deal with. There is no professional 'cab rank' requirement for solicitors requiring them to take on work but is important that the decision to accept or reject instructions is not based on grounds that would be offensive to any anti-discrimination or equal opportunities legislation or policies. Many firms have adopted procedures that they will decline work where it would be uneconomic, outside the competence of the practice or where the client has a record that suggests that the firm does not want to deal with him or her. Sadly, an increasing number of these situations involve assaults, abuse or threats of violence against the firm's personnel.

Vetting will tend to be more cursory in relation to repeat work and established clients. The more onerous checking in relation to new clients will include 'know your client' checks in relation to money laundering provisions which were revised in 2000 in updated guidance from the Law Society.[2] Developments are fast-moving in this field and firms need to ensure that they are aware of the regime's requirements which are increasingly based on a European perspective. It should be remembered that the penalties for involvement with illegal or improper business or even for failure to report are seen as criminal and can result in imprisonment.

There is an interesting recommendation in the questionnaire that firms take additional steps in relation to instructions passed on by another firm. Any professional difficulties that a previous firm experienced could re-surface for the new firm and procedures in this area do appear to be sensible. Recommended procedures include enquiring the reason for the transfer and investigation as to whether there are 'outstanding claims or complaints in relation to the business transferred'.

Conflicts of interest

The other issue at the outset of a potential matter and the decision as to whether the matter should be taken on at all is conflicts checking. The requirement at F1a of Lexcel extends to maintaining: 'an index of matters (to) facilitate identifying any conflict of interest'.

The index of matters is usually based on a client and file numbering system, so that all dealings for any given client can be identified, and each matter can be distinguished. Problems can arise where a fee-earner starts to run an incidental matter under an existing file. General files, most commonly found in commercial departments for miscellaneous advice to clients, can also be problematic if they are used to by-pass normal file opening procedures.

There is arguably no completely foolproof way of checking for conflict of interest situations. Commonsense checking around the office should never be discounted as one of the most effective steps to take, but as firms grow it would be unwise to rely on this alone. Most firms will in addition rely on accounts computer checks or perhaps circulate details of all new instructions for perusal by all colleagues. The guidance notes to the section stress that what matters most is that whether manual or computerised, procedures should be: 'in place, understood and consistently applied throughout the practice'.

The professional position on conflicts of interest has become more stringent in recent times following the House of Lords decision in *Prince Jefri* v. *KPMG* [1999] 2 AC 222 and care is needed. The situations where the same firm may act for both seller and buyer in a conveyancing transaction are more restrictive under the new Rule 6 which provides that conveyancing transactions where it is possible to act for both parties have become more uncommon.

The SIF questionnaire suggests that the policy against conflicts of interest should include 'an absolute prohibition against undisclosed financial arrangements between partners and clients' and that there should be an up-to-date record of partners' financial interests. Some may be surprised to discover that it is recommended that this extends to staff but one could understand an objection if it transpired that there was a close personal link between a staff member and an opponent in litigation. The questionnaire is not in favour of 'Chinese walls' arrangements for overcoming conflicts.

Key dates

Many of the difficulties of the SIF in its darkest days were caused by the deluge of claims relating to the introduction of automatic strike-out provisions in civil litigation. This exposed in many firms an over-reliance on the fee-earner's management of their own diary. The odd slip had always been a problem but now became in many instances a disaster. The imposition of a compulsory back-up system probably should have been a compulsory requirement years ago. It is found in F1 of Lexcel and has been a mainstay of the Legal Services Commission requirements since the inception of franchising.

The format of the back-up system could be a central diary or a computerised alert system. Responsibility for making the entries should be made clear. In most cases it should be the fee-earner who has the primary responsibility. Key dates have been defined as any date, the missing of which could give rise to a claim in negligence. It is advisable that each firm or department within the firm should spell out what it considers to be key dates. They will include most obviously:

- limitation periods;
- strike-out dates;
- hearing dates;
- opposing party deadlines;
- appeal deadlines;
- dates for filing of evidence;
- earliest dates for applying for decree absolute;
- registration deadlines;
- completion dates;
- notice periods in landlord and tenant;
- rent reviews;
- statutory filing requirements.

In all cases a reminder or 'countdown' should show up at an appropriate stage before the final date. There would be little value in a single reminder that the limitation period expires the same or the next day.

There are some interesting suggestions in relation to amendments to key dates by SIF which are borne out of long and expensive involvement in the failure of systems. These are that correction fluid should never be used but the entry should be crossed out and initialled with the new entry clearly shown. If approval is needed for entries this should also be apparent.

Undertakings

Breaches of undertakings remain a principal area of professional negligence claims. It should follow that procedures for monitoring the giving and performing of undertakings are important in all practices. According to *The Guide to the Professional Conduct of Solicitors 1999* an undertaking is:

> any unequivocal declaration of intention addressed to someone who reasonably places reliance on it and made by a solicitor or a member of a solicitor's staff in the course of practice.[3]

It should be noted that in some cases a promise to give an undertaking at a later stage has also been construed to be an undertaking in its own right. Most firms will place limitations on the giving of undertakings and it is important that these are found in a policy on the subject. The requirement in Lexcel is that firms 'ensure proper authorisation and monitoring of undertakings given on behalf of the practice'. The guidance note to F1 provides that the restrictions could be:

- providing the approved wording;
- designating who may and may not give undertakings;
- approval procedures;
- maintaining records of undertakings and their discharge.

Most firms distinguish the general conveyancing undertakings to redeem charges from others, especially those relating to costs or the obligation to repay other liabilities.

There is no need for a central register of undertakings to be established, though they have become standard practice for many, less so for standard conveyancing undertakings. The real dangers are long running matters where undertakings are lost in extensive file clips which have been built up over substantial periods of time. The simplest system to adopt is that partners only may give undertakings and that the giving of an undertaking has to be prominently stamped on the file, dated and authorised by partner initials. The more garish the colour of the sticker, the better.

Recommendations in relation to the content of undertakings are that they should not relate to matters outside the control of the firm and must in all cases be phrased in such a way to avoid any confusion as to their full extent. SIF use the familiar mnemonic (SMART) of their being:

Specific in their extent;
Measurable to avoid misunderstandings;

246

Agreed and confirmed;

Realistic, in that the firm will be able to deliver on them;

Timely, with clear guidance on when they will take effect or expire.

Oral undertakings should always be confirmed immediately in writing and the Law Society has recommended that firms should not accept undertakings by e.mail.

Lexcel has further reporting requirements in relation to risk management. There is a provision at F5c that the client should be informed in writing of any changed circumstances once the matter is under way that might affect the degree of risk that they are exposed to or their view of the cost–benefit analysis of proceeding. Likewise at F7, dealing with the end of the matter, it is provided that the fee-earner should notify the risk manager if the final assessment of the outcome achieved differs from the initial assessment with a written explanation. This should not be taken to mean that every unsuccessful litigant needs to be reported since the instructions will generally be to have had the matter resolved, which it will have been. This applies instead to the situation where the client will have failed to gain the benefit of the process that they might have anticipated. An obvious example in litigation would be where the reason for the client losing the claim was that it was struck out for want of prosecution.

Other recommendations of SIF in relation to risk management appear and are dealt with elsewhere, in particular the proper confirmation of terms of business with clients and the proper management of a complaints policy in Chapter 18 and effective delegation practice in Chapter 10. Risk management sits easily with the general area of supervision which is deserving of separate treatment.

Supervision

Supervision as a general concept appears in all the main quality standards. It is a wide ranging topic and is therefore found in different areas of the Lexcel standard. One of the main developments in the first version of LAFQAS when it appeared in 1998 was a considerable addition to the requirements of supervision in section L. Investors in People lays great emphasis on the role of the manager, especially in relation to development, but is less specific in relation to day-to-day work supervision.

There is one general requirement in Lexcel which is not found elsewhere:

> Practices will ensure that there are appropriate documented arrangements for supervision. (D7)

This is deliberately wider than the specific duties in relation to case work and seems to be intended to emphasise the importance of supervision generally. It should be read in conjunction with the requirements for named supervisors of the areas of the practice which is found in A1:

> There will be a named supervisor for each area of work (a supervisor may be responsible for more than one area).

The requirements of the Legal Services Commission are considerably more prescriptive than Lexcel. Typical of this general approach is the preliminary issue of who may be a supervisor. So far as Lexcel is concerned the supervisor needs only: 'appropriate experience of the work supervised and be able to guide and assist others' (A1).

Under CLSQM L2.2, however, there is a requirement for the supervisor to have gained their:

> experience, knowledge and understanding in the relevant category of work over a minimum period of time in the preceding five years. This minimum period of time is generally assessed as three years full time (defined as 350 hours per year for a full time employee) or five years part time (defined as 1050 hours over five years).

The limited discretion in the Legal Services Commission requirements appears not to have been liberally applied and it was recognised by Steve Orchard, chief executive of the LSC, at a Legal Aid Conference in Nottingham in May 2000 that these strict requirements had led to problems, especially in areas such as consumer contract and debt where many rural firms would be unlikely ever to develop a sufficient practice to meet the requirements. Recognising this as a factor in the decline of availability of services, an increased use of the so-called 'portfolio route' to showing sufficient expertise was planned. Legal aid supervisors have also had to undertake a basic three technical training courses per year in the areas that they supervise and there is a requirement at L2.4 that they should 'cascade' their knowledge of the subject. In addition they are also required to attend training on major new areas of their practice subject and ensure that this is passed on in some suitable manner to their colleagues and should also know the limits to their expertise and so be discerning on which work they should turn away. Panel membership is approved in general terms by the Commission and where an appropriate specialist panel exists it is usually a requirement that the supervisor belongs to it. Despite the fact that most such panels are creations of the Law Society the Lexcel standard is not so prescriptive on this point.

The practical skills of supervisors appear as a requirement in both

Lexcel and CLSQM, but much more specifically in relation to legal aid. Lexcel confines itself on this requirement to the training provisions in D5c that:

> skills and knowledge required for the management and organisation of the practice (as well as for legal practice) are provided for in training and development.

There was originally a proposal that all legal aid supervisors would have to attend approved supervision training but this did not eventually materialise, nor did a formal validation process for legal aid supervision training. Supervisors who could show that they had supervised:

> at least one full time caseworker (or equivalent) for a minimum period of at least 1 year in the preceding 2 years immediately prior to the application (L3.1)

would be deemed to be qualified to supervise. There is the power for an auditor to specify attendance on a course as corrective action if they felt that supervisory arrangements were lacking, but many auditors seem to have taken the view that training should be compulsory in any event and many delegates on supervision courses have attended as a result of an audit-based request.

Supervisory practice

The acid test for this area of requirements must be how effective supervision actually is in practice. Most of the emphasis on this in Lexcel will be found in F10 which starts with requirements that there should be documented procedures to include:

(a) availability of a supervisor to guide and assist others;
(b) appropriate procedures to allocate work in relation to the qualifications and experience of fee-earners and their workloads.

It will tend always to be the case that supervisors run the risk of being the busiest fee-earners. Since they are likely to the most experienced and senior person in that area of work they are also likely to be in higher client demand, so the tension between fee-earning and management responsibilities is a familiar problem. It is fair, however, that a supervisor should be truly available and not so permanently busy that access is unduly restricted. Managing this balance may mean designating certain periods of the day as supervision time, striking a 'quid pro quo' that the supervisor should, other than in real emergencies, be left to get on with their fee-earning work at other times during the day. The position in multi-office practices will need greater attention, a fact highlighted in CLSQM at L4.2. This may mean at very least regular phone calls if not personal visits to the office.

The allocation of work is an opportunity to check pressure and potential dangers. Firms should have some procedure where the supervisor, in most circumstances, should authorise a matter opening form. This is not to say that fee-earners should be confined for ever to the range of instructions that they can currently manage or they will not develop as they should. What is important is that the supervisor can know the risk points and know which matters are likely to require greater hands-on checking through the complexities of the matter or the inexperience of the person handling. A clear statement as to the work that the firm will and will not take on is helpful.

Independent file reviews are also given prominence in F10 with provisions that are broadly in line with section M of CLSQM. The independence of checking is stressed in the provisions. Lexcel provides that there need to be arrangements for:

(c) the management of case files to be reviewed periodically and the review will (except where there is only one fee-earner in the practice) be carried out by a fee-earner who has not been involved in the day-to-day conduct of the matter;

(d) a record of the review to be kept on the case file and on a central record;

(e) ensuring that any corrective action identified is carried out promptly.

File reviews are certainly one of the more time-consuming aspects of a case management system to introduce in practice and views on their usefulness differ. The concept that there should be independent checking of matters is often one of the elements that meets with the clearest support with partners in theory, though they might find the time taken on the task to be excessive. File reviews under Lexcel can be limited to procedural reviews only, but have to be undertaken by a fee-earner. CLSQM requirements are for reviews to extend to legal issues and procedural compliance.

The time taken on reviews adds to the importance of striking a balance between too onerous a programme which takes an unreasonable amount of fee-earner time to implement, and too superficial a commitment which produces little insight into the problems being experienced by advisers. If the programme is pitched appropriately it will make a significant contribution to the continuous improvement which should be one of the aims of any quality programme. The flexibility to choose how many files should be reviewed for different fee-earners is stressed in the guidance notes to F10 and the Legal Services Commission guidance note at M1.1. The factors to be taken into account would include the experience of the fee-earner and the extent of problems which tend to come to light as reviews progress. If a firm finds a pattern of very few and mostly minor problems it would be justified in seeking to reduce the number of files checked, but the converse could also be the case. It is important that file reviews are seen as a management tool which should be undertaken for their own value to the practice rather than, as often seems to be the case, primarily to satisfy the audit requirements.

Nothing in any quality standard commits the named supervisor to undertake all these responsibilities in person, and the procedures should make it clear that file reviews in particular could be a shared responsibility. There is a suggestion that any other reviewer should be capable of meeting the supervisor standards in CLSQM at M1.1, but there will be discretion on this at audit. Where the task is delegated it is important that the supervisor retains overall control and is made aware to what is emerging from the process, as by being handed the forms of review before they are filed. A copy of the form also has to be placed on the matter file and each firm will need procedures for 'corrective action', whereby steps required at the review are confirmed to have been taken. The usual requirement is that the reviewer checks to see if the corrective action has occurred but this need only be on a sampling basis in most instances.

Other requirements in CLSQM are that reviews have to be substantive and the file must be examined, so print-out reviews are inadequate. Records must be kept as to which files have been reviewed and a note must appear on the matter file recording the review itself and any 'corrective action' required. The procedures must cover the frequency and numbers of files to be reviewed, while supervisors' files are also subject to review, but the frequency of review will probably be reduced. The wording of F10 means that partners' files are also included in review requirements for Lexcel.

Miscellaneous techniques

There are various other elements to supervision which firms might find helpful, of which the most common relates to post checking. The presence of a partner or other senior member of staff to oversee what is opened is often a very effective first alert to problems which might develop. Most in training will have received the 'see me' comment on the top of the letter with clarification sought by a partner. It is a concern with the increasing use of e.mail that this daily checking can be by-passed, as is often the case with faxes also.

Post signing is again a matter for firms to determine for themselves. There is no rule that partners only may sign post though this remains the practice in some firms or specialist departments within them. Given the difficulties that this can impose in most offices attempting to send the post out in time it is a sensible compromise to suggest that letters of advice by staff have to be seen by partners, but otherwise checking is more through file reviews. The practice of maintaining an extra copy of letters of advice by junior fee-earners, especially while they serve any probationary period of their employment, enables more specific feedback to be provided on their expertise and communication style.

Departmental meetings are highly recommended as long as they do not become a waste of time. A limited standing agenda should be developed and meetings should never be allowed to overrun. For legal aid firms who have to show that know-how is being 'cascaded' proof of meetings and the agenda that was used at them is invaluable.

Finally, regular print-out review is good practice though, as stated above, it will not be accepted as an independent file review. There are provisions in CLSQM at N1.2.5 that 'files are checked for inactivity at pre-determined intervals' which can be met by print-outs being marked up as they are considered. This procedure is often in place for good financial housekeeping and if the accounts department maintains two or three months' worth of print-outs per fee-earner, or if they are returned to the department or person dealing, there will be evidence for any auditor that this requirement is being addressed.

Main points

- Risk management will need active consideration throughout the firm.
- There needs to be one named person responsible for risk management.
- Clear supervisory procedures need to be in place.

References to Lexcel

A1 Supervisors
B1 Business planning
D7 Supervision
F1 Conflicts of interest and risk management
F4 Acceptance of instructions
F5 Progress of matter
F7 Final review

F9 Undertakings
F10 Supervision of case work

Notes

1 Moore, M. and Dodd, M. (2001) *Lexcel Office Procedures Manual*, Law Society Publishing.
2 *Money Laundering Legislation: Guidance for Solicitors* (2000) (being re-written at time of writing).
3 *The Guide to the Professional Conduct of Solicitors* (1999), Law Society.

17

Case management

- Index of matters
- Taking instructions
- Progress of the matter
- Documents
- At the end of the case
- Services from others
- File management
- Variations in ISO 9000

Many of the provisions which can be grouped together as case and file management procedures arise under either risk management or client care and are dealt with under those topics. There remain, however, a number of requirements which will influence how the firm's fee-earning activities should be organised. These will include issues such as the recording of instructions on the file, the traceability of all necessary information and the arrangements for securing the services of external experts and counsel.

It is within these areas that all the legal quality standards owe the greatest debt to ISO 9000 (formerly BS 5750). That standard confines itself to the process of an organisation and for the most part does not deal with other areas of management. ISO 9000 requires any organisation to document its key processes in such a way that the requirements of the standard are satisfied and then show that these procedures are in consistent use.

The difficulties that lawyers have experienced with ISO 9000 have usually stemmed from its terminology. The standard was drawn up in the late 1970s as a manufacturing and engineering device primarily and grew in its importance to service organisations only later. In response to this a joint project of the Law Society and the British Standards Institution developed an adaptation of the code for use by law firms. Thus 'contract review' became taking instructions, 'design review' became case planning and 'non-conforming product' became 'client complaints'.

Document management is one of the principal requirements of ISO 9000 which has been adopted more latterly by CLSQM and Lexcel. The purpose of these requirements is that all personnel should at all times be working to the latest versions of any procedures. The basic requirement is to have a manual covering all the core processes which need to be regulated. This will form the 'controlled documentation' which will be subject to the provisions. To ensure that control is maintained there will need to be rules that there are formal procedures for determining the contents of manuals and their amendment, and lists of all the copies in current issue so that updating can be firm-wide. The status of each page need to be shown as by numbering all pages sequentially (e.g. 'page 3 of 23') and giving an issue date or number.

The organisation of the procedures is a matter of choice in most firms provided that all the requirements of the standard are addressed. The conventional approach is to have a quality manual where the firm's general approach to quality is found. This sets out in general terms what must happen in fee-earning work in all departments, how the practice is managed and how quality is administered.

An office manual will be more familiar to most firms. It sets out the more detailed procedures by which the firm operates. It may be helpful to supplement this with a set of departmental procedures in addition to the general rules on fee-earning found in the main quality manual. This is where the differences between the departments are highlighted. A typical general rule for taking instructions from clients that 'it is essential that any fee-earning personnel act upon the clients' full and considered instructions' might benefit from more details on the actual arrangements for taking instructions which apply in each department for each work type. There may be checklists in some departments but not others, of which some may be compulsory and others optional. This level of variation will need to be set out somewhere in the system and it is advisable to keep the procedures as relevant as possible to the actual users. The net effect of this approach would often be a pyramid (see Figure 17.1).

The documented systems could now simply be on the computer system if everyone concerned would have sufficient access to the data. Under the 1994 version of ISO 9000 the heading became 'document and data control' reflecting the increasing use of computer systems for this purpose. The one qualification to this is in CLSQM with its requirement at W1.3 that: 'multi site organisations must hold a copy of the manual at every location where a franchise is held' which would

Figure 17.1   *Case management pyramid*

appear to require a hard copy to be available. There are clear advantages in maintaining the system on computer on a 'read-only' basis in that updates become much easier to administer. One computerised program in use in a large legal aid practice has a device for users to add comments to any of the provisions for consideration by the quality controller. This also contains checks that certain steps on the matter can only occur if, for example, a client care letter has been sent from the program.

In Lexcel the provisions on document control appear at E2 and add the requirement that there should be an annual review of the documentation even if no changes are planned. The same requirement for annual review appears in CLSQM at W1.2. The general rule in ISO 9000 is that it is possible to store up a number of changes if they are not too significant in order to control the administrative burden of placing all amendments with holders.

Index of matters

There are various requirements which relate to 'traceability', the concept that all information and paperwork should be stored so as to enable easy retrieval. The first of these in the context of a law firm is that each matter should be unique and identifiable whether for the same or different clients. In Lexcel the requirement can be found at F1, linked to the issue of conflicts of interest which we examined in Chapter 16. There is a linked provision at F2 requiring all files which are supported by particular funders – the Legal Services Commission is the obvious example to be identifiable. The equivalent provisions in CLSQM add requirements in relation to the opening and closing dates of files to assist in the Commission's auditing procedures (N1.1).

The index of matters is usually based on a client and file number-ing system and will be fairly standard practice in most firms. Problems tend to arise, if at all, where a fee-earner starts to run an incidental matter under an existing file. General files, most com-monly found in commercial departments for miscellaneous advice to clients, can also be problematic if they are used to by-pass normal file opening procedures.

Taking instructions

Experience tends to show that the matter that starts on a sound footing, with client and adviser in agreement on priorities, costs and other such issues, is one that is more likely to proceed smoothly. Conversely, 'problem files' can often be traced back to an unsatisfac-tory commencement. F4 of Lexcel, together with the various require-ments in relation to confirming instructions, are therefore significant provisions for the firm that wants to improve its services through the adoption of case management procedures. There will need to be provisions for agreeing with the client and then recording on the file:

- the client's instructions and objectives;
- a clear explanation of the issues raised and the advice given;
- action to be taken by the practice and the likely timescale;
- strategy decided upon and any case plan.

There are also sections dealing with what must be confirmed to the client in writing which, in addition to the information required under the client care code (see Chapter 18), includes key dates which must be entered onto the back-up system. The contents of P1 in CLSQM are broadly the same and deal with various aspects of public funding such as the effect of discharge or revocation of a certificate. Any limit to the service to be provided should be set out; a common example is advo-cacy at the industrial tribunal for the legally aided client.

It is important to note that there is little in the way of how these provisions must be met within the standards. The obligation is instead to ensure that instructions are properly taken, noted and confirmed. There is, in particular, no obligation to use checklists, though any checklists used should certainly be documented for the purposes of ISO 9000 in particular. Where certain departments use checklists and others do not, separate departmental procedures become invaluable in setting out the checklists merely for those who are affected by them.

Progress of the matter

Section F5 of Lexcel deals with the various elements of progressing matters and addresses one of the principal criticisms directed against solicitors. All too often matters start well with a flurry of activity by the firm, only to be followed by a long period of 'drift' when the client can easily feel as if nothing is happening on their matter. The problem is exacerbated if the firm has adopted the sensible policy of interim billing. The effect is that the client receives regular bills but is unable to perceive any progress.

The equivalent procedures in CLSQM are found in section S. Again, the wording may differ somewhat, but the effect of the provisions is much the same. The principal rule is that: 'information on progress of the matter (or reasons for the lack of progress) is given to the client at appropriate intervals'.

In addition to the requirement that costs information is provided at six-monthly intervals at least, any changes in the risk profile of the matter or the likely cost benefit to the client must be raised. Certain major developments should not wait: one example given is that there should be immediate reporting to the client in relation to any adverse costs order against the client (Lexcel F5f).

The concept of the 'case plan' holds great potential in many matters. It is best explained as being simply a strategy for the matter. For the most part a case plan can emerge quite satisfactorily from the letter to the client confirming instructions. At any early stage it may be difficult to plan with confidence the full development of any matter, not least because the first stage might be to research the evidence. As the case plan develops, so it might change in a sequence of letters confirming the position with the client.

There are clear requirements in legal aid matters for a 'separate' case plan (i.e. one that is not simply contained in a letter to the client) where the matter is:

- multi-claimant, i.e. 10 or more certificates have been granted;
- subject to High Court jurisdiction, or
- the firm's likely total costs, including disbursements and VAT, are likely to exceed £25,000.

For ease of supervision some reference to the case plan is advisable, one of the simpler systems in operation being that any case planning sheet is given a distinctive colour to stand out on the correspondence or documents clip. Many file summary sheets will have a space for case plans and updates to them to be identified.

Documents

F6 records what is referred to in the original text of ISO 9000 as 'traceability', the important principle of documents and other items being capable of being found within the office. For the most part this is achieved by requiring all papers to be on the matter file that they relate to, but attention is also needed with items of evidence.

In one firm a defective tyre which had allegedly caused a collision was stored in the office. On inspection it was asked what was in place to show which file this item related to if, coincidentally, another allegedly defective tyre should become involved in another matter. To overcome the potential difficulties, a procedure requiring clear labelling of the client and matter name and number is standard practice. There are clear benefits here to risk management, another provision being that files or computers with sensitive data on them should not be left in unattended cars. To avoid the considerable wasted time of looking for files which have been taken from the office, fee-earners might be required to note which files they have taken, as by a note to their personal diary if that stays in the office at all times. It is also useful to require a 'log' to be kept on the first or principal file for each matter recording what other files, bundles and items of evidence form the full contents of that matter.

At the end of the case

A clear end to any matter is desirable and the final piece to the risk management jig-saw. The principal aspects are well set out in Lexcel F7 with its requirements that the firm:

(a) reports to the client on the outcome and explains any further action that the client is required to take in the matter and what, if anything, the practice will do;

(b) accounts to the client for any outstanding money;

(c) returns to the client original documents and other property belonging to the client if required (save for items which are by agreement to be stored by the practice);

(d) if appropriate, advises the client about arrangements for storage and retrieval of papers and other items retained, (in so far as this has not been dealt with already, for example in terms of business);

(e) advises the client whether they should review the matter in the future, and if so, when;

(f) carries out a concluding risk assessment in relation to the case;

(g) notifies the practice's overall risk manager if the final assessment differs from the initial assessment, and provides a written explanation.

An increasing number of firms are charging their clients for storage facilities to bring themselves into line with banks and other such institutions, especially if the documentation subsequently goes elsewhere. As the standards suggest, this might be better dealt with under the initial terms and conditions of business. The risk management procedure is completed with the end of that matter. Final assessment should only be taken to be materially different if the client did not succeed in their main aim, e.g. to have a matter litigated. If the case was heard, but lost, this should not usually generate a risk management alert, but if the hearing was missed through a diary error this would be a very different proposition and would require reporting. Prompt reporting of matters which could give rise to a claim becomes all the more vital if firms at any stage change their insurers.

The Franchising Specification adds nothing to these fairly straightforward provisions. The requirements of ISO 9000 mainly concern 'after-care and follow-up'. This is defined as any continuing commitment to the client after the immediate matter has been ended. Provisions are very much more common in industry. The contract to supply equipment of most types usually carries the obligation to provide service for a defined period, for example. Solicitors do not, by and large, provide after-care services and if this is the case within the firm this should be stated. Nothing in ISO 9000 says that such procedures must exist, merely that if they do they are documented. Common exceptions in law firms are wills reviews at five-yearly intervals or annual company secretarial services in a commercial department. Where departmental procedures are adopted after-care is probably best dealt with there, even if only to state that it does not apply.

The easiest way to ensure compliance with the provisions on ending matters is through the completion of a closing sheet. This can often be worked into the main file summary sheet as is the case in the form appearing in the *Lexcel Office Procedures Manual*.[1]

Services from others

When Pannone Blackburn, as it then was, developed the first ISO 9000 system for a law firm word leaked out to the local Bar that they would now appear on a list of approved 'sub-contractors'. There were those who found this demeaning, while others saw in it an opportunity for review work. Would natural justice apply to decisions to enter and exclude? The answer, of course, was 'no'.

Since that time the concept of approved lists has become standard and it should be noted that the latest revisions to ISO 9000 talk now of 'suppliers' rather than 'sub-contractors'. The main requirements are that the firm considers who it wishes to use and that clear instructions are given for any advice requested. This must in turn be considered for its usefulness and relevance.

Selection criteria could include membership of recognised bodies, recommendations, etc. The involvement of the client in the decision to appoint experts or counsel, and their right to choose the adviser, are regarded as being important by the Legal Services Commission. There is potential for conflict if the client's views offend the anti-discrimination policy that the firm is required to have. In these unfortunate situations the policy prevails, so a client stating that he or she does not want a black barrister, for example, would be told that this preference could not be respected. There is, however, some allowance on this in the latest version of CLSQM with its inference that the client's preferences should be taken into account in situations where the client knows a particular medical examiner or 'where in sensitive cases the appropriate use of female/ethnic minority group experts might be preferred' (U1.1.2).

The list of approved counsel and experts can be firm-wide or departmental. The only requirement in any of the codes is for approved advisers to be recorded, but there is potentially more usefulness in a list of non-approved outsiders. This serves as a warning to others not to instruct. There is a timely warning as to the combined dangers of the law of defamation and data protection legislation in the guidance notes to F8 of the Practice Management Standards. It will usually be the responsibility of all departments to keep up-to-date lists of approved counsel and other professional contacts for their sphere of work. One format is to have three lists as shown in Figure 17.2.

Those experts who have provided an effective service to the firm in the past may be entered onto the 'A' list. If the service proves to be satisfactory the fee-earner contracting the services may recommend that they be entered onto either the 'A' or 'B' list as appears appropriate. Any caveat should also be recorded. Experts and others providing unsatisfactory service may be entered onto the 'C' list. There will need to be a procedure for determining who authorises insertions and amendments.

How experts receive their instructions will need some attention. The usual rule is that they receive instructions through letter, brief,

A	B	C
Approved without reservation	Approved with reservation	Not approved for use by the department

Figure 17.2   *List of professional contacts*

telephone conversation or at a meeting. Where instructions are provided orally they should be confirmed subsequently in writing. In all cases a clear note of instructions or a copy of them must appear on the matter file.

There is a need for a critical review of any advice received. On receipt of advice from a sub-contractor the fee-earner receiving it should consider its suitability and value. If it is thought to be inappropriate it should be referred back to the adviser. Consideration might subsequently be given to the non-payment of the fee and to recommending that that individual be considered for inclusion on the 'C' list.

File management

The final element of section F needing attention here appears at F9 providing that:

(a) the status of the matter and the action taken can be easily checked by other members of the practice;

(b) documents are arranged in an orderly way;

(c) key information is shown clearly on the file (e.g. at the front of the file) which will include details of any undertakings given on behalf of the practice.

It is a good standard to set that any file with the firm should be readily intelligible to a colleague with minimal difficulty and without needing to revert to the client for missing details. This should do little more than underpin normal principles of good file management. The main rules are that all major steps should be noted on the file and all correspondence, attendance notes, etc. filed away. There is no compulsion to have any particular arrangements for files, though the highlighting of key information is advised. Many firms adapt general file summary sheets for particular departments to show the state of progress of the matter, but this is not compulsory.

For the sake of completeness it is worth mentioning here that there are provisions on access to information sources and know-how at E3 of Lexcel. The provisions in CLSQM are in addition more specific in relation to the public funding reference materials which must be available.

Variations in ISO 9000

The differences in the requirements of the original ISO 9000 standard on the one hand and Lexcel and CLSQM on the other have reduced considerably with the most recent revisions. There remain a few provisions which are particular to ISO 9000 and which are not found elsewhere.

The first relates to purchasing. Whereas the practice management standards and franchising extend only to 'barristers, expert witnesses, etc.' ISO 9000 will additionally extend to suppliers of office equipment, stationery and the like. This again illustrates the original industrial origins of the standard. In making a car, the suitability of brakes bought in from elsewhere is critical, but it is difficult to extend this by analogy to law firms buying paper and pens. Firms seeking ISO 9000 registration will, however, need to keep a record of approved office suppliers, together with records of orders for checking as supplies are received.

There are also distinctions between the provisions on file reviews and internal audits within the standard. It is important to distinguish between the two functions as it is usually preferable to separate them in practice. The objective of internal audit is to gain evidence of whether the system is felt to be working and is usually conducted on a quantitative basis. Data is collected to show where improvement to the system is needed, either in terms of improving the documented system itself or in training for personnel applying it. The orthodox view of quality assurance is that through internal audit all systems should eventually become self-regulating. From audits stem the corrective and preventive action that will lead to an improving system.

File reviews play a different, but complementary, role. They are concerned not so much with observing systems as ensuring that legal advice is accurate, that appropriate strategies are being pursued and that activity is maintained on the file. They are more likely to be conducted on a qualitative basis. Whereas the task of internal audit can be delegated to an administrator, file reviews need to be undertaken with someone of appropriate expertise – a fee-earner in the case of F10 of Lexcel. In firms that are registered to ISO 9000 and the other standards the internal audit programme often enables senior person-nel to spend less time checking on administrative file management procedures at file reviews, which could be seen as beneficial.

If internal audits are the key to an improving quality system, the records of the development of the system are clearly an integral part of achieving this. One of the perennial criticisms of ISO 9000 was that an organisation only had to perform consistently to be awarded the standard. The fact that the standard achieved was low, or that the out-put of the organisation was little more than rubbish, would not mat-ter. This was always exaggerated since there was always a requirement in the standard that a 'quality' system did exist. An organisation stip-ulating a response time of a year to correspondence for example, would be asked what this had to do with quality and it would not have been allowed. The revision of the standard which appeared in 1994 laid greater emphasis on preventive action, a theme now taken further in the current changes. The whole object of a quality assur-ance system should be to achieve improvements which, in ISO 9000, are achieved as shown in Figure 17.3.

It is also a requirement that there should be an annual manage-ment review, the contents of which are largely determined by the operational level as shown. It is helpful in any organisation in relation to the management of quality and seeking improvements and is good practice under any system.

Finally, there are requirements that 'quality records' should be maintained under ISO 9000. The file itself is a quality record but these provisions usually relate more to the maintenance of management records and audit reports.

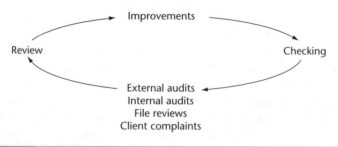

Figure 17.3   *Quality assurance system*

> **Main points**
>
> - Firms need appropriate procedures for all elements of case and file management.
> - Procedures may vary between departments.
> - Most of the procedures are core to Lexcel, CLSQM and ISO 9000 but there are some additional requirements to be found in ISO 9000.

References to Lexcel

F1 Index of matters
F6 Traceability
F7 End of matters
F8 Use of experts
F9 State of files

Notes

1 Moore, M. and Dodd, M. (2001) *Lexcel Office Procedures Manual*, Law Society Publishing.

18

Client care

- A client care programme
- Compulsory requirements

Outstanding client care should be seen as one of the principal goals of any quality improvement programme. There is considerable overlap between quality and client care since both focus on the client or customer reaction to the service provided. In a service profession where there will always be a choice of advisers, the quality of service provided is bound to be seen as the main differentiating factor between firms. Service quality is also increasingly recognised as being a critical factor in retailing. The marketing director of Sainsbury's observed that brand values emerging from national slogans were integral to their development policy, but that 'each customer's view of Sainsbury's comes not from national advertising but from how they were treated during their last visit to the store'. As another petrol retailer memorably put it in a recent campaign: 'it's a people thing'.

Notwithstanding the widespread recognition of the importance of client care, there is ample evidence of it often being disappointing in practice. Successive annual reports of the Office for the Supervision of Solicitors and the Solicitors Complaints Bureau before it, as well as the Legal Services Ombudsman, conclude that a regime of true client care could not be said to have taken general hold within the profession. Much the same conclusion emerges from the academic research on the topic which has appeared in recent years:

> it appears that most firms, even those who have established a complaints procedure, have yet to adopt a culture of client care which is founded on the notion that it is beneficial to operate a complaints procedure and to use reports of client dissatisfaction as feedback mechanisms to improve the legal services offered.[1]

This 1995 report entitled *Client Perceptions* surveyed about 1,000 respondents who had complained to the then Solicitors Complaints Bureau. There was widespread concern at the findings:

- 89 per cent said that they had not been made aware of the existence of an in-house complaints procedure;
- despite this, 50 per cent had approached their solicitors first before going to the Solicitors Complaints Bureau but satisfaction levels with the outcome of complaints investigations by firms and the way that they were handled were very poor;
- some two-thirds expected the firm to take the matter seriously and to put things right, but only 8 per cent said that they felt that the firm had done something substantial to resolve matters.

Commenting on the number of firms that nonetheless claimed to have complaints procedures the report went on to state that:

> this discrepancy may indicate a difference between the meaning of 'client care' for client and solicitors. For Rule 15 to resolve complaints and, more importantly, for it to reduce the numbers of complaints of inadequate professional service, solicitors must comply with both the spirit and the letter of the rule.

The challenge seems still to be to go beyond mere compliance with the professional rules and to embrace client care systems and techniques with enthusiasm. One of the findings of a team of researchers from Bristol University in a report of 1998 entitled *An Investigation into In-House Complaint Handling by Solicitors* was that there were confusing messages from the Law Society to firms as to whether they were being encouraged to develop the necessary regime and systems, or being threatened with sanctions for not doing so.[2] A clear theme of this excellent report was again that many firms were approaching the tasks of running a complaints system in a rather tokenist spirit of bare compliance. Perhaps, however, this picture should not be too surprising. It is surely understandable that a profession that is based on rules compliance in the content of its advice to clients might apply the same philosophy to rules which it receives from its governing body. The unfortunate and fairly clear consequence is a failure of client care culture. In the words of an anonymous solicitor quoted in the Bristol research: 'We are a service profession without a service culture'.

A client care programme

Client care has received considerable attention from the Law Society in recent years. Practice Rule 15 came into effect in 1991 requiring certain information to be given to the client at the outset of the matter unless it was inappropriate in the particular circumstances. In an attempt to enhance the general level of client care the Office for the Supervision of Solicitors produced a guide on client care in 1997, *Keeping Clients: a Client Care Guide for Solicitors*, which was circulated to all firms.[3] It was written by Patrick Stevens in conjunction with Martin Mears, the former Law Society president, and received general acclaim for its practical suggestions on how firms could develop better client care standards. Curiously the term 'client care' was not defined in this publication and was therefore left instead to readers' common sense and intuition. A good working definition is:

> A policy by the firm to ensure that all clients receive service which meets or exceeds their expectations.

Various points emerge from any such definition, but in particular it may well be that perfect client care, rather like 'total quality management', is an elusive ideal. Given the nature of legal work and the difficulties and anxieties of many clients, total satisfaction may be unachieveable for many practices, but this should not be taken to mean that it is not a worthwhile goal.

A preliminary issue for firms, therefore, is the level that they aspire towards. Given the client base they have and the competition they face, is it good enough simply to meet clients' expectations or should they, like so many other service businesses today, seek to exceed expectations or 'delight' their clients? The higher standards would be associated with the philosophy of total quality management. Either way, measurement of satisfaction, as through client surveys, will make any programme more substantive.

However it is defined, there is clear advice that firms should have a policy for client care and not leave the subject to the good manners and common sense of its personnel. This advice can be found most recently in the guide *Handling Complaints Effectively* which was produced by the Office for the Supervision of Solicitors and distributed to firms in 2000.[4] The sample 'client care charter' at pages 17–19 of that guide sets out headings on 'our commitment to you' and 'how you can help us' and would be a good starting point at least for firms wishing to adopt a policy. There is a suggestion in B1.7 of Lexcel that the firm's client care policy could form an element of its marketing plan.

Client care procedures will be shaped largely by the profess-ional rules and guidelines now contained in the Solicitors' Costs Information and Client Care Code 1999 which accompanies the revised Practice Rule 15 which took effect in September 1999, but it should go further than this. One researcher active in this area,

Tamara Goriely, lists seven requirements for a client care regime.[5] These are:

- adequacy of information on likely costs at the outset;
- listening to the client;
- understanding the problem for which advice is sought;
- keeping the client informed on progress;
- providing clear advice;
- attitude to complaints;
- feeding back information from complaints to achieve improvements.

One of the challenges for firms in improving client care is that there is more to achieving client care than simply having systems in place. Certain of the areas above, such as listening to clients and providing clear advice, are purely skills. No amount of careful drafting of manuals or procedures will assist where skills are lacking. Above all there must be a sense of the importance of client care at all levels of the practice. Systems play a part, but they are not the total story. The firm that is determined to develop the best standards of client care will therefore need to address three interlocking components (see Figure 18.1).

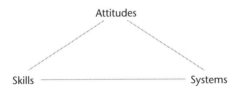

Figure 18.1   *Improving client care*

Concern and courtesy are high on any list of important attitudes to adopt. These may be obvious to most, but clearly not all. Client surveys reveal time after time that perceived delay in responding to telephone calls and letters will cause disappointment. Where it is impossible to return a call the task should be delegated to a colleague, such as the fee-earner's secretary. The colleague might confine themselves to explaining when a call will be possible. Above all clients expect a sense of urgency about their problem and the way that it is being handled. There are still too many advisers who seem to treat each set of instructions as a rather abstract academic exercise.

Other elements relate to the skills needed to practise effectively, mostly skills of communication. The ability to listen, suspend judgement, avoid stereotyping and then to phrase advice so that it is intelligible and palatable to the client are all to be encouraged. These now form a more significant part of the initial training of solicitors in the Legal Practice Course and the accompanying Professional Skills Course. It is a point often conceded that it may well be certain more senior members of the profession who are more in need of such training.

One of the most persistent problems of service delivery appears to stem from the differing perceptions of fee-earners and clients on what a 'quality' service truly is. Professional advisers tend to concentrate on quality of expertise. This has been variously described as quality of 'input' and 'real' quality, but the concern seems to be at odds with most clients. The available research tends to show that clients are likely to take technical expertise for granted; what will concern them more is quality of 'output' or 'perceived' quality. Most consumers of professional services will probably be ill-equipped to judge the expertise of the adviser, but they can readily judge the manner in which the service is delivered. Other personal factors such as the confidence and demeanour of their advisers are also important. In these terms an expert lawyer who relates poorly to clients will probably struggle to impress. On the other hand the importance of expertise should never be overlooked. Communication skills and a positive attitude to clients are all well and good, but only if expert advice and services are being provided. The clear goal has to be quality of expertise and quality of service output; one without the other will be problematic.

Another way of looking at the importance of client care is to examine the role of the marketing concept in practice, dealt with in Chapter 15. The ethos that makes the client or customer the starting point for planning services and their delivery is a useful insight for what is failing in many firms. Traditionally the professional adviser could expect deference from their clients, but no longer. Commercial standards of service delivery will be expected and the firm that fails to meet such standards will experience problems.

Finally, it is interesting to note that Goriely lists attitudes to complaints systems as an important component to client care. This would seem to be in line with the Bristol report that having a paper system is of little benefit if there is not the commitment to gain the benefit from it that should be expected.

Compulsory requirements

A revised Practice Rule 15 took effect in September 1999. The main reason for the revision was to harmonise the original Rule 15 requirements in relation to responsibility for matters and the requirements in relations to costs information which were rather confusingly found elsewhere in the Written Professional Standards on Costs. The original Rule 15 provided that:

(1) Every principal in private practice shall operate a complaints handling procedure which shall, *inter alia*, ensure that clients are informed whom to approach in the event of any problem with the service provided.

(2) Every solicitor in private practice shall, unless it is inappropriate in the circumstances:

    (a) ensure that clients know the name and status of the person responsible for the day to day conduct of the matter and the principal responsible for its overall supervision;

    (b) ensure that clients know whom to approach in the event of any problem with the service provided; and,

    (c) ensure that clients are at all relevant times given any appropriate information as to the issues raised and the progress of the matter.

(3) Notwithstanding rule 19(2) of these rules, this rule shall come into force on the 1st May 1991.

The main provisions of the rule were more concerned with ensuring that clients knew who would be dealing with the matter, how it would be supervised and whom they should approach in the event of problems. Curiously, many in the profession seemed to think that Rule 15 was more to do with publicising hourly rates than anything else and the general level of appreciation of what the rule actually required was poor. Many firms attending workshops on client care organised by the Office for the Supervision of Solicitors complained about the negative impact of setting out full complaints procedures at the outset of a matter, but it is clear from above that this was not necessary, merely that clients knew in the first instance whom to approach in the event of difficulties.

A letter to the *Gazette* in July 1999 expressed the resentment that many practitioners have for the compulsory complaints regime and the common misunderstanding about what precisely is required.

> If . . . the Marks and Spencers and Tescos of the world . . . were under a duty to give their customers in writing at the point of every sale details

of how to complain – highlighting that it would not cost them a penny, however much trouble they caused, justified or not – then their complaints ratio might well increase alarmingly.[6]

The next issue contained a letter from Mike Frith of the Office for the Supervision of Solicitors:

> I would also correct his mistaken impression – one which he is far from alone in holding within the profession – that he is required at the outset of his instructions, to give his clients full details of how to complain. He is not, nor does Practice Rule 15 demand that he do so. All Rule 15 requires, in this respect, is that he has in place a complaints procedure and that the client is told to whom he can address any problems – the word 'complaint' is not even mentioned in that context.[7]

The new rule contains broadly the same provisions in relation to all of the above. The costs position now has the status of a practice rule, so the enforcement provisions for persistent non-compliance are potentially more stringent. Beyond this the new code is more wide-ranging than its predecessor. In relation to complaints it makes it clear that all forms must have a complaints handling procedure which must be 'available on request'. Many of the detailed provisions on costs information are shaped by the Woolf regime, the obligations to consider cost benefit and risk most obviously.

Practice Rule 15 and the Solicitors' Costs Information and Client Care Code 1999 are the basis of compliance with Lexcel and also with the CLSQM:

> Practices will have written procedures to ensure compliance with the Solicitors' Costs Information and Client Care Code 1999 and to provide for regular communication with clients, third parties and the court as necessary in relation to costs (Lexcel F3).

There are also references to the Code in the guidance notes to F4 (Taking instructions) and F10 (Supervision of casework). For the most part the CLSQM is in line with the requirements of the Code and the Lexcel standards, though the wording is slightly different. Many firms may find it confusing that so many rules are contained in so many sources, but there is remarkable similarity between them. This is not coincidental since each of the provisions were drawn up in the light of any other rules then in place. Beyond the basic requirement that the name and status of the person acting should be disclosed in addition to the supervisory arrangements the main requirements can be summarised as follows.

Initial costs information

There was a surprising amount of opposition to the whole concept of having to give costs information to clients at the outset of matters when Practice Rule 15 was first mooted. Although this often ran along the lines of the difficulties of saying anything precise at an early stage the reservations of many practitioners were clearly more based on an embarrassment with talking about money at all. Many feared that revealing the likely expense of the matter would deter too much work. Since that time most will have concluded that it is better to have fewer clients who do pay than more who do not.

For many clients the hourly rate is probably an unattractive way to communicate the information. Quite apart from the fact that the figure can seem uncomfortably high it lays too much emphasis on effort and not enough on outcomes or results. By contrast the rate for the job might seem much better value and we are likely to see a continuing decline in the use of hourly rates as the basis for fee quotes to clients in years to come.

A curious myth has developed within the profession that as long as clients have been informed of the applicable hourly rates, the adviser has met their obligations under the rules. This was not in fact the case under the Information on Costs for Clients Regulations of 1991. This stated that solicitors should, on taking instructions, give clients the best information possible about 'the likely cost of the matter'. The payment of fees and other charges, along with eligibility for legal aid and/or insurance were also covered. This is made all the more clear under the new Code. The principal rule at 4.a is that:

> the solicitor should give to the client the best information possible about the likely overall cost, including a breakdown between fees, VAT and disbursements.

Rule 4.b requires explanation of the likely time input if time is to be a factor in billing, which would equally mean that it does not have to be dealt with if this is not the case. Take, for example, domestic conveyancing which, for right or wrong, is conventionally dealt with on some form of fixed fee basis. If a fee has been agreed, the time input by the solicitor is then of no direct concern to the client in relation to the fees to be paid. The only qualification to this would be that it is prudent to be as specific as possible as to the circumstances in which the estimate will have to be exceeded and additional charges will accrue. Stating the maximum fee-earner time allowed for in providing the estimate, for example, improves the position of the firm in the occasional transaction which develops unexpected and time-consuming complications.

There are helpful illustrations in 4.c concerning what is meant by 'best information possible', which is stated to include:

- agreeing a fixed fee, or
- giving a realistic estimate, or
- giving a forecast within a possible range of costs.

These illustrations will be found along with the other elements of costs information in the list of points to be covered under F3b of Lexcel. For the most open-ended matters, most obviously complex litigation which everyone knows is likely to settle well before a trial looms, the illustration suggests:

> explaining to the client the reasons why it is not possible to fix, or give a realistic estimate or forecast of, the overall costs, and giving instead the best information possible about the cost of the next stage of the matter.

It is also provided that advisers should be very careful to distinguish estimates from quotes. Clients provided with estimates often regard them as being watertight quotes and careful wording in any confirmation of terms is clearly very important. It will be good practice not simply to rely on the written confirmation but to make the basis of the information very clear at any client interview as well. Written confirmation of all points covered in the first interview is always advisable; the Code provides that it is 'good practice to record in writing all information required to be given by the Code'.

Further points to note in relation to initial costs information are the general duty to ensure that costs information is not inaccurate or misleading (3.a), the need for an explanation as to how the firm's fees are calculated save where the overall costs are clear or fixed (4.f) and the need to consider cost/benefit in pursuing any possible course of action (4.k). There have always been clients who were so incensed by the circumstances that they found themselves in that they wanted to litigate out of principle and the new rules make it all the more important to make clear to such clients the potential costs of these principles. The issue of potential costs liability in litigation has to be dealt with for those involved, or who may potentially become involved, in contentious matters along with other possible sources of funding such as legal aid, insurance and trade union benefits.

There is growing concern about the potential risks of not meeting the requirements set out in rule 4 of the Code. The case of *Pilbrow* v. *Pearless de Rougemont* [1999] 3 All ER 355 received extensive publicity.

A client asked to see a solicitor on his matrimonial affairs and was duly advised. Unfortunately for the firm at no stage had it confirmed in writing that the adviser was unadmitted. It was held that there was no obligation to pay the professional fees for advice provided since, in the view of the Court of Appeal, there had been a failure of contract: the firm had not provided what the client had requested.

In another matter an unsuccessful litigant was held justified in not paying for his costs where the possibility of after the event insurance had not been raised with him at the outset of the matter. These developments have led Tony Girling, a former president of the Law Society and now a highly regarded consultant and trainer on professional issues, to advise that firms insist that they receive written acceptance of terms and conditions before acting. It would seem that the additional requirements now found in the Solicitors' Costs Information and Client Care Code 1999 create risks for the unwary that need to be guarded against.

The difficulty of applying the strict requirements to commercial work is a potential problem with the regime now in force. The Code provides that there is no need to provide the 'full information required by the Code if it would be inappropriate in the circumstances' which would probably extend to the common situation where the established commercial client provides instructions and simply tells their advisers to 'get on with it'. Formal confirmation of the fees on this set of instructions is not provided since both parties know full well that at the end of the matter both will sit down and agree a fee which is acceptable to both. If this cannot be done the client would have to look elsewhere and the firm would lost a client, so there is a mutual interest in coming to an agreement that both are happy with. Whereas the former Practice Management Standards required the full information required by the Code unless the work was of a 'repetitive manner' there is greater flexibility in the new Lexcel Standards as they are more in line with the Code.

Since many of these provisions are still relatively novel and work patterns can continue to develop, regular reviews of letters of confirmation of instructions to ensure compliance with the Code are advisable. It should be borne in mind that both Lexcel and the CLSQM require at least an annual review of quality system documentation, which in most firms would include the drafts of client care letters (Lexcel E1 3b: CLSQM W1.2) The additional step of adding to any office manual a summary of the rules and the issues to be covered in an early interview with clients will also be advisable. Many firms have developed checklists to be completed at all such interviews for future reference on file. Whatever may be appropriate within any given firm or department, the advice must be to manage compliance and not take it for granted. There will be those who can simply be led to the water, but others may need to be made to drink.

Continuing costs information

For many legal aid firms one of the foremost difficulties of adapting to successive franchising regimes has been the need to send out letters summarising the costs position every six months. Many continue to doubt the appropriateness or value of this, not least because of the volume of telephone enquiries which seem inevitably to follow. 'Why are you telling me this? I thought that I was on legal aid.' The justification of the Commission was that the client should realise how much public money was being spent on them and that they should not be in any different position to private paying clients. In addition, the information will become of direct relevance to a legally aided client if the statutory charge eventually becomes applicable. The position is indeed in line with the requirements for private paying clients as found in rule 6 of the 1999 Code:

> The solicitor should keep the client properly informed about costs as a matter progresses. In particular, the solicitor should:
>
> (a) tell the client, unless otherwise agreed, how much the costs are at regular intervals (at least every six months) and in appropriate cases deliver interim bills at agreed intervals . . .

Again, the spirit of the rule is not simply to follow the general six months' rule which follows, but to have regard to the client's circumstances and the developments in the matter which may cause the client to re-think their strategy. Major developments and their implications for costs should be notified promptly. It is to be hoped that, with so much emphasis on better cash management in recent years, the encouragement to issue interim bills should be superfluous.

It should be stressed that the six monthly update is the minimum requirement only and the Code provides that significant changes should be brought to the client's attention without delay. For the purposes of Lexcel audits a costs review should be taken to be more than simply an update on the costs position, but a review of whether any initial costs estimate may then need revision. This seems also to emerge as the suggestion in 6.b. The draft of the continuing costs letter precedent should therefore include a section indicating whether the adviser considers it necessary to review any of the original advice supplied on likely overall costs. Changing legal aid entitlement also needs to be picked up in the event of a 'material change in the client's means' which comes to the solicitor's attention under 6.d.

Complaints handling

Guidelines on client care tend to urge that complaints should not be seen as being simply a problem, but also as an opportunity to reassure that client and learn how to avoid problems with others. It was referred to as 'free research data' in the *Keeping Clients* publication,[8] but it is quite clear that although many may agree with this in principle they are still far from making this a reality in their own firms.

The picture of formal systems which few fee-earners or other staff within the firm use or even know about is confirmed by the Bristol University research mentioned above. The investigation into in-house complaints handling by solicitors and Practice Rule 15 by Christensen, Day and Worthington concluded that there was a general lack of commitment to explore complaints and respond adequately to them.[9] Complaints were often marginalised by the fee-earners concerned as coming from 'the wrong type of client' or being only likely when a bill was received, in which case the client was probably 'trying it on' in relation to payment. Similar scepticism attached to matrimonial clients who were thought bound to complain as a result of basic dissatisfaction with the process in which they found themselves. This basic lack of engagement by a firm with the complaints received made a satisfactory outcome from the client's point of view more unlikely.

With regard to solicitors' attitudes to complaints systems, there was a continuing belief in the potential harm to the solicitor/client relationship arising from the emphasis on complaints in most Practice Rule 15 letters. This was seen as being likely to cause dissatisfaction where it might not otherwise exist. The general conclusion was that the profession remained 'steadfastly unconvinced' as to the benefits of a Practice Rule 15 regime.

On the management of complaints systems there was widespread evidence of a system being in existence, but not in use. A formal register of client complaints might have been established a year or two beforehand, but the firm had since received no formal complaints. There is an adage of the quality world which suggests that: 'If you get no complaints you are not asking the right questions', and the only likely explanation for a nil complaints record is that complaints are not being addressed.

Definitions of 'complaints', rather like the term 'client care', are thin on the ground. This lack of general definition contributes to some of the more common misunderstandings. There are, for example, firms where the partner responsible will take the view that only issues leading to potential negligence should be regarded as a complaint. The spirit of the Rule requires a very much more comprehensive view of the issue than this. It is perhaps for this reason that there is a requirement in the Practice Management Standards that each firm will have documented arrangements for complaints handling, including a 'definition of complaint' (F11a). A definition will be found in CLSQM in the guidance notes to V1.2: 'a complaint is any expression of client dissatisfaction, however it is expressed'.

This definition would be wide enough to cover even the most trivial of concerns and is therefore probably too wide for general use. Other commentators, such as Stephen Hammett in a former version of *The Law Society's Solicitors' Office Manual*, have stressed the need for common sense in judging when a complaint is not simply a 'grumble', which may lack precision but is probably more practicable.[10] If minor difficulties are excluded a working definition would be:

> any expression of dissatisfaction with the service provided or the fees charged which cannot be resolved informally between fee-earner and client.

On the issue of definitions, however, a word of caution here for legal aid firms is important. The wording on complaints procedures at section V of CLSQM is that firms need to report and record centrally 'every complaint made'. Despite a submission during the consultation process that this should read 'formal complaint' the wording was unchanged, so it must be presumed that the Legal Services Commission do wish even the 'grumbles' as defined above to be recorded, given their wide definition of what constitutes a complaint. This seems to be the experience of various legal aid firms who have discovered to their surprise that they have been found non-compliant for having minor client problems on file but not recorded, even though they may have been misunderstandings which have been resolved to the apparent satisfaction of the client with minimal effort.

Much of the impetus for complaints systems was driven by the public sector in the 1990s. This created some useful guidelines on complaints systems such as the following from the Citizens' Charter Task Force. Internal complaints handling should:

(a) be easily accessible and well publicised;
(b) be simple to use and understand;
(c) allow speedy handling with clear time limits and progress reports;
(d) ensure a full and fair investigation;
(e) respect people's desire for confidentiality;
(f) address all points at issue and provide response and redress;
(g) feed information to management to enable improvement.

The extent to which complaints procedures have needed to be publicised to clients depends on which quality systems the firm adheres to. In the original Rule the requirement on communication was simply that clients should know 'whom to approach in the event of any problem with the service provided'. Likewise in the 1999 Code:

> Every solicitor in private practice must ensure that the client . . . is told whom to contact about any problem with the service provided (7.a.iii).

As we have seen, this is not the same thing as requiring the full complaints procedure to be set out in the initial client care letter and can quite adequately be dealt with in a sentence or two in the first letter, and is probably more appropriately done so on this basis. When a problem does arise, however, each principal in private practice must: 'ensure that the client is given a copy of the complaints procedure on request' (7.b.iii).

The previous version of the Practice Management Standards required greater prominence for the details of complaints procedures in initial correspondence, but F4 on complaints handling now brings the standards into line with the Solicitors' Costs Information and Client Care Code 1999.

Other requirements of complaints handling are to have a written complaints procedure and to ensure that the client is told the name of the person in the firm to contact about any problem with the service provided.

Most solicitors seem to fear the impression that can be conveyed by long first letters that deal with what should happen if or when things go wrong. It is important to stress, therefore, that this need not be the case. The draft letters which accompanied the 1999 Practice Rule 15 revision were up to five pages in length. It may well be better to develop a client leaflet which can incorporate details of complaints procedures without detracting from the more important things that clients will want to read about in a letter. This is certainly the case at Girlings Solicitors of Kent whose terms and conditions appear in the 2000 revision of the *Lexcel Office Procedures Manual*.[11] Other firms have produced separate leaflets or letters which are made available when a complaint is received. Such literature can be left on display in the reception area, particularly if there are other leaflets or booklets for client use.

Complaints procedures benefit from being organised into three levels, probably reducing to two with sole practitioners. These can be represented by a triangle if the numbers of each category are measured: see Figure 18.2.

| Figure 18.2 | *Complaints procedure* |

At the first and most obvious level there will be all manner of informal problems which crop up from day to day and which are generally resolved there and then. Most firms will prefer not to make these the subject of formal reporting arrangements since there will be numerous misunderstandings which are easily resolved amongst them and the bureaucracy of reporting is unlikely to be worth the data which emerges. As we have seen, however, legal aid matters should report even this level of difficulties within the formal system. As an illustration of this distinction a comment that 'you solicitors charge a lot for what you do' would probably be accepted as part of the everyday dialogue that is likely and such explanation as is possible will be given. If, on the other hand, the client says 'I am not paying this bill for £2,000: you said that it would be £1,000 at most' then a complaint seems to have developed. Even at this level it seems sensible to encourage the adviser to try to deal with the problem as informally as possible. If, through explanation or reminder of conversation or correspondence, they can satisfy the client that the bill arose fairly, there seems little point in requiring the formal system to be engaged. The real problem develops where the client cannot be persuaded in this way. At that stage the complaint must be regarded as a formal one and some form of reporting must ensue.

If the reporting of complaints is to be encouraged it is important that management adopt a realistic and supportive attitude to the issue. It is advisable to involve the fee-earner concerned in the investigation to help ensure that the appropriate response is made. Nobody likes to be the subject of a complaint, whatever may be said about the value of the data. Although we never win kudos for reporting the most complaints we should also not be discouraged or penalised either. Ideally the firm should adopt as neutral an attitude as possible to the reporting of complaints. The production of lists of how many complaints have been received by each department or fee-earner may be needed for an effective risk management policy but should be circulated and used with tact for this reason. Fee-earners will need reassurance that the reporting of complaints by them will not be held against them in some way.

It is worth stressing the importance of an immediate response, even if this is only an acknowledgement and an explanation of the timetable of events to follow, probably accompanied by the firm's written complaints procedure as required by the 1999 Code. The efficiency with which the complaint is dealt with is likely to have a considerable bearing on the acceptability of its eventual finding, even if the view is taken that the firm was not in the wrong in any way.

One of the useful insights in the Bristol University report is the attitude to judging complaints that firms adopt. More firms believe that they are genuinely fair and objective than seems to be the case so far as clients are concerned. How does this apparent contradiction arise? The answer seems to be the difference of judging a complaint in a semi-judicial manner, as opposed to what might be called a 'pragmatic' approach. Under the first approach we employ our legal skills and instincts to assess whether the client has established a problem. We probably put the onus on them, whether on balance of probabilities or beyond reasonable doubt, who knows. The client has raised this problem, however, and it is for them to prove it. We examine the file and perhaps speak to the fee-earner concerned (though not, interestingly, the client in most cases, it would seem) and probably conclude that there is nothing to merit censure of the fee-earner, so the complaint must therefore be dismissed.

The pragmatic approach employs a wholly less legal and a more overtly commercial approach to the situation that exists. The complaint is a fact of life: it exists and there is no point in denying its existence. A few complainants might be negotiating to get their bill reduced, but most are likely to hold genuine grievances whatever the eventual outcome. The customer may not be right, but he or she is convinced that they are right, and if the firm wants repeat business from them or hopes for positive things to be said about them by this client, the complaint has to be accepted to some degree.

The truth is that client and adviser are often at cross purposes. Lawyers reviewing files look for legal errors. Clients, the research suggests, are more likely to be concerned with how they are communicated with and handled as people. The adviser who checks a file for legal errors when a complaint is received has probably already missed the problem that the client is trying to bring to their attention. An excellent example is the familiar complaint for delay. The lawyer's view of delay can be shaped by time limits: if the claim is still within the permitted period for issue there is nothing wrong with the file. The client, however, could be excused for missing the nuances of statutory limitations periods. So far as they are concerned the matter is taking too long and nothing appears to be happening. This divergence of views is a frequent example of the tension between 'real' and 'perceived' quality mentioned above. Failure to recognise this distinction and address it will almost inevitably result in disappointment with the complaints process so far as the client is concerned.

As in negotiating, an outright rejection will cause only bitterness and resentment. An acknowledgement of the problem and its genuineness to the complainer, accompanied by an apology, will almost certainly ameliorate the situation. Is an apology not an admission of fault or liability, however? The answer is that it need not be. The Office for the Supervision of Solicitors *Guide to Complaints Handling* suggests that: 'if you must have the last word, say sorry'.[12]

A word of caution now needs to be added to this eminently sensible advice, which is that each firm should check how comfortable its indemnity insurers are with expressions of regret. They may have different views on the line between admitting regret and fault and the risk of cover being withdrawn through compromise of the position is worth taking seriously.

Assuming a free hand in relation to this a common problem will be that the legal steps were correct, but the client has failed to understand what was happening:

> Having looked into this file I can assure you that the fee-earner concerned followed normal procedures and could not be criticised for the legal steps that they took on your behalf.

In this response it is possible to sense the relief of the writer. They have looked at the file and there is no issue of negligence. Perhaps the partner is the one who deals with issues of negligence and so is understandably focused on looking for cases that might need referring to the insurers in any event. The client must be a trouble-maker, the wrong type of client or perhaps even a 'nutter'. There has been a response, however, so if the firm is ever inspected a formal complaints procedure can be shown to be in existence. Any subsequent appeal to the Office for the Supervision of Solicitors will merely confirm what a nuisance this client is. By this stage, however, the goodwill of the client has almost certainly been lost for ever. The story will be told to numerous contacts of the client in the inevitably one-sided manner that they are bound to adopt and, if it does go further, more time and effort is going to be needed to answer any continuing enquiry. This in itself will be to the overall cost of the profession, be it the local law society or the Office for the Supervision of Solicitors.

How much better to try to address the client at their level of concern:

> Having looked into this matter I can appreciate that matters should have been explained more clearly and I apologise for not having kept you sufficiently in the picture of what we were doing for you and why. It probably is important to stress that the steps taken were absolutely necessary and were those that any competent lawyer would have taken in the circumstances, but you did of course need more explanation and I am sorry that you did not receive this.

This will be more likely to dissipate the problem and provide the client with the reassurance that they are likely still to be seeking.

The cost of not dealing satisfactorily with client complaints is one argument for an appeal procedure other than the Office for the Supervision of Solicitors. It was clear in the Bristol University report that complainants are much more likely to believe in the fairness of an appeal if they see some objective input to it.[13] The Office for the Supervision of Solicitors is, sadly, always likely to disappoint certain complainants as a result of its perceived close links with the profession. Likewise, another partner from the same firm may not represent the sort of independent view that many expect.

It is encouraging to see local law societies taking an initiative in this regard. One example is the scheme established by the Birmingham Law Society who took great pride in reducing to just two the numbers of complaints which it was unable to resolve with the result that a complaint to the Office for the Supervision of Solicitors followed from the 123 received between May 1999 and October 2000.

There certainly seems to be value in involving lay representatives in any such process. Where there is no local law society scheme or where the firm does not participate in it for any reason there is no reason why a firm should not set up its own appeals committee consisting of a different partner – perhaps the senior partner at this stage as opposed to a client care or managing partner – along with one or other outsiders to the firm who can be seen to be adding a client perspective. In such circumstances the complainant's agreement to the involvement of any outsiders would be necessary to ensure that client confidentiality requirements were not breached. Although this may be a second or appeal stage in a partnership, it could be the most effective way to deal with the first stage of a formal complaint to a sole practitioner or principal.

The management of complaints systems form a useful summary of the main points on managing client care. The establishment of satisfactory definitions, systems and procedures are important, but without the accompanying determination to make them work they will not achieve the benefits which should be expected from them.

Main points

- Enhanced levels of client care should be one of the main aims of the quality programme.
- Client care is only improved where there is a true commitment to it and not mere lip service.
- Client care is made up of attitudes, skills and systems.
- In a competitive marketplace client care is ultimately the main difference between rival firms.

References to Lexcel

B1 Marketing plan
F3 Client information
F4 Confirmation of instructions
F5 Information on progress of matters
F11 Complaints handling

Notes

1 Jenkins and Lewis, (1995) *Client Perceptions*, Law Society.
2 Christensen, C., Day, S. and Worthington, J. (1998) *An Investigation into In-House Complaint Handling by Solicitors*, Bristol University.
3 Stevens, P. and Mears, M. (1997) *Keeping Clients: a Client Care Guide for Solicitors*, Office for the Supervision of Solicitors.
4 *Handling Complaints Effectively* (2000) Office for the Supervision of Solicitors.
5 Goriely, T., [1993] 'Quality of legal services: the need for consumer research', *Consumer Policy Review*, vol. 3. no. 2.
6 [1999] *Gazette*, 7 July, p.16.
7 [1999] *Gazette*, 14 July, p.16.

8   Stevens, P. and Mears, M. (1997) *op. cit.*
9   Christensen, C., Day, S. and Worthington, J. (1998) *op. cit.*
10 Hammett, S. (1993) *The Law Society's Solicitors' Office Manual*, Law Society.
11 Moore, M. and Dodd, M. (2001) *Lexcel Office Procedures Manual*, Law Society Publishing.
12 *A Guide to Complaints Handling* (2000) Office for the Supervision of Solicitors. See also correspondence following Ombudsman's Casebook [2000] *Gazette*, 19 October, p. 50 from J. Alcock ([2000] *Gazette*, 2 November, p. 16) and subsequent replies.
13 Christensen, C., Day, S. and Worthington, J. (1998) *op. cit.*

Index

Index